Palgrave Macmillan Studies in Banking and Financial Institutions

Series Editor

Philip Molyneux
Bangor University
Bangor, United Kingdom

The Palgrave Macmillan Studies in Banking and Financial Institutions series is international in orientation and includes studies of banking systems in particular countries or regions as well as contemporary themes such as Islamic Banking, Financial Exclusion, Mergers and Acquisitions, Risk Management, and IT in Banking. The books focus on research and practice and include up to date and innovative studies that cover issues which impact banking systems globally.

More information about this series at
http://www.springer.com/series/14678

Djurdjica Ognjenovic

Deposit Insurance Schemes

Funding, Policy and Operational Challenges

palgrave
macmillan

Djurdjica Ognjenovic
Zagreb, Croatia

Palgrave Macmillan Studies in Banking and Financial Institutions
ISBN 978-3-319-51142-9 ISBN 978-3-319-51143-6 (eBook)
DOI 10.1007/978-3-319-51143-6

Library of Congress Control Number: 2017933086

Printed on acid-free paper

This Palgrave Macmillan imprint is published by Springer Nature
The registered company is Springer International Publishing AG
The registered company address is: Gewerbestrasse 11, 6330 Cham, Switzerland

Foreword

The funding deposit insurance scheme (DIS) is one of the most important elements in creating and maintaining a credible safety net and enabling DIS to fulfill its role when deposits become unavailable due to bank failure. When funding is not designed properly, the financial capacity of the DIS is weak and its available funds are non-proportional to its liabilities, resulting in either temporary liquidity gaps or severe insolvency. Deposit insurers around the globe often complain regarding the legal limitations related to funding and the scarcity of timely information which limit their repayment effectiveness. To a certain extent it is all true.

The financial management practice in the deposit insurance authority is equally important. If risk awareness, financial planning and fund investment policies are poor, the DIS may face insufficiency of available financial resources when needed.

For policy makers, it is crucial to design DIS features based on an international guidance enabling funding from all available sources in an efficient manner. For deposit insurance practitioners, funding is the topic of utmost priority on a daily basis and professionally, the most challenging issue to be resolved.

Surprisingly or not, deposit insurance has become a topic of great interest and discussion among the policy makers, academics and practitioners almost entirely due to events and consequences related to the recent international financial crisis in 2008 and onward.

This is, therefore, a crucial moment to re-investigate whether deposit insurers are ready to assume the biggest role ever in the support of stronger national and international financial safety nets. Are DISs today more financially robust than earlier? Is their financial capacity stronger than before? Can all new rules, guidelines, procedures and operational changes prevent undercapitalization of DISs in the future?

Preface

The main motive for writing this book was to provide a comprehensive overview on DISs, with a focus on funding a DIS from policy and operational perspectives, gained over more than 20 years of practical experience in countries all over the world, and to answer questions of how to establish and maintain a credible deposit insurance fund (DIF) that would be able to contribute to the stability of the financial sector, regardless of its mandate, in the most efficient way.

All deposit insurance authorities manage large sums of money, collected within a relatively predictable timeframe aiming to ensure sufficient liquidity in case of unforeseeable events such as bank failure. The challenging dynamics and changes in the financial infrastructure, especially within the EU, force DISs to undertake legal and institutional changes and transform themselves into more robust financial safety net players. Are they ready?

On a daily basis, deposit insurance authorities, regardless of their mandate, worry about the funding and ask themselves the same questions:

- Are there sufficient financial resources in the DIF?
- How to ensure liquidity if needed and where?
- Should a target fund be established?
- What would be the optimal size of a DIF?

How to fulfill the mandate efficiently and more cost-effectively?

The book addresses all these questions and provides examples and solutions on specific issues and topics related to establishment, financial management and optimal DIS funding. The book discusses challenges currently faced by the European Union (EU) members in their attempts to comply with an improved EU regulatory framework on deposit insurance and bank resolution.

In order to provide recommendations and enable every national jurisdiction to apply identical methodological and analytical steps, examples are prepared using theoretical banking sector data in the same manner as it would be done in the real-case scenario. The same methodology can be applied in any DIS in any geographical area, with a small or large banking sector, with a narrow or broad mandate and regardless of a DIS's institutional development and legal form.

The book is divided into seven chapters, where chapters 1 and 2 address major policy issues on funding and key DIS design features.

Chapters 3, 4 and 5 are focused on operational challenges related to funding a DIS on a daily basis, which the deposit insurance practitioners face in their everyday work and in collaboration with other safety net players, with a major focus on target funding and ideally optimal funding.

Chapters 6 and 7 of the book address issues related to the challenges faced by EU member countries when complying with EU regulatory framework on deposit insurance and bank resolution.

For simplicity and in order to avoid confusion arising from regulatory differences existing in different jurisdictions, as well as in the terminology used in the available literature, the following terms will be used in this book, in the context of deposit insurance and bank resolution:

Bank is any deposit-taking credit institution licensed and supervised by the national supervisory authority that collects deposits from the public and is the subject of deposit insurance.

Problem bank is a bank that is identified as such by the supervisory authority due to breaches of prudential norms or its unsound financial condition where one or more supervisory measures are or will be prescribed, and the condition of which may be rehabilitated or may result in failure over time.

Failing bank is a bank undergoing insolvency proceedings or other form of resolution process due to severe financial conditions and non-viability of its business under the going-concern basis and whose depositors are entitled to receive covered deposits compensation from the deposit insurance authority under the existing DIS framework.

Contents

List of Figures

List of Tables

Acronyms

List of acronyms used in this book:

BCBS	Basel Committee for Banking Supervision
BIS	Bank for International Settlements
BRRD	Directive 2014/59/EU of the European Parliament and of the Council of 15 May 2014 establishing a framework for the recovery and resolution of the credit institutions and investment firms
CAR	capital adequacy ratio
CDIC	Canadian Deposit Insurance Corporation
DGS	deposit guarantee scheme
DGSD	Directive 2014/49/EU of the European Parliament and of the Council of 16 April 2014 on deposit guarantee schemes
DIF	deposit insurance fund
DIS	deposit insurance scheme
EAD	exposure at default
EBA	European Banking Authority
ECB	European Central Bank
EDIS	European Deposit Insurance Scheme
EFTA	European Free Trade Association
EL	expected losses
EU	European Union
FDIC	Federal Deposit Insurance Corporation
FSAP	Financial Sector Assessment Program

GDP	gross domestic product
IADI	International Association of Deposit Insurers
IFRS	International Financial Reporting Standards
LCT	least cost test
LGD	loss given default
MIS	management information system
P&A	purchase and assumption
PD	probability of default
SCV	single customer view
SIFI	systemically important financial institution
SRM	Single Resolution Mechanism
SSM	Single Supervisory Mechanism

1

Deposit Insurance at a Glance

1.1 Introduction

It is often said that there are no two identical deposit insurance schemes (DISs) in the world. If that is true, the question is whether it is possible to establish universal standards and principles that would work for all DISs and how authorities can ensure that the design of a national DIS is the right one fitting domestic needs and circumstances. Moreover, does the difference in the mandate and powers of DISs affect their funding challenges or limit funding options?

To look for answers one must observe historical developments and how and why DISs were established in the first place. Evolution of DISs was not painless, as the idea was born after many depositors around the world had suffered financial losses due to bank failures. Over the years, the number of explicit DISs grew and had officially reached 113 by 2014 (IADI 2016b, 1). The role and mandate of DISs have been evolving over the years. Consequently, DISs must ensure overall financial robustness to face all challenges, in the most efficient and effective manner.

D. Ognjenovic, *Deposit Insurance Schemes*,
DOI 10.1007/978-3-319-51143-6_1

This chapter explores the differences among DISs, important historical developments, different DIS models, significance of the Federal Deposit Insurance Corporation (FDIC) and the current role of the DIS within the financial stability safety net and in the bank resolution process.

1.2 What Is Deposit Insurance

Deposit insurance is a legally established and recognized system, an explicit protection of selected categories of deposits of eligible depositors, deposited with a bank, up to the prescribed amount, in case of their unavailability or bank failure. In most jurisdictions, the trigger for the deposit insurance authority's liability to execute a payout to depositors is a formal recognition of the bank's failure through some form of insolvency proceedings or resolution process.

However, sometimes insolvency proceedings occur having met certain formal preconditions which could take time and/or which judicial authorities might have the right to challenge and overrule the decision of the bank's supervisory authority on bank failure, prolonging the formal declaration of the insurance event. In such circumstances, depositors may become upset when they don't have access to their money due to legal intricacies. Therefore, over the years authorities have intended to modify and accelerate the trigger for deposit insurance, thus enabling depositors to have a fast access to their deposits.

The European Union (EU) deposit insurance regulatory framework, by Directive 2014/49/EU of the European Parliament and of the Council of 16 April 2014 on deposit guarantee schemes (DGSD), is based on the principle of 'unavailability of deposits', which obliges national DISs to execute a payout even if the bank is still formally operating and does not necessarily have severe insolvency issues, upon the declaration of unavailability of deposits by the relevant administrative authority or a ruling by a judicial authority (Directive 2014/49/EU 2014, L 173/157). Consequently, if a bank is still operating, payout of unavailable insured deposits by the deposit insurance authority may create a number of legal challenges. Therefore, jurisdictions tend to prescribe simultaneous occurrence of 'unavailability' of deposits and 'formal failure and closure' of a bank.

Definitions of deposit insurance have been evolving over time, mostly due to numerous varieties of deposit insurance models existing nowadays and natural evolution of DISs.

Some (Kyei 1995, 6) identify two types of deposit insurance:

(i) explicit guarantee where formal deposit protection arrangement exists and
(ii) implicit guarantee where it is taken for granted, mostly based on past experience, where the government is bound to take steps and protect the banking system and depositors who deposited their money in banks.

Based on the choices how to establish deposit insurance (Garcia 1999, 4) a DIS may be classified into a maximum of six categories:

(i) an explicit denial of protection,
(ii) legal priority of depositors' claims during liquidation
(iii) ambiguity regarding coverage,
(iv) implicit guarantee,
(v) explicit limited coverage and
(vi) full explicit guarantee (blanket guarantee).

For many years New Zealand was one of two countries in the world (along with Argentina) that explicitly denied deposit insurance. However, due to the latest international financial crisis, in October 2008, New Zealand authorities responded with a temporary introduction of a DIS which expired in December 2011 (Treasury 2011, 1). During the three-year period, 72 banks were members of the established scheme introduced under the Public Finance Act and depositors of nine failed banks were compensated. In New Zealand, there are still ongoing discussions on the pros and cons of the establishment of a permanent DIS; however, at present, the government has made a decision against it. As such, New Zealand's view on the role of deposit insurance in the financial stability is specific.

Before 1979, deposits in Argentinean banks were unconditionally guaranteed by the government. An explicit DIS was introduced by, at that time, the military government as an optional scheme for private banks. In 1991, an explicit DIS in Argentina was abolished and 'replaced' by a more stringent and transparent supervision. However, in 1995 the DIS was re-established and since then it has existed in the form of an explicit DIS (Torre 2000, 3–6).

Australia, similar to the neighboring New Zealand, had not introduced deposit insurance until the financial crisis in 2008. Before that, depositors were protected through the preferential priority claim on the assets of a failed authorized deposit-taking institution. Several smaller banks failed during that period, so depositors did not suffer any financial loss, nor their confidence faded. However, as a consequence of the international financial crisis, the Australian Government introduced a DIS with a temporary guarantee of AUD 1 million per person, which was decreased to AUD 250,000 in February 2012 (Government 2008, 1). Australian authorities, contrary to New Zealand's, did not abolish the DIS.

Most countries with an established DIS have improved its legal and operational features over time, usually through broadening of the mandate and powers and strengthening of the DIS role within the financial safety net. Contrary to them, Hungary took a different path and decreased the power of the established DIS from the bank resolution fund with the least cost mandate to a simple paybox DIS (NDIF 2005, 4).

Although implicit deposit insurance as well as explicit blanket guarantee are sometimes classified as DISs, the modern definition of a deposit insurance rather refers to an explicit DIS, which is established by the law with a prescribed coverage level and other rules. For that reason, throughout this book, whenever we discuss the DIS, we have in mind the explicit DIS.

1.2.1 Diversity of Terminology

Academics and practitioners use numerous synonyms for specific terms related to deposit insurance, mostly as a result of linguistic and legal peculiarities of different countries, as well as due to the translation of

English terms and definitions into local languages and vice versa. For example, the terms 'deposit insurance', 'deposit protection' and 'deposit guarantee' are widely used as synonyms, although the terms 'insurance' and 'guarantee' are not synonymous. Another good example is that the terms 'insurance premium', 'insurance fee' and 'insurance contribution' are also used as synonymous.

Inconsistent usage of terminology throughout documents and papers can create confusion, misunderstanding and misinterpretation.

The American deposit insurer, the famous FDIC, has the longest deposit insurance institutional existence and experience and is often used as a role model for other countries when introducing or redesigning a DIS. Many authorities consult the FDIC legal documents and policy papers when looking for problem solutions. However, the legal system and practice in the United States differ from legal systems, infrastructure and practice in Europe and in other countries. A very common practice of 'copy-paste' laws results in a number of issues when the deposit insurance is implemented and in case of a bank failure, due to the fact that the law with copied and directly translated text on deposit insurance did not fit into the local legal framework properly.

The International Association of Deposit Insurers (IADI) created and published a glossary of deposit insurance terms (IADI 2016a, 1).

Core Principles for Effective Deposit Insurance (Core Principles), developed by the IADI, in collaboration with Basel Committee for Banking Supervision (BCBS), provide a list of some key terms. Nevertheless, some important definitions are still missing (IADI 2014, 8–10). One such example of a missing definition is the term 'deposit insurance fund(s)'. Core Principles provided a definition of the target fund size, which is derived from the term 'deposit insurance fund' (DIF). Similarly, IADI's glossary also does not provide a definition of the DIF. Such an important term should be clearly defined as it refers to other important topics.

DGSD provides a list of key terms with definitions used in the main text of the document. These terms somewhat deviate from the terminology used internationally, without clear reasons for the creation of new expressions for terms that have been used all over the world for many years.

Another confusing term which creates a lot of misunderstanding is 'bank resolution'. This term does not even have one single meaning. What is bank resolution actually? Some jurisdictions define bank resolution as a method of closure of the bank, while for the European Union member countries 'bank resolution' is a much more complex term used for actions on a failing bank based on public interest, where the bank, although being close to failure, may survive and continue operation.

How does bank resolution relate to deposit insurance? The most recent international financial crisis urged countries to use ad hoc solutions and modify the existing tools and methods for which sometimes the legal framework did not exist at the time of intervention. Deposit insurance has become closer and more interrelated to bank resolution than ever. The European Union, in its attempt to unify methodology and procedures, created a specific toolkit for dealing with bank failures, as a consequence of severe banking crisis in its member countries when the existing resolution mechanisms did not work or were very costly and adopted Directive 2014/59/EU of the European Parliament and of the Council of 15 May 2014 establishing a framework for the recovery and resolution of credit institutions and investment firms (BRRD) (Directive 2014/59/EU 2014, L 173/190-348).

1.2.2 Implicit Deposit Insurance

Some authors (Demirguc-Kunt et al. 2008, 3) argue that every country offers implicit deposit insurance regardless of how vigorously it denies it and that the adoption of an explicit DIS does not eliminate an implicit guarantee. This statement could be confirmed only if every country experienced bank failure where authorities never allowed their citizens to suffer losses of unpaid deposits.

The main characteristic of an implicit deposit insurance is the absence of a law and other rules related to deposit insurance. Depositors assume that their deposits are protected either because nobody told them differently or because the government intervened in a similar manner in the past. Governments usually prevent bank failure offering assisted financial support and restore its operation either by bailing out the bank in some way or by 'bailing out deposits' if the bank fails, enabling payout of deposits from the budget or transferring deposits into another healthy bank. These solutions are mostly decided on an ad hoc basis, in order to preserve public confidence and social welfare, and to prevent severe damage to the financial system of the country.

Another characteristic of the implicit deposit insurance is that there is no procedure for the compensation of deposits. If there is an implicit assumption of a DIS, the national government may undertake inconsistent actions and apply different rules in respective bank failure cases in order to make deposits available to depositors, such as, for example, when assisting the transfer of deposits onto another healthy bank in full or limited amount, to recapitalize the bank with budgetary resources or to introduce moratorium on deposits for a limited period of time and cover the bank's losses and buy the bank's assets. However, these actions do not guarantee the standard approach of the government's intervention. Any bank in the future may be allowed to fail where depositors would have to claim their deposits through normal insolvency proceedings.

However, all these different actions and attempts may create uncertainty and lead to unequal and preferential treatments for different categories of depositors (small versus large depositors, individuals' versus legal entities' deposits) which are not known from the beginning. Depositors may have high expectations of assumed protection based on past experiences, and their disappointment may lead to severe bank run if the news on bank failure leaks out.

It may be argued that actions taken by governments are impulsive acts in order to maintain financial, social or political stability, when no explicit DIS had been established. Depositors do not know in advance whether they will suffer losses in case of bank failure. In addition, there are no guarantees that the government will intervene every time, as there is no legal obligation for a deposit insurance. Any form of protection depends on the government's free will (and financial resources).

Sometimes, the government might even wish to interfere, but fiscal implications would be too high. Depositors, in turn, may feel much more vulnerable compared to the limited explicit deposit insurance.

Clearly, without an established DIS, there are no available financial resources ensured and preserved for the purpose of payout. Banks don't fail according to a predetermined schedule so that the government may ensure sufficient funds in the budget and intervene when needed.

Regular government interventions in cases of bank failures are not in line with the postulates of modern economies. Today, governments' interventions are justified in extraordinary and isolated cases, as a last resort, only when the entire banking system is jeopardized in times of financial crisis and when all private solutions have already been exhausted.

If implicit deposit insurance exists, it may lead to a moral hazard where bank owners and management are relaxed and eager to take higher risks as the government will intervene with financial assistance to a bank if it faces liquidity or solvency issues.

As a financial stability measure, implicit deposit insurance was more dominant in developing countries, countries with no historical bank failures and countries with the dominant state ownership of banks.

1.2.3 Unlimited (Blanket) Explicit Guarantee

Blanket guarantee is a temporary or a permanent scheme or a policy measure where deposits are protected in full, that is, in an unlimited amount and scope, and such arrangement is explicitly stated in the legislation in the form of either a law or a government decision. Nowadays, blanket guarantee is considered as rather an 'anti-crisis' measure than a type of a DIS.

Over the years, national authorities have used this measure in times of financial crisis in order to stabilize deposits' withdrawal and prevent a run on healthy banks (Laeven and Valencia 2008, 5).

Blanket guarantee can increase moral hazard, and it is not easy to remove the measure once the financial system stabilizes. If the moment chosen for the removal of a blanket guarantee is not right, depositors may again fear for their deposits.

In addition, this measure is a type of an offset to bank failure due to the fact that if a bank failed during the explicit blanket guarantee regime, it would transform from an only declarative 'blanket' protection into a full financial protection. Therefore, if a blanket guarantee is introduced, banks usually don't fail. Its main purpose is to 'stabilize' the shaken confidence of depositors. It may also be used in support of the rehabilitation process of large systemic banks.

In autumn 2008, as a response to the international financial crisis, the following countries introduced an unlimited explicit guarantee on a temporary basis: Austria, Australia, Denmark, Germany, Hong Kong, China, Ireland, Iceland and the Slovak Republic (Schich 2008, 18). Some of them, such as Ireland, announced the duration of an unlimited blanket guarantee while other countries did not specify it, allowing a certain level of flexibility to assess the most appropriate timing for its abolishment.

In addition, the following countries used a blanket guarantee on a bank-selected basis, at a certain point of time when resolving individual banks: Chile, the Czech Republic, the Dominican Republic, Lithuania, Paraguay and the United Kingdom (in a well-known case of the failed Northern Rock, in 2007) (Laeven and Valencia 2008, 22).

However, blanket guarantee has a strong stabilizing power and depositors are given the assurance that they will not suffer any losses. It is valuable as long as the government 'fulfills' its promises. If the government announces a blanket guarantee and, at the same time, depositors suffer losses when the bank fails, it may be challenging to restore the lost confidence any time in the future.

In a way, blanket guarantee will be a successful measure as long as depositors have confidence in the government that is behind the guarantee of their deposits. Similarly, if a DIS is established as the public DIS and associated with the government, depositors will trust the explicit DIS as much as they trust or distrust the government.

Blanket guarantee as a stability measure has not always been successful. There are arguments on blanket guarantee failure to improve the public confidence despite significant fiscal costs (Honohan and Klingebeil 2003, 1550).

In addition, blanket guarantee, as a measure of financial stability, is successful only if credible. Blanket guarantee will not restore depositors' confidence in cases where fiscal policy is unsustainable or if the government lacks credibility (Laeven and Valencia 2008, 5).

Clearly, it should be used as a breathing device prior to the severe deterioration of market conditions. If used in combination with liquidity support, when market conditions already worsen, blanket guarantee can only increase fiscal costs and fail in restoring depositors' confidence.

More specifically, blanket guarantee is unsuccessful in reversing the flow of foreign liabilities.

Either as a consequence of the spread of the international crisis or as an internal financial sector meltdown, a number of countries introduced a blanket guarantee as a stability measure in the period from 1992 to 2000 as a part of an overall stability package, at substantial fiscal costs. Among them Indonesia, Japan and Ecuador are identified as countries where the blanket guarantee measure was not 'successful' (Laeven and Valencia 2008, 8).

The credibility of the blanket deposit guarantee depends on the strength of the government's fiscal position, size of the government's balance sheet related to the banking system's balance sheet and on its ability to access international capital markets (Moody's 2008, 24). Whenever blanket guarantee was not credible, authorities had to announce deposit freezing in order to stop the run on banks.

1.2.3.1 'Blanket Guarantee' in the Former Socialist Federal Republic of Yugoslavia, Ljubljanska Banka Case

Before 1991, a specific type of unlimited explicit guarantee existed in the former Socialist Federal Republic of Yugoslavia (SFRY). Explicit unlimited guarantee was 'declared' through a uniformed printed statement on the last page of citizens' savings books with the following text: 'Deposits are guaranteed by the Socialist Federal Republic of Yugoslavia'. This was the perfect example of an explicit unlimited guarantee for citizens' deposits but the guarantee itself was 'blanket' and coverage was not specified. At the same time, bank failure concept was unknown.

In the former SFRY, an explicit government guarantee for foreign exchange deposits was introduced with legal amendments of the *Law on Foreign Exchange Operations*, originating in 1969. The Republic of Croatia also kept the same wording transposing the Federal law into the Republican 'Law on Foreign Exchange System, Operations and Exchange of Gold', back in 1993. A similar guarantee clause was put in the savings contracts when citizens were opening the foreign exchange account and deposited money. The level of domestic savings was negligent at that time due to several devaluations of the national currency over the years; therefore, the 'guarantee' was important for foreign exchange savings.

However, neither of the two laws prescribed any details on how the guarantee would be exercised. At that time, it was sufficient to announce that the government was 'backing up' banks and guaranteeing the deposits. Moreover, banks were in a so-called 'social ownership' and until then not a single bank had failed.

Therefore, the first test for an explicit DIS was in 1991 when SFRY ceased to exist and split into six new countries (Serbia, Croatia, Slovenia, Bosnia and Herzegovina, Macedonia and Montenegro) with inherited financial sectors, laws and problems.

The Slovenian-based Ljubljanska banka case showed all weaknesses of the existing explicit blanket guarantee, although at the end the bank did not formally fail at all.

The dispute over Ljubljanska banka between Slovenia and Croatia was resolved only in 2014 through European Court for Human Rights' Grand Chamber's Ruling (ECHR 2014, 39) stating that there had been a violation of Article 1 of Protocol No. 1 (protection of property) of the European Convention on Human Rights (no one shall be deprived of enjoying their possessions and property) and a violation of Article 13 by Slovenia, under which Slovenia was responsible for Ljubljanska banka's debts toward depositors.

Depositors were requested to submit their claims directly to the Slovenian Succession Fund starting from December 1st 2015 until the end of 2017 (SRSN 2015). After the verification process applicants will be entitled to receive their money within three months since the submission of applications. The Slovenian government will repay more than €385 million to more than 230,000 depositors from Croatia and Bosnia who claimed more than €260 million in principal (Reuters 2015). Depositors were also entitled to an interest rate (for 1991 the contracted interest rate, for 1992 interest rate at 6 percent and from 1993 onward interest rate at 1.79 percent).

But, how did all of it start?

Ljubljanska banka is a Slovenian-based bank which had over the years grown into one of the largest banks operating in SFRY with branches in all SFRY republics. Its Croatian branch was established in Zagreb in 1969 with limited operation. The branch received the legal entity status in

1978 when its operations expanded. Until 1992 (after the split of SFRY), the bank had more than 2,000 employees in Croatia in 3 branches and 30 premises.

The Slovenian court overturned the status of a legal entity of the Croatian branch of the bank already in December 1989 (before the breakup of SFRY), based on the bank's internal acts. The Croatian part of the bank continued its operations based on special instructions approved by the Croatian National Bank which allowed full business activities such as collection of deposits and approval of loans. The Croatian National Bank withdrew its instructions for Ljubljanska banka—the Main Branch Zagreb operation—when its business account was closed down. Slovenia was the first former SFRY country which declared independence in June 1991. Soon (in 1994) the first Constitutional Act was passed whereby Slovenia declared the guarantee only for savings in Slovenian banks deposited in Slovenia (thus only for the Slovenian portion of Ljubljanska banka's deposits), without mentioning who guarantees for the savings of depositors deposited in the same bank on the territories of other Republics. Ljubljanska banka's business account was functional in Croatia through accounts in Slovenia until 1994.

Many Croatian, Serbian and Bosnian citizens initiated legal proceedings against the bank at their national courts due to the denial of their depositors' status and lack of reactions from both the bank and the Slovenian government.

In July 1994, Slovenia amended the Constitutional Act whereby Nova Ljubljanska banka was established; that is, Ljubljanska banka was broken up into the 'old' and 'new' bank (concept also known as the 'bridge bank' or 'good and bad bank'). Old Ljubljanska banka kept the liabilities of the former bank, but assets were transferred into Nova Ljubljanska banka.

In 1991, when Croatia declared its independence, it also declared that all foreign exchange savings deposited in Croatian banks became a public debt of the Republic of Croatia.

At that time, Croatian depositors held approximately DEM 900 mil (i.e. €450 mil) in Ljubljanska banka's Main Branch in Zagreb. Ljubljanska banka had a legal status of a Slovenian, not a Croatian, bank and deposits deposited at its Main Branch in Zagreb were not considered as deposits deposited in a Croatian bank.

Therefore, Croatian depositors of the Slovenian Ljubljanska banka who deposited their money in Croatian branches found themselves in a 'legal limbo' because their deposits were guaranteed neither by the Republic of Croatia, nor by the Republic of Slovenia. Both countries used the so-called 'territorial principle' of guarantee, guaranteeing only for its own banks on its own territory, not on the territory of other countries.

However, the Republic of Croatia, realizing the scope of possible problems and potential losses for its citizens, enacted a law which allowed the Croatian citizens to transfer their claims from Ljubljanska banka's Main Branch Zagreb into Croatian banks, within a limited period of time. Such transfer was not automatic, but rather voluntary, and each depositor of Ljubljanska banka had a choice to do it or to retain the status quo and hope that Slovenia would change its laws and mind and allow access to the deposits.

Deposits of those depositors which were transferred into Croatian banks automatically fell into the category of the Croatian public debt (due in ten years with a 5 per cent interest rate, paid in two annual installments).

Depositors had a difficult choice to make. Ljubljanska banka was a big bank with a long history and Croatia was a newly established state, with a huge public debt and a challenging economic situation as a result of the recent war with Serbia. Therefore, many depositors, although Croatian citizens, were reluctant to transfer their deposits from Ljubljanska banka into Croatian banks, based only on the promise made by the Croatian Government that their deposits would be available in ten years' period of time.

Croatian banks were liquid at that time, and soon several of them decided to 'release' the transferred foreign exchange deposits to depositors and convert them into 'new foreign exchange savings', that is, regular savings accounts. That was a 'win–win' situation and a good deal for banks that were offering the conversion. They were buying the 'public debt' from depositors, at the same time 'de-freezing' deposits and allowing depositors the same interest rate that was offered to their regular customers. Banks were earning money on the difference on the interest rates offered by the Croatian government (5 per cent annually) and the interest rates they offered to depositors (which were lower than 5 per cent annually). As a result of conversion, depositors could dispose freely of the total deposit amount (which would otherwise be at their disposal in ten years' time).

Soon, all other banks followed the initial idea, after realizing that depositors were not withdrawing deposits.

Public debt on old foreign exchange savings soon became a tradable good and the 'owner' could use it to buy real estate. Therefore, many, but not all, depositors decided to transfer their foreign exchange savings into Croatian banks, in the amount of DEM 544.4 mil, while others were reluctant to do it. As a result, more than 130,000 Croatian depositors had claims against Ljubljanska banka for their foreign exchange deposits until final decision was reached. As a consequence of the amended Slovenian Constitutional Act, chances of being repaid were reducing more and more over time. The Republic of Croatia decided to assist its citizens in their attempts to obtain deposits from Ljubljanska banka. Therefore, in its bilateral contacts with Slovenia, Croatia always raised the issue of Ljubljanska banka's depositors and ministers of finance of the two countries and governors of central banks regularly held meetings, however without significant improvements and a satisfactory solution for the Croatian depositors for years.

Finally, based on the former SFRY states' Succession Agreement (UN 2001, 35), all depositors' claims from banks from other republics were subject to succession negotiations. Succession discussions and negotiations were slow and without a quick result for depositors who, at that moment, had already been waiting for years. During its accession to the European Union, Croatia again raised the issue of depositors of Ljubljanska banka as a political pressure on Slovenia, but as a consequence and a counterpolitical measure Slovenia did not want to ratify the Croatian succession.

By the end of 2015, Croatian citizens, depositors of Ljubljanska banka's Main Branch Zagreb, had not received compensation of their foreign exchange savings deposited in the bank prior to 1991, that is, for 24 years. The first payout of unavailable deposits in Ljubljanska banka's Main Branch Zagreb occurred in spring 2016.

This case has taught us many important lessons, though one of the most important lessons learned is that neither implicit assumptions that the government protects savings in banks nor explicit and blanket guarantee provided by the government can be taken for granted as an absolute guarantee. Unclear and complex legal solutions always lead to problems in practice. In this case, what had started as an explicit government guarantee turned into a political issue between the two countries and an international legal battle lasting for too many years.

1.2.4 Explicit Deposit Insurance

Explicit DIS is a legally established deposit insurance with a prescribed coverage amount and details on the responsible deposit insurance authority, its mandate and financing. It is approved by the law (either by 'lex specialis', that is, a separate act on DIS), or as a part of another senior law such as, for example, the Banking Act or is based on other legal grounds (e.g. a government decree). In other words, there is an established system in place which guarantees, in theory and also in practice, for deposits deposited in banks, in accordance with the uniformed rules and procedures elaborated in national legislation.

Deposit insurance regulatory framework is complementary to the bank supervision and bank resolution, resulting in numerous varieties of the mandate and an institutional setup.

Some national jurisdictions opted for the creation of a comprehensive banking legislation with one law which covers everything related to banks from their establishment and licensing through their operation and supervision to their closure and resolution, including deposit insurance.

In some countries several laws regulate the subject of deposit insurance (for instance one law regulates DIS and another law usually regulates the establishment and operation of deposit insurance authority).

Most of the countries opted for 'lex specialis' law on deposit insurance where one separate law regulates the deposit insurance issue, including characteristics of the system and authority entrusted with the deposit insurance mandate. In general, this might be the most appropriate option, although authorities will take into account the national legislative practice when choosing the right legal model.

Whatever is the case, the legal act should define main elements of the DIS so that anyone who reads the law has a clear idea what is regulated, how, by whom and how much. The general public will be aware of the established DIS and how the system works and affects them. Accompanying subordinate legislation should define the remaining details. The law on DIS should provide clear definitions and prescribe at minimum key features of the DIS so that the reader may be able to understand the characteristics of the DIS and the level and scope of the depositors' protection.

More specifically, the law on DIS in any country should contain clear provisions on DIS's legal structure, governance, mandate, coverage amount and scope, payout trigger, legal deadlines and procedures, powers and responsibilities of DIS's governing bodies, accounting and reporting requirements, sources of funding (regular, special, extraordinary), cooperation and information exchange with the banking regulator and so on.

Moreover, the law would need to indicate the date of effectiveness of the deposit insurance, as well as provide the principles for review and increase of deposit insurance coverage level. The law should be structured in a logical way, in line with the national legislative and nomothetic rules, and in a transparent way.

Some jurisdictions prefer to prescribe rather general provisions of a law as the procedure for legal amendments is too long and too complex. However, in such cases, it should be ensured not to make changes in the subordinate legislation too often and without justification. Other jurisdictions opt to prescribe all details in the law on DIS. The best option is somewhere in the middle.

A deposit insurance authority will, in addition to the law on DIS, develop and approve internal acts, which may be classified as general subordinate legislation and technical subordinate legislation. The statute (charter) of the deposit insurance authority, rules on internal organization, code of ethics, rules on board's meetings and similar subordinate legislation are of general nature and not only associated to deposit insurance authority.

Other, more 'technical' subordinate legislation may be in the form of guidelines, policy, rules, procedures, decrees, orders and instructions which will depend on the legal system of the country. Some of this subordinate legislation is approved by the board and some is within the purview of the management. Usually, if the subordinate legislation is obligatory for the third party (e.g. banks), it must be approved by the board. If the subordinate legislation prescribes or instructs something that is relevant only to the staff of the deposit insurance authority, such laws are developed and approved by the management. Specifics of each country shall be taken into account when developing the subordinate legislation. Subordinate legislation will at minimum regulate details on banks' reporting and other information submission, investment rules and procedures, payout process, emergency funding, budgeting, providing information to the public and so on.

1.3 DataBases on DIS

Although over the past years many authors have researched and collected information on the established DISs, the research was random and irregular. Results of such research were non-consistent or non-comparable with each other or over time, although they were obtained by the same authors. The reason for this is owed to the fact that the collection of data was not a primary aim but rather a secondary one to writing the paper on DIS. Another reason is the development of deposit insurance over time.

In addition, lack of transparent information available to research resulted in the collection of data via questionnaires where answers were provided by the questioned national authorities. Even today many DISs lack transparency and don't publish even basic information in a publicly available form. Due to the lack of uniformed terminology or misunderstanding and misinterpretations, answers were submitted in good faith, but they were not always accurate, thus not sufficiently reliable.

A few decades ago, deposit insurance was not that much of an intriguing topic and papers written on deposit insurance were short, simple and often based on a brief conclusion of a simplified comparison of different DISs and their features. Therefore, in the past, databases were a rather spontaneous work of deposit insurance enthusiastic researchers and not the result of a strategic decision to create comparable and useful information base on DISs.

In the past, when there were few established explicit DISs, authors could easily detect them and compare their main features. In 2000s, the number of explicit DISs grew rapidly and it was not always easy to classify them properly.

As a result, there are only two comprehensive systemically collected databases on DIS, one in 2003 (Demirguc-Kunt et al. 2005, 1–81) and another in 2014 (Demirguc-Kunt et al. 2014, 1–43), but the volume of the collected data is not the same. As a result, there are some inconsistencies in the collected data regarding the existing DISs or their classifications and so on. Nevertheless, both databases are the most reliable source of collected information on the existing DIS (Fig. 1.1).

Countries pioneering in the establishment of DIS were Czechoslovakia (1924), the United States (1934), Cuba (1952), Turkey (1960), Norway, India (1961) and the Philippines (1963) (McCharty 1980).

By 1980 there were only 13 countries with an established explicit DIS (in alphabetical order): Argentina, Canada, Chile, Germany, India, Japan, Lebanon, the Netherlands, the Philippines, Spain, Turkey, the United Kingdom and the United States.

By 1995 there were already 47 explicit DISs around the world (Kyei 1995, 3).

Based on end 2013 data from 190 countries around the world, 112 countries established an explicit DIS (Demirguc-Kunt et al. 2014, 32), although in accordance with IADI, there were 113 countries with an

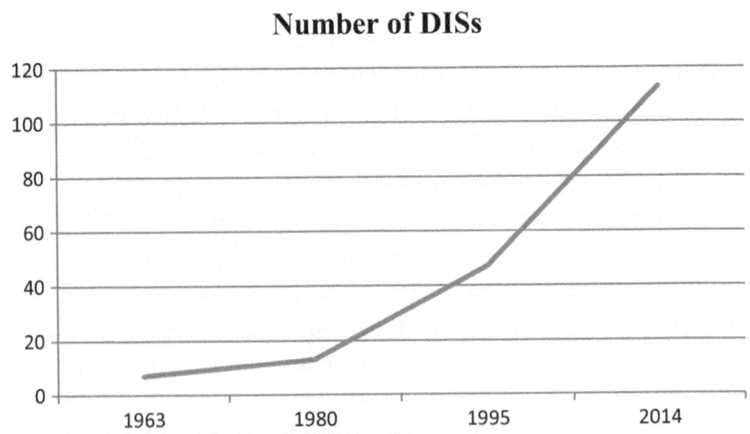

Fig. 1.1 Development of explicit DISs

established explicit DIS by 2014 and 125 countries with an either explicit or implicit DIS by 2016 (IADI 2016c, 1).

1.4 Origins of DIS

It is interesting that the idea of deposit insurance, although developed in the United States in the nineteenth century, actually originated in China, a country that resisted the introduction of deposit insurance for many years and only by the end of 2014 presented publicly its first draft law on DIS.

Chinese merchants from the port city of Canton, called Hongs, who were licensed for foreign trade in exchange for security duties, had experienced problems by the end of the eighteenth century and were not able to pay their foreign creditors which caused a number of incidents and even some international scandals. The Chinese government interfered and forced the remaining merchant houses to assume collective liability for the foreign debts of their failed colleagues. They did so and over the next ten years they were repaying the accrued debts. As a result, the 'Canton Guaranty System' (Grant Jr. 2014, 54–138) was introduced in 1780 and had run until 1842 when it collapsed along with the failure of the merchants due to the Opium War.

However, the mutual guaranty system became known outside the Chinese boundaries. At the same time, the development of banking in the United States led to the first banking failure in 1809 and to the banking crisis in the state of New York in 1829 (a hundred years prior to the Great Depression and economic crisis which led to a formal introduction of DIS in the United States and the establishment of the FDIC). At that time, private banks were allowed to print the money, and they did it, sometimes (like it happened to many central banks later) more than they could cover. The reformer Joshua Forman was convinced that the confidence in banks could be restored by the introduction of the 'Safety Plan', that is, bank-obligation insurance program (Grant Jr. 2014, 218–252). The main idea of his plan was for banks to assume collective liability, similarly to the Chinese merchants, to insure banknotes and deposits and to contribute to an insurance fund. In addition, the board of commissioners was granted bank examination powers. Forman also proposed a list of investments for the banks' equity, which was rejected.

From 1831 to 1858 five additional states adopted a similar insurance program for banks: Vermont, Indiana, Michigan, Ohio and Iowa. These insurance programs were closed in 1866 due to the 'free banking' movement and establishment of the national bank system in 1863.

Again, in the period from 1908 to 1930 eight states adopted the deposit insurance programs known as 'deposit guarantee' and even had experience with bank failures. In cases of bank failures, in some states, depositors received interest-bearing certificates with dividends paid from the liquidation of bank's assets. In other states, depositors were repaid in cash. However, those state insurance funds were unable to cope with the first signs of depression in 1921, which resulted in their failure to repay depositors and in the failure of established systems.

1.4.1 Czechoslovakia Gets the Credit as the First Country Ever to Establish a DIS

Although Forman is the one who should be credited for the development of deposit insurance in the United States which led to the establishment of the FDIC a hundred years after and whose role in the historical development of deposit insurance around the globe is huge, Czechoslovakia was actually the first country that established the first DIS on a national level, in 1924 (McCharty 1980, 579–581).

Czechoslovakia, at that time, set up sophisticated credit insurance and DIS with two special funds:

(i) a Special Guarantee Fund was established for the purpose of assisting banks and
(ii) a General Guarantee Fund was established to encourage savings by increasing the safety of deposits and ensuring the best possible development of banking.

At the beginning, two funds were separate and when they incurred losses, the government intervened. The Ministry of Finance administered both funds but banks also had their representatives at the administrative board. Both the government and banks contributed with funds. When banks suffered losses, they were able to obtain financial assistance from the fund, but it was not at no cost. Banks were obliged to implement reorganization and improve their financial condition.

The General Guarantee Fund provided deposit guarantee in banks and savings banks. Member banks had to pay contributions. In addition, the fund also grew through income from investments. The scheme was completely terminated in 1938.

Although there are not many sources on this DIS, it clearly sets the same principles of deposit insurance that still exist in many countries around the world.

In modern times, the Czech Republic established a DIS in 1994 by establishment of Deposit Insurance Fund and Slovakia established a DIS in 1996 as a non-government Deposit Protection Fund, funded exclusively by banks.

1.4.2 Establishment and Role of the FDIC

The FDIC is the 'oldest' and most experienced deposit insurer in the world. It has been evolving and transforming itself since 1934; it has had many ups and downs, experienced grey and glory days, but nevertheless, it has played and still plays one of the most important roles in the global spread of deposit insurance and serves as a role model for the 'ideal deposit insurance'. Many countries study the FDIC and its operation when intending to establish or reorganize the existing DIS.

Although a few other national DISs played a significant role in the development of the deposit insurance, for many deposit insurance experts and practitioners it is the FDIC that must be given credit for the internationalization of DIS. The FDIC symbolizes 'alpha DIS' in the world of financial stability.

The establishment of the FDIC was not a smooth process due to the strong resistance at that time. It was not until the Great Depression that the federal DIS was finally established. On average, more than 600 small rural banks failed every year between 1921 and 1929, but in 1930 that number doubled and finally in 1933 approximately 4,000 banks failed (FDIC 1998, 5). As a result, depositors' confidence was at jeopardy as never before.

In 1933, it took only a 40-minute debate to pass the law known as Emergency Banking Act which was later amended by Section 12B on creation of the FDIC and definition of its duties, organization and functions and limited coverage up to USD 2,500 per each depositor. The scheme was envisaged as temporary but was soon transformed into a permanent one. Officially, it became effective in January 1934 and the FDIC became operational in July 1934.

The scheme was established as mandatory for banks, although banks' membership was conditional. The FDIC examined the banks prior to granting them membership and the main condition was positive solvency. It was a DIS with obligatory-conditional membership.

At the time of establishment of the FDIC, 12,987 banks (90 per cent of all commercial banks) and 214 mutual savings banks (36 per cent of all mutual savings banks) became members of the FDIC and participated in the DIS. As an immediate consequence of the restored public confidence in banks, total deposits increased by USD 7.2 billion which represented a 22 per cent increase (FDIC 1998, 31).

The Treasury contributed to the FDIC with USD 150 mil capital and initial contribution of the banks was set at 1 per cent of insurable deposits. Soon (by July 1934), the coverage amount had been increased up to USD 5,000 per depositor per bank.

The period from 1934 until 1941 was characterized as a great success for the FDIC. During that time 370 banks failed, which incurred losses for the FDIC in the amount of USD 23 mil. However, at end of 1941, the FDIC collected USD 553.5 mil from its member banks, resulting in the coverage ratio of 1.96 per cent (the highest in the FDIC history).

Many argue that the establishment of the FDIC was not the only reason why the banking sector stabilized. At the same time, the attitude of banks and bankers changed since many banks that survived still remembered the times of crisis and were averse to risk taking. In addition, banks had to comply with numerous high supervisory standards and strict prudential norms at that period. All of that jointly resulted in a sound and stable banking sector.

In its historical overview the FDIC called the upcoming period from 1942 until 1970 the period of war and recovery. During the three war years only 28 banks failed. Banks were highly liquid and well capitalized. The FDIC moved its headquarters to Washington DC but also suffered from staff shortages and was unable to fulfil its annual plan of banks' examination. Although the annual growth of loans increased, banks were very conservative all the way until mid-1960s and did not take excessive risks.

The FDIC provides details on the size of the FDIC funds, number of bank failures and development of coverage level in a chronological manner (FDIC 1998, 32–72).

By 1948, the FDIC's funds had grown to more than USD 1 billion and it was then decided to return the initial funding in the amount of USD 150 mil and USD 139 mil, increased by interest, to the Treasury and Federal Reserve Banks, respectively. Despite that fact, the FDIC's financial resources had grown to more than USD 4.4 billion by 1970. The coverage amount had increased gradually several times up to USD 20,000 in the same period.

The period from 1971 until 1991 was called the 'costly evolution'. During that time the FDIC became insolvent in the amount of USD 7 billion. That period was characterized by the foreign exchange and interest rate volatility, higher risk undertakings by banks and a large number of banks on the market, which all contributed to an increased competition and consequently numerous bank failures.

In 1971, the FDIC for the first time used an open-bank assistance tool and provided a loan to a failing bank. Soon, the FDIC granted loans to 130 problem banks. The coverage amount grew to USD 100,000 by 1974. During the 20-year period, more than 1,400 banks failed, which was far less than 1933 records, but banks were much larger and their losses were bigger, resulting in a meltdown of the FDIC's funds (which had grown by USD 18.3 billion by 1987) to insolvency in the amount of USD 7 billion.

A new era that began in 1992 and lasted until 1998 was known as a turmoil period, both for banks and the FDIC. The new legislative changes were introduced in 1991 and one of them was the risk-based premium which replaced the linear premium that was applied in the past. Target coverage ratio of 1.25 per cent was set and the FDIC was due to reach it within 15 years. The FDIC was empowered with prompt corrective actions and an obligation to conduct least cost test and opt for least cost resolution. Too big to fail and systemic risk were defined. The FDIC's borrowing facilities increased from USD 5 billion to USD 30 billion.

Since 1999 until the end of 2014 the FDIC once more went through difficulties. Banks were again in the process of consolidation, which resulted in a larger risk exposure of the FDIC. Many still argue about the FDIC role and its 'usefulness' as well about the overall costs of bank failures and whether the FDIC can handle a 'mega-bank' failure. In 2008, only 25 banks failed in the United States, but in 2009 and 2010 the number of failed banks increased to 140 and 157 respectively. In 2011, the number of failed banks was 92. In 2012 and 2013 only 51 and 24 banks failed respectively (Fig. 1.2).

Today the FDIC employs more than 8,500 employees. It has three main functions:

(i) to insure deposits,
(ii) to protect depositors of insured banks through its supervisory function and

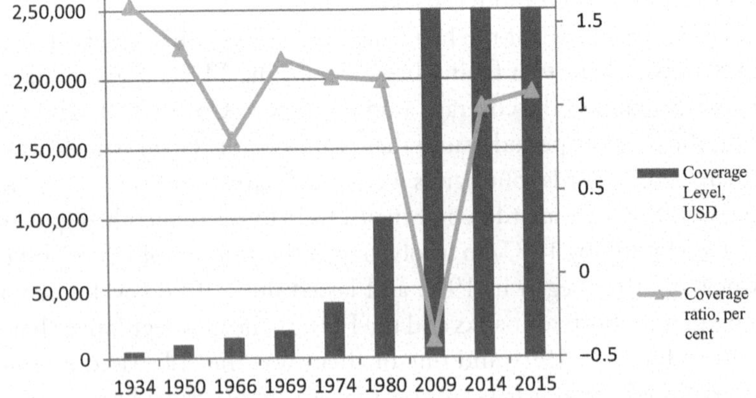

Fig. 1.2 FDIC coverage level and coverage ratio (Source: Data taken from FDIC, Annual Report, Appendices VII 2015, p. 139)

(iii) to resolve failed banks. Deposit insurance is permanently increased to USD 250,000 per depositor.

In the past the FDIC used different resolution tools (including bridge bank and open bank assistance); however, today it uses only two resolution tools (FDIC 2014, 16–20):

(i) Purchase and Assumption and
(ii) Deposit Payout.

Deposit payout is executed only if the FDIC does not receive any bid from solvent banks for purchase and assumption. The FDIC is obliged to comply with the least cost methodology and choose the bidder who offered the better price for the failed bank's assets and liabilities. In addition, the FDIC acts as a receiver (bankruptcy trustee) during the receivership process. As stated in its acts, manuals and guidelines, the primary goals of the resolution process (and primary tasks for the FDIC) are to provide depositors with a timely access to their insured funds and resolve the failing institution in the least costly manner.

The FDIC is informed prior to the formal closure of a bank on the likelihood of a failure of a bank. Such formal notification enables it to conduct due diligence on the potentially failing bank and develop a resolution strategy, analyzing asset and liability composition of the bank, its liquidity, marketability, time and other factors (e.g. potential fraud).

Based on the information gathered and analysis conducted, the FDIC decides how to structure the sale of a failing bank. In order to market the bank, the FDIC sets up the virtual data room and collects the bids from potential acquirers. Bids are compared to costs of liquidation of the bank, that is, to the amount of insured deposits that will be paid if the bank is liquidated. Valuation of bids must end prior to the formal closure of the bank, that is, within 90 days, during which period the FDIC conducts all activities related to the preparation of the resolution of the failing bank.

The finalization of the resolution process is the formal closure of the failing bank when assets and deposits are transferred into the acquiring bank. Depositors automatically become depositors of the acquiring bank

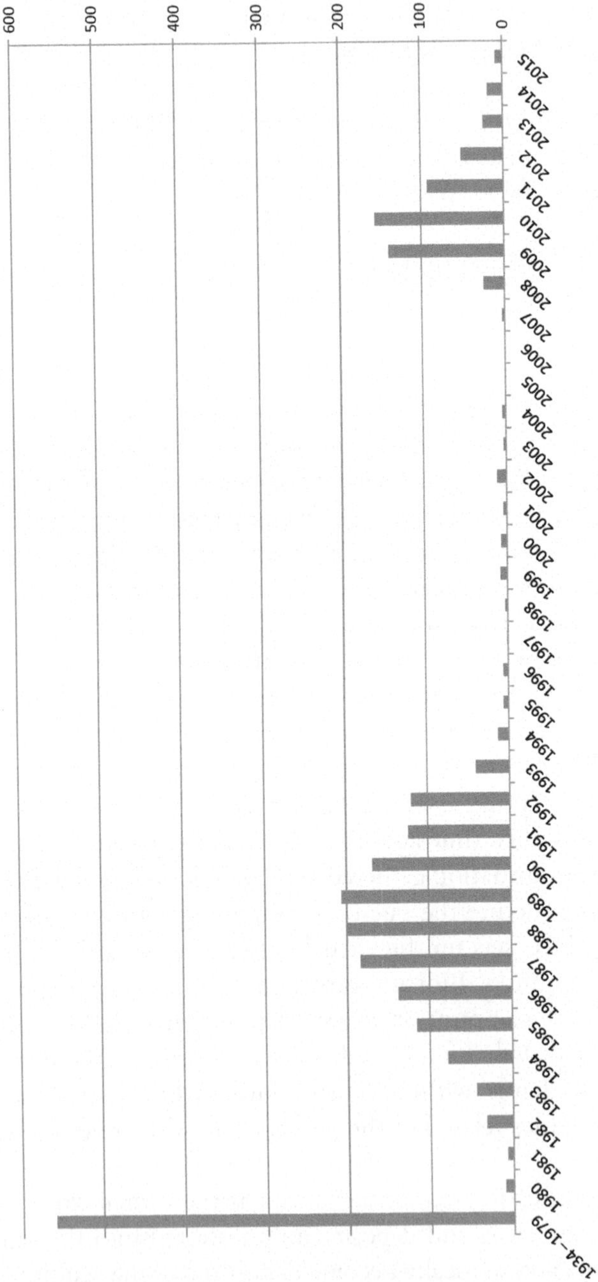

Fig. 1.3 Number of resolved banks by FDIC (Source: Data taken from FDIC, Annual Report, Appendices VII 2015, p. 145)

having uninterrupted access to their deposits. The closure of a failing bank is usually on Friday, allowing the FDIC to finalize everything over the weekend and enabling the acquiring bank to reopen on Monday, as usual.

Purchase and Assumption (P&A) is a resolution tool where a healthy bank purchases some or all assets and some liabilities, including the insured deposits. There are several types of P&A transactions used by the FDIC (2014, 16–20) such as:

(i) Basic Purchase and Assumption,
(ii) Whole Bank Purchase and Assumption,
(iii) Purchase and Assumption with Optional Shared Loss and
(iv) Bridge Bank Purchase and Assumption.

In addition, there are several types of deposit payouts used by the FDIC such as:

(i) Straight Deposit Payoffs where the FDIC mails checks to depositors,
(ii) Insured Deposit Transfer where the FDIC uses payout agent bank and transfers insured deposits to the agent who conducts the payout,
(iii) Deposit Insurance National Bank, established without capitalization, up to two years (Fig. 1.3).

1.5 Deposit Insurance and International Financial Crisis in 2008

Prior to the 2008 international financial crisis, the role of deposit insurance was mainly limited to the individual bank failures and fast and efficient payout of insured deposits in such cases. In some countries (USA, but also in Canada, Turkey, South Korea, Malaysia and a few others) deposit insurance had already played a significant role in contributing to overall financial stability, as a result of painful past experiences with national banking crises in those countries.

In autumn 2008, when the international financial crisis spread all over the world, disturbed depositors were nervously withdrawing their deposits from banks regardless of their financial condition and soundness.

During the financial crisis, 48 jurisdictions enhanced the existing deposit insurance arrangements as part of financial stability measures where 19 jurisdictions declared full depositors' guarantee (i.e. 'blanket guarantee'), 22 jurisdictions increased deposit insurance coverage permanently and seven jurisdictions increased coverage on a temporary basis (IMF&IADI 2010, 3).

Soon after the announcement of measures mostly through increased coverage, depositors were finally convinced that their deposits were protected and it was the moment that stopped further panic and withdrawal of money caused by the fear of financial system meltdown.

Yet, that was not all.

It was just the beginning of initiatives related to policy implications on a more important role deposit insurance could play in supporting financial stability (Hoelscher 2011, 4–10). The European Union enhanced its deposit insurance legal framework with the development of new DGSD that was adopted and published in the first half of 2014, after several years of discussions and negotiations, and it is considered to be an important step toward the creation of a single banking union in Europe.

In addition, countries with explicit public deposit insurance have experienced consistently lower declines in deposit growth during the 2008 crisis period (Han and Melecky 2013, 9).

Deposit insurance, by its definition, contributes to financial stability and supports other safety net pillars, although in the past that role was not sufficiently validated. Its primary focus was to protect small depositors in case of an individual bank failure through fast and efficient deposit payout. Discussions on deposit insurance tasks and what it can and can't do differ substantially in the period prior to and following 2008 international financial crisis.

Since autumn 2008, when the financial stability of many countries was jeopardized due to the spread of bank failures, regardless of the soundness of banks, deposit insurance was one of the key elements that contributed to an enhanced financial stability.

Due to the changed role of deposit insurance, many of its design features have changed largely, as well. There is a shift in the mandate of paybox DIS toward paybox plus DIS where DIFs are used for financing bank resolution as an alternative to deposit payout.

The coverage amount is set differently after the crisis compared to the period before 2008. Deposit insurers tend to shorten the payout timeframe as much as possible. Deposit insurers and bank supervisors formalized their relationship and become 'partners' in an effort to enhance national financial safety nets. And, more than anything else, funding became standardized with a focus on establishing the target fund size and building a more robust funding base.

Traditionally, deposit insurance was a guarantor of those depositors (less sophisticated savers and their 'small deposits') who were not able to fully understand banking risks. It had certain elements of social protection, as well. Banks operate by assuming different levels of risks. Even in a sound financial system with a strong prudential framework, banks fail from time to time.

It was always challenging to determine the line that divides 'small deposits' from 'large deposits' and to establish an optimal coverage level. In other words, authorities of many countries often asked themselves the same question—how 'small is the small' when determining the coverage level?!

The appropriate and optimal level of coverage amount was one of the key elements of prudent deposit insurance. Coverage level should not be too small (because it would not be sufficiently prudent) or too big (to create moral hazard).

For many years the coverage amount was determined in relation to GDP per capita, which was used as a standard benchmark. In the past, it was considered appropriate if the coverage amount was set within one to two times to GDP per capita. If the coverage amount was set below one to GDP per capita, that was considered too low. If the coverage amount was lower than expected, depositors would fear a lack of actual protection and, despite the existence of deposit insurance, their losses would still be high in case of bank failure.

Conversely, when the deposit insurance coverage amount was set to more than two times to GDP per capita, it was considered as too generous, which could have triggered a riskier attitude of bank managers who were ready to grant loans more generously knowing that depositors would be paid from the DIFs.

In autumn 2008, as a reaction to the crisis, national jurisdictions spontaneously increased the coverage amounts, almost as ad hoc reactions, disregarding the ratio of coverage level to GDP per capita (Hoelscher 2011, 8–9)

Surprisingly, the measure was successful (it stopped the panic and deposit run on banks) and proved to be justified. Therefore, the whole concept of one to two GDP per capita adequacy of coverage level suddenly became outdated. Not only that the higher coverage did not trigger any moral hazard or riskier banking, but on the contrary, as a surprise to earlier beliefs and theories, the increased coverage actually prevented further deterioration of the crisis and collapses of banks and stabilized the banking systems, in general.

Based on the new rule of thumb for setting the coverage level that was widely accepted, the coverage amount was supposed to protect at least 80 per cent of depositors and 20 per cent of the total amount of insured deposits. This method is known as '80:20 rule' (IADI 2013, 7–8).

During the 2008 crisis, many countries introduced a higher coverage which did not correlate to GDP anymore. The level of GDP per capita was abandoned as the benchmark used for determining the optimal coverage amount. Instead, it became more important what depositors 'felt' was the right protection amount and whether there was a critical mass of depositors that might have felt unprotected if the coverage amount was set too low.

More stringent supervisory measures followed changes in deposit insurance policies and practice, which, in addition, possibly mitigated moral hazard.

In addition to coverage amount, payout time was always a critical DIS feature. Before 2008, in most countries it was accepted to initiate payout of insured deposits within 30 days from an official failure of a bank. At present, most countries tend to shorten the payout time to seven working days or less and invest in developing management information system and pre-failure preparation in order to execute payout as soon as possible without disruption to the payment system.

During the financial crisis, as experience proved, the deposit insurance and its coverage amount became key features for ensuring financial stability. Regardless of a number of other financial stability measures which the financial authorities were undertaking in 2008, such as, for example, asset guarantee and financial assistance to problem banks, it was not until the DISs were enhanced and coverage amount increased that depositors stopped the withdrawal of their deposits. That was a surprise for the policy makers and even for deposit insurers. It was the first time that the financial stability was attributed to deposit insurance and its stabilizing role for the financial system became so vital for its mandate.

It was just the beginning of an overall enhancement of other key features of DIS, and many countries followed that example with amendments to their national laws on deposit insurance by an overall improvement of the legal framework.

On a larger scale, all over the world, the legally prescribed payout time frame was shortened, deposit insurance was given a place in national anti-crisis committees, exchange of information was improved with banking supervisors and, as a consequence, funding arrangements were improved.

Before the latest financial crisis, initial and backup funding was modest, while regular funding was ensured from member banks. After the crisis, funding was revised and extraordinary (backup) funding arrangements were revised and enhanced either in the form of a more explicit backup funding ensured from national governments or in the form of more and more popular standby credit facilities and payment commitments (within the EU).

The reactions of the public were immediate and visible to everybody. From that point on, deposit insurance became recognized as the fourth pillar of the financial safety net (Schich 2008, 4–12).

Some argue (Iwanicz-Drozdowska et al. 2016, 201–219) that only one component of the DIS, that is, the component related to the comfort of increased coverage level, contributed to the financial stability, and that it is only because of the psychological assurance, while the financial capacity of DIS failed to improve at all.

Nevertheless, the empowered DISs must re-confirm and justify their stronger position within the financial safety net and the role that is undertaken in ensuring financial stability through the enhancement of funding.

1.6 Role of DIS in the Safety Net

Deposit insurance is a recognized pillar of the financial safety net protecting both the depositors and the system itself from consequences of a bank failure. It helps building confidence to offset the financial crisis. Although there is no generally accepted definition of the key elements of the financial safety net, sometimes three and sometimes four pillars are defined, but in both cases deposit insurance is the pillar of the financial safety net. However, we may understand that for creating and ensuring public confidence, thus minimizing disruption in the financial system and preventing a bank run, there is a need for an established and efficient DIS, clear rules on lender of last resort, strong prudential regulatory and supervisory framework and efficient bank resolution framework. All four components are interactive and the success of one of them would depend on the success of other three. In other words, if, for instance, supervision is robust, problems in banks will be detected early rather than later, thus resulting in lower costs for deposit insurance if the final result is the failure of a bank. Or if there is only a limited resolution framework in place, supervisors don't have many options how to deal with failing banks.

The strength of the financial safety net depends on the strength of its weakest component. In other words, even if only one component of the safety net is insufficiently strong, the overall safety net will be weak.

National jurisdictions should strive to build and strengthen all four pillars of their safety net simultaneously. It is important to understand that all of them contribute to the same goal.

Therefore, it is necessary to take into account each pillar's individual and overall role within the financial sector. Sometimes the dividing line of responsibilities is not clear and interests can overlap. In cases when governance of institutions is weak, conflict of interest may overpower the ultimate goal of preservation of financial stability.

Institutionally, financial safety net responsibilities are divided among several financial and public authorities. The central bank plays the role of the provider of liquidity support. In addition, in most cases it is also responsible for prudential regulation and banking supervision. Alternatively, prudential regulation and banking supervision may be placed outside the central bank. The Ministry of Finance is a part of the financial stability scheme because the state is the absolute guarantor and often the last resort in the case of bailing out systemically important institutions or in the case of financial crisis. Financial safety net is incomplete without deposit insurance component.

Exchange of information between these entities is important, especially when they need sufficient time to execute the functions. Such cooperation may be more or less formalized, through mutually agreed protocol on the scope and timing of exchanged information. Regular joint meetings facilitate the quality of cooperation.

1.7 (Mis)understanding Bank Resolution (Traditional Approach)

'Bank resolution' is the term which deserves special attention, due to the complexity of the subject, and also due to different interpretations of the definition as well as its application and implementation in national jurisdictions. It is not uncommon that even two experts or practitioners from two different countries are not thinking of the same process when they talk about the bank resolution, although they both agree that the resolution relates to failing or soon failing banks.

One (resident of Europe) under the term *resolution* understands measures undertaken regarding the problem bank or failing bank in order to ensure continuation of bank's main functions, which is in the public interest, and which can result in a recovery of its financial health or closure of some of its parts.

Other (resident of the United States) understands that the resolution of a bank results in the disposal of its assets and eventually the closure of the bank.

Can both of them be right?

There are number of differences between the EU and US bank resolution regimes, such as, for example, the type of banks, resolution authority, whether or not there is a requirement to develop a recovery plan, who develops the resolution plan, the concept of resolution strategy, type of support from the resolution fund and so on (BBVA 2014, 150).

There are no clear lines between bank rehabilitation (remediation), restructuring and resolution, neither in national legislation, nor in literature and especially not in the implemented practice.

The most recent developments in the EU related to the establishment of single resolution mechanisms and adoption of a BRRD also contributed to the need for clarification of what is understood under the term 'bank resolution'.

In order to understand what resolution is, it is important to clarify and differentiate the problem and failing bank. In simple terms, any bank can, during its operation and life cycle, become a problem bank (troubled, distressed) for different reasons, which can be of internal or external nature or due to the bank's non-compliance with prudential norms.

Sometimes national legislation provides a clear definition of a problem bank and lists circumstances when the bank is classified as a problem bank; however, many jurisdictions don't provide such a clear definition.

Nevertheless, supervisors are legally empowered with different tools and mechanisms which can be imposed to a problem bank. Such measures may be in the form of imposed actions or forbearance or combination of the two within the prescribed time frame.

Problem bank may recover its condition if its problems are properly and timely treated. Sometimes problems are only minor and temporary but, in reality, it may also happen that problems, once when they become visible and revealed by supervisors, are already so deep and complex that any financial intervention would only prolong the 'diseased life' of the bank for a short period of time and increase the final financial cost of its death significantly.

Bank can become problematic due to liquidity issues which can turn to insolvency. Bank can become insolvent although the structure of its balance sheet and regular cash inflow do not cause liquidity problems at all. Severe conditions, if not treated for a long time, may result in non-viability of a bank and its eventual failure. Nevertheless, this is not always a rule, nor is the process that simple.

Because of all that, it is not possible to define a problem bank generally without understanding what had caused the problems and how severe these problems are. However, it is not easy to understand the real condition of the bank without a thorough and deep analysis, quantitative and qualitative due diligence, inclusion of financial projections of profitability, solvency and cash flows, in addition to a full understanding of the bank's business model and its comparative advantage on the market.

In other words, problem (distressed, unhealthy) and even failing bank may rehabilitate its condition over time and become a healthy bank again with the use of private or public financial assistance. Similarly, the condition of a problem bank may deteriorate over a short or longer period of time so that it is impossible to re-establish its health and financial stability, resulting in small chances for returning to regular operation.

Financial condition (financial health) of a bank can improve or worsen over time, with or without formal external interventions. Banking authorities (either supervising institution or a specialized resolution authority) may intervene in different phases of the bank's distress with different tools (depending on the national banking legislation), ranging from imposed administrative measures to appointment of a temporary administrator (conservatorship) and replacing bank management, sometimes imposing recapitalization to bank's shareholders (private solutions) or recapitalization of the bank with public financial resources.

The final outcome of interventions over the problem bank may be positive (bank is rehabilitated and/or restructured and continues its operation) or negative (bank is dead and ceased to exist, that is, bank is resolved, disposed of and closed).

Therefore, interventions, including financial assistance with private or public funding, where the final goal and outcome is to recover and rehabilitate the existing bank, may be understood as bank rehabilitation (recovery) where restructuring of its business processes and operations is key for the successful improvement of financial soundness.

However, when banking authorities intervene and apply particular tools with a goal to close down the bank efficiently and without distress for depositors and the financial market, such actions could be called resolution of a failing bank.

Based on this classification, resolution of a bank would result in the end of existence of a bank in its previous legal form, that is, 'death' of a bank. Resolution tools are usually related to the withdrawal of the banking license and closure of the bank, either through legal insolvency proceedings (most likely run by the court) known as bank liquidation or bank bankruptcy or through administrative proceedings known as receivership.

Sometimes, the term 'winding up' is used as well. In reality, the bank will be closed down, its assets will be sold and creditors repaid. Yet, the most important thing is that the bank does not continue its operation as the same legal entity that was licensed and authorized by the supervisor. The difference between liquidation and bankruptcy arises due to different jurisdictions and national legislations which prescribe different legal procedures in the case of liquidation and bankruptcy, persons who are allowed to initiate the process, authority which is responsible for the management and supervision of the procedure and so on. In general, the main difference between liquidation and bankruptcy is related to the assessment of initial conditions of a failing bank.

If there is an assumption that assets may be liquidated (sold) and creditors repaid from the liquidated assets, then liquidation will be initiated and formal liquidator will be appointed. Liquidator can, during the liquidation procedure, determine that the financial distress of the bank is much higher and/or that the real value of the bank's assets is much lower than presented, resulting in the fact that the liquidation process could turn into a bankruptcy procedure in the end.

Bankruptcy will be initiated if it is clear from beginning that the value of assets is much lower than the amount to be repaid to creditors. In addition, any creditor can initiate bankruptcy proceedings, while liquidation can only be initiated by supervisor (regulator) or the bank itself (self-liquidation).

In many countries, both liquidation and bankruptcy proceedings are strict legal insolvency proceedings handled by commercial courts, although in some countries liquidator and bankruptcy trustee may be appointed by other authorities (supervisor, regulator, deposit insurer, resolution authority), or they even share the responsibilities. However, there are many different forms of insolvency proceedings among jurisdictions, though all of them have one similarity—final repayment of creditors from the liquidated bank's assets and closure of the existing legal form of the bank.

In addition to bank closure and often in combination with the bank closure, other resolution tools may be used as well, such as the partial or whole transfer of assets and liabilities into another healthy bank. Such transfer may occur prior to the bank's closure, at which point it is called an open purchase and assumption (open P&A) or after the bank's closure when it is called a closed purchase and assumption (closed P&A). When a partial P&A is applied, the remaining assets and liabilities are then liquidated in a normal closure procedure.

When the failing bank is big, complex and/or of systemic importance for the system and when transfer of assets and liabilities can't be finished in a short prescribed time, assets and liabilities are temporarily transferred into a specialized newly established bank that is called a bridge bank, in order to preserve assets that could be sold later. In the second phase, which usually lasts for a limited amount of time (in most cases up to one year, although some jurisdictions prescribe shorter or longer time frame), assets and liabilities are sold to another healthy bank or a potential investor who acquires the shares of a bridge bank and recapitalizes it, transforming it into a regular bank. A bridge bank is usually established and operated under special legal requirements, which are not the same as for other licensed banks. For example, a bridge bank does not have to comply with all prudential norms and its credit operation and collection of new deposits are often limited.

Many authors define and understand bank resolution regardless of the outcome of the intervention, but rather according to mechanisms and tools that are used. In other words, in many countries, restructuring and recovering of the bank's condition can be understood as a resolution tool, as well.

Some (Scott 2002, 11) classifies resolution mechanisms as liquidation (legal mechanisms which result in the withdrawal of the banking license and closure of the bank), assisted acquisition (business transfer of assets and liabilities, that is, P&A and withdrawal of banking license) and nationalization (the government temporarily assumes ownership of a bank, restructures it and sells at a later phase, banking license is not withdrawn). According to Scott, conservatorship (temporary administration) and suspension (bank holiday) are not a resolution mechanism, but rather interim steps taken by the authorities in order to analyze and understand better the financial condition of the problem (troubled, distressed) bank.

Some (McGuire 2012, 6–10) classify resolution mechanisms as liquidation (closure), conservatorship (temporary administration), P&A and nationalization.

Some (Hoelscher et al. 2006, 15) classify resolution tools as private solutions (mergers and acquisitions, recapitalization and sales) and public solutions (intervention authority, P&A, bridge banks, public sector capital support and liquidation).

Resolution can be defined (Parker 2010, 2) as a decisive action to solve the problems of the bank, where resolution can be conducted as private solutions (recapitalization, sale of bank shares, merger) and assisted solutions (P&A transactions, insured deposit transfer, deposit payout in liquidation).

All the above-mentioned authors are from the United States, and their classifications are based on the FDIC's experience in bank resolutions.

> The FDIC defines resolution as 'the disposition plan for a failed institution, designed to protect insured depositors and minimize the losses to the insurance fund that are expected from covering insured deposits and disposing of the institution's assets. Resolution methods generally include P&A transactions, insured deposit transfers, and straight deposit payoffs. Resolution can also refer to the assistance plan, through open bank assistance, for a failing institution' (FDIC 2014, 37).

Traditional bank resolution process in the United States is divided in two stages:

(i) Resolution stage
(ii) Liquidation stage

The FDIC is informed about the bank's failure officially via a failing bank letter which is the official start of the resolution process lasting up to 100 days. The FDIC then sends its team of specialists to assess the value of the failing bank and its assets and to prepare a resolution plan, conduct the marketing of the bank and collect bids from potential bidders.

Received bids are evaluated on the basis of the least cost principle, after which the resolution method is approved and the bank is formally closed. The FDIC is then appointed as receiver (liquidator, trustee) responsible for the liquidation of the remaining assets. Deposit payout is conducted only when the FDIC does not receive bids for purchase and assumption.

However, there is also a new resolution approach in the United States, regulated by the Dodd-Frank Act, for systemically important financial institutions (SIFIs), over USD 50 billion in assets. This is one of the key differences from the EU BRRD approach where any bank can be resolved or rehabilitated in accordance with the BRRD. There are other differences as well; SIFIs in the United States do not have to develop recovery plans but must develop resolution plans. In Europe, banks must develop recovery plans, yet resolution authority will develop resolution plans. The FDIC is responsible for the resolution of SIFIs, while in the EU these will be national resolution authorities and the Resolution Board for the European Monetary Union.

Core Principles define resolution as 'the disposition plan and process for a non-viable bank'. Such definition clearly states that resolution is the plan and the process undertaken for the failing bank (non-viable bank whose condition will not improve) (IADI 2014, 10). Therefore, IADI defines bank resolution as the 'death process' of a bank.

Further, IADI definition states that resolution may include 'liquidation and depositor reimbursement, transfer and/or sale of assets and liabilities, the establishment of a temporary bridge institution and the write-down or conversion of debt to equity. Resolution may also include the application of procedures under the insolvency law to parts of an entity in resolution, in conjunction with the exercise of resolution powers.'

1.7.1 Deposit Insurance and Bank Resolution

Deposit insurance and bank resolution are complementary pillars of the financial stability safety net in any country. Their mandates may be strictly separated through legal and institutional arrangements, but their tasks are always to preserve financial stability and prevent instability, that is, lack of depositors' confidence, bank run and financial contagion. Even if there are two different legal entities responsible for deposit insurance and bank resolution respectively, their cooperation must be close because there is no clear borderline between the two. Deposit insurance and bank resolution may be combined within one authority where the bigger emphasis may be given to either the deposit insurance or bank resolution.

Historical evidence shows that many countries experienced high costs of bank failures due to the inertia of actions, legal obstacles and ineffective resolution regimes which, at the end, resulted in the transfer of costs into deposit insurance in payouts of insured depositors.

As a result, based on expensive lessons learnt, the established resolution frameworks are ever evolving, empowering the deposit insurance authorities with a stronger role in the resolution process. The trend is, therefore, in favor of the stronger role of the DIS in bank resolution.

There are many varieties how deposit insurance may take part in the bank resolution process and what powers could be given to the deposit insurance authority. A DIS may be involved only in some stages or actively participate in the whole process, even in decision making on resolving a failing bank. However, the role of DIS in the bank resolution process depends on the overall financial net infrastructure and on the role of the bank's supervisory authority in banking resolution process.

Banking crises are cyclical and bank failures are isolated and non-predictable events in the long run. When once 'cleaned' through either insolvency proceedings or some forms of bank resolution and, as a result, when the majority of the banking sector is safe and sound, there is less justification for two specialized institutions. Their tasks may be combined under the same umbrella. Deposit insurance exists even in a stable environment focused on building up its funds and preparing for the isolated individual banking failures. Therefore, it is logical to give some, if not all, resolution powers to deposit insurers.

However, a problem may arise due to the specifics and specialties of expertise required for bank resolution. The knowledge and know-how on bank resolution is built through experience, not ex-cathedra. It often happened that experts, who were involved in bank resolution, changed their profession, worked as auditors or managed the banks instead, for simple reasons such as lack of bank failures.

In many countries, especially smaller ones, resolution powers are even placed within the supervisory authority. If that is the case, the relationship between the supervisor and the deposit insurer may be very complex due to the possible inertia in the exchange of information and lack of collegial cooperation. The relationship sometimes even feeds rivalry between authorities.

Another tricky moment in their division of responsibilities arises due to the costs of resolution. Namely, deposit insurers often argue that costs of bank resolution could and would be lower if the deposit insurance was endowed with resolution power, since supervisors were slow and did not react on time. Supervisors argue that the resolution legal framework and the complexity of problems in a failing bank are limiting factors that influence possible actions and interventions. It is a vicious circle where deposit insurance often pays the bill at the end.

It may be argued further whether roles and activities of deposit insurance and bank resolution should be fully separated or one is a natural complement to the other. Nevertheless, the role of deposit insurance in bank resolution depends on the mandate given to the DIS.

If the mandate of the DIS is narrowed to paybox, then the DIS's role is simple and minimized to the realization of the payout of covered deposits. With the expansion of the DIS mandate, the role of the DIS in bank resolution becomes more important. A DIS involvement may, for example, be limited to financing other resolution methods up to the amount of covered deposits. This is the case if some form of transfer of assets and liabilities from a failing bank takes place, that is, in case of P&A resolution tool. In such arrangement, the deposit insurance authority provides financial resources up to the amount which is necessary that the acquiring healthy bank accepts the covered deposits from the failed bank, which would otherwise be paid in full amount from the DIF. Therefore, a deposit insurance authority must ensure that its cost is lower than the total covered deposits. A DIS will be called a 'loss minimizer' if it is able to select the least cost resolution strategy, without the interference of other safety net players.

The deposit insurance authority may share responsibility on bank resolution with another legal entity, if there are such legal and institutional arrangements in place (e.g. the banking supervisory authority may be responsible for making a decision on bank resolution alone or jointly with the deposit insurance authority and then 'transfer' the responsibility for 'execution' and implementation of the approved resolution process fully or partially to the deposit insurance authority).

A DIS may also assume full responsibility for bank resolution, with the aim to minimize the risks for the system and make all decisions related to the selection of resolution tools in the most cost-effective way. A DIS is called a risk minimizer if it is able to minimize the risks of contagion for the system through proactive, timely interventions in a problem (or failing) bank, with some or full range of supervisory (including prudential) powers and is empowered with a mandate to remove a failed bank from the system in the most efficient and effective way.

In reality, the combinations of powers and mandate to be entrusted with a DIS are numerous. Core Principles advocate for the operational independence of the DIS and for cost effectiveness of the DIFs, assuming that the DIS undertakes a bigger role in bank resolution and has a vote on the usage of DIFs for bank resolution.

If the bank resolution framework is weak and doesn't allow for flexible solutions, decisions made outside of the DIS may affect the operational independence of the DIS and consume DIFs.

An established banking resolution regime should ensure a broad range of resolution tools and instruments at disposal to the resolution authorities. Limited solutions don't provide options and impose greater financial costs.

In addition, when several entities are responsible for the resolution, the legal framework should clearly prescribe their individual objectives and responsibilities with no gaps, overlaps or inconsistencies. A written cooperation agreement or protocol, in the form of a type of memorandum of understanding with details on the formally agreed exchange of information and cooperation, may specify and clarify each individual task and expected activities throughout the whole process.

Core Principles advocate for the least cost principle to be applied, although the wording describing the criteria allows a discretion, stating that one or more of the available resolution methods should allow the flexibility for resolution at a lower cost. In general, if the least cost principle is implemented, the resolution method which is the least costly must be executed. This approach has been successfully implemented by the FDIC for years already, due to the early intervention of the FDIC at a failing bank and due to a large number of banks in the market which may be interested in some form of assumption of the failing bank's assets and liabilities. However, in countries with a smaller number of banks and in case when problems with a failing bank were not detected on time and its financial condition caused depletion of the attractiveness of assets, the number of other banks interested in the purchase of 'what is left' would not be sufficient to successfully execute what could be the least cost resolution option.

Furthermore, resolution procedures shall follow a defined creditor hierarchy where shareholders bear first losses and insured deposits are protected from losses. Depositors should not be discriminated on the basis of their nationality or residence. No court should reverse decisions on the resolution of non-viable banks.

Regardless of the resolution method used, depositors should always have a fast access to their deposits and authorities should have that in mind when designing and implementing the resolution process.

1.7.2 The FDIC's Resolution Tools

The FDIC has never been a paybox DIS and since its establishment it has been given banks' supervisory powers and the role of banks' examiner. Gradually its role expanded to receivership, that is, being responsible for legal activities over failed banks, selling assets and collecting funds in order to pay creditors maximizing the recovery with a clear distinction between its receivership role and deposit insurance role.

The FDIC used different bank resolution tools over time such as open bank assistance, P&A and deposit payout (FDIC 2014, 20–23). Open bank assistance, that is, financial assistance to problem banks, has not been used since 1992 and there are two main resolution tools used at present, such as P&A and deposit payout.

P&A is the most commonly used resolution tool by the FDIC.

Since 1991, the FDIC has been obliged to conduct the least cost test and choose the least cost resolution method. Consequently, it markets the failing bank, collects the bids from potential acquirers and selects the least cost method, which is often P&A, that is, the transfer of insured deposits and selected bank's assets into another sound bank.

The FDIC is responsible for a quick and smooth resolution process. Therefore, the use of P&A is the most common resolution transaction method used by the FDIC. There are several varieties of P&A tools, such as:

(i) Basic P&A where typically cash, cash equivalents and marketable securities are transferred into another bank with the possibility of transferring non-current assets (premises) optionally, and on the liabilities side are transferred insured deposits.
(ii) The whole bank P&A where the acquirer purchases the maximum amount of the failed bank's assets.
(iii) P&A with optional shared loss where the FDIC agrees to share losses with the acquiring bank (for losses on the collection of loans in the future).
(iv) Bridge bank where the FDIC acts as an acquiring bank on a temporary basis, usually no longer than 2 years, through a new temporary chartered bank which is created and controlled by the FDIC. This temporary bank is created to 'bridge the gap' between bank failure and the time it takes the FDIC to evaluate and market the failed bank to a third party. After the envisaged time, the bridge bank must be either sold or liquidated.

Deposit payout is executed if the FDIC did not receive a less costly bid offer for purchase and assumption or if no bids was received at all.

During the recent international financial crisis, 2008 till 2011, the FDIC resolved a number of banks. The FDIC resolved 25 institutions in 2008, 140 in 2009, 157 in 2010, 92 in 2011, 51 in 2012 and 24 in 2013 (FDIC 2014, 3).

1.8 Conclusion

Since the eighteenth century and the Canton Guaranty System which inspired the establishment of the DISs known at present times, there has been a variety of historical evidence from all over the world on the role that DISs played when banks failed. Without a doubt, the biggest number of banks failed in the United States resulting in the fact that the FDIC became the largest and the most advanced DIS in the world. Other national jurisdictions recognized the importance of the DIS for gaining and maintaining public confidence and consequently for the overall financial stability. Therefore, nobody questions whether a DIS is needed anymore; it has rather been discussed what type of DIS is the most suitable one for the country and its specifics. The primary role of any DIS regardless of its mandate is to enable depositors to have a fast access to their funds entrusted with the banks, at times when these deposits are at jeopardy. Whether a deposit insurance authority must wait for another entity to initiate insolvency proceedings or it may react as soon as deposits become unavailable in a fast and cost-effective manner, a DIS is the key pillar of financial stability. A DIS may be empowered with a simple paybox mandate, which compensates the covered deposits when an insurance case occurs, or with a full range of resolution powers where a DIS is, in some form, involved in the bank resolution process. There are numerous forms and types of DISs, and only the most recent international financial crisis branded a DIS with an unquestionable stability adjective it deserves. In order to justify its new status a DIS must be sufficiently financially robust.

Bibliography

Australian Government. 2008. http://www.guaranteescheme.gov.au/. Accessed 2016.

BBVA. 2014. *Regulation Outlook: Compendium on Bank Resolution Regimes: From the FSB to the EU and US Frameworks*. Madrid: BBVA.

de la Torre, Augusto. 2000. *Resolving Bank Failures in Argentina*. Policy Research Working Paper. Washington, DC: The World Bank.

Demirguc-Kunt, Asli, Baybars Karacaovali, and Luc Laeven. 2005. Deposit Insurance Around the World: A Comprehensive Database. http://documents.worldbank.org/curated/en/593131468330040612/Deposit-insurance-around-the-world-a-comprehensive-database. Policy, Research Working Paper; No. WPS 3628. Accessed 2016.

Demirguc-Kunt, Asli, Edward J. Kane, and Luc Laeven. 2008. *Deposit Insurance Around the World: Issues of Design and Implementation*. Cambridge, MA: MIT Press.

Demirguc-Kunt, Asli, Edward Kane, and Luc Laeven. 2014. Deposit Insurance Database. http://siteresources.worldbank.org/INTRES/Resources/469232-1107449512766/Deposit_insurance_database_preWP.pdf. Accessed 2016.

Directive 2014/49/EU. 2014. Directive 2014/49/EU of the European Parliament and of the Council of 16 April 2014 on Deposit Guarantee Schemes. http://eur-lex.europa.eu/legal-content/EN/TXT/?uri=CELEX:32014L0049. Accessed 2016.

Directive 2014/59/EU. 2014. Directive 2014/59/EU of the European Parliament and of the Council of 15 May 2014 Establishing a Framework for the Recovery and Resolution of Credit Institutions and Investment Firms and Amending Council Directive 82/891/EEC, and Directives 2001/24/EC, 20. http://data.europa.eu/eli/dir/2014/59/oj. Accessed 2016.

ECHR. 2014. European Court of Human Rights' Grand Chamber's Ruling 16th July 2014, ECHR 218 (2014). http://www.echr.coe.int/Documents/CLIN_2014_07_176_ENG.pdf. Accessed 2016.

FDIC. 1998. *A Brief History of Deposit Insurance in the United States*. Washington, DC: FDIC.

———. 2014. *Resolutions Handbook*. Washington, DC. FDIC.

———. 2015. Annual Report, Appendices VII. Annual Report, Washington, DC. FDIC.

Garcia, Gillian G.H. 1999. *Deposit Insurance: A Survey of Actual and Best Practices*. WP/99/54. Washington, DC: IMF.

Grant, Frederic Delano Jr. 2014. *The Chinese Cornerstone of Modern Banking*. Leiden: Martinus Nijhoff Publishers.

Han, Rui, and Martin Melecky. 2013. Financial Inclusion for Financial Stability: Access to Bank Deposits and the Growth of Deposits in the Global Financial Crisis. Policy Research Working Paper Series 6577. The World Bank.

Hoelscher, S. David. 2011. *Deposit Insurance Policies and Financial Crisis*. http://www.iadi.org/docs/David%20Hoelscher%20%20Paper%20Deposit%20Insurance%20Policies%20and%20the%20Financial%20Crisis%205%20%2011.pdf.

Hoelscher, David, et al. 2006. *Bank Restructuring and Resolution*. London: Palgrave McMilllan.

Honohan, P., and D. Klingebeil. 2003. The Fiscal Cost Implications of an Accommodating Approach to Banking Crises. *Journal of Banking and Finance* 21: 1539–1560.

IADI. 2013. *Enhanced Guidance for Effective Deposit Insurance Systems: Deposit Insurance Coverage*. http://www.iadi.org/en/assets/File/Papers/Approved%20 Guidance%20Papers/IADI_Coverage_Enhanced_Guidance_Paper.pdf. Accessed 2016.

———. 2014. *The Revised Core Principles for Effective Deposit Insurance Systems*. Basel. IADI.

———. 2016a. http://www.iadi.org/en/core-principles-and-research/publications/glossary. Accessed 2016.

———. 2016b. http://www.iadi.org/en/deposit-insurance-systems/. Accessed Sept 2016.

———. 2016c. http://www.iadi.org/en/deposit-insurance-systems/dis-worldwide/. Accessed 2016.

IMF&IADI. 2010. Joint Report to Financial Stability Board: Update on Unwinding Temporary Deposit Insurance Arrangements.

Iwanicz-Drozdowska, Malgorzata, Jakub Kerlin, Pawel Smaga, and Marta Tomasik. 2016. EU Guarantee Schemes: Status Quo and Policy Implications. *Journal of Banking Regulation*, Vol. 16, 3: 201–219.

Kyei, Alexander. 1995. *Deposit Protection Arrangements: A Survey*. WP/95/134. Washington, DC: IMF.

Laeven, Luc, and Fabian Valencia. 2008. *The Use of Blanket Guarantees in Banking Crisis*. IMF Working Paper, WP/08/250. Washington, DC: IMF.

McCharty, I. 1980. Deposit Insurance Theory and Practice. *IMF Economic Review* 27(3): 578–600.

McGuire, C. 2012. *Simple Tools to Assist in the Resolution of Troubled Banks*. Washington, DC: The World Bank.

Moody's. 2008. *Moody's Sovereign Analytics: Sovereign Defaults and Interference: Perspectives on Government Risks*. https://www.moodys.com/sites/products/DefaultResearch/2007100000522782.pdf. New York. Accessed 2016.

NDIF. 2005. http://www.oba.hu/images/stories/downloads/oba/en/NDIF_Serving_Depositors_for_15_Years.pdf. Accessed 2016.

Parker, D. 2010. *Closing a Failed Bank, Resolution Practices and Procedures*. Washington, DC: IMF.

Reuters. 2015. http://www.reuters.com/article/slovenia-banks-idUSL5N0YJ 4G920150528. Accessed 2016.

Schich, S. 2008. Financial Crisis: Deposit Insurance and Related Financial Safety Net Aspects. *OECD Financial Market Trends* 2: 1–39.

Scott, D. 2002. *Policy Research Working Paper 2843: A Practical Guide to Managing Systemic Financial Crises: A Review of Approaches Taken in Indonesia, the Republic of Korea, and Thailand.* Working Paper. The World Bank.

SRSN. 2015. http://www.srsn.si/en/media_room/news/article/1328/5655/7f342e5c505624a4529ec61b649350d5/. Accessed 2016.

The Treasury. 2011. http://www.treasury.govt.nz/economy/guarantee/retail. Accessed 2016.

UN. 2001. *Agreement on Succession Issues.* https://treaties.un.org/doc/source/RecentTexts/29-1.pdf. Accessed 2016.

2
Key Design Features of an Explicit DIS

2.1 Introduction

Explicit DIS differs from an implicit one in its origin (legal versus no legal basis) and in the clear definition of its mandate, policy objectives and design features. These elements formulate a unique form of the DIS through an established legal structure, institutional setup, governance, coverage level and coverage scope, sources of funding and information exchange with other authorities, payout trigger, time frame and procedures, powers and responsibilities of the DIS governing bodies, accounting and reporting requirements. Individually and jointly, all the listed elements of an explicit DIS always create a somewhat unique national DIS. A minor difference in one of those features may result in noticeable differences in terms of the efficiency and credibility of an established DIS.

The main DIS elements are always prescribed by the legal framework; however, their full effectiveness depends on implementation. It is somewhat easy to judge the success of any established DIS if it had the opportunity to execute all its functions, especially the payout. Some jurisdictions established the DIS but never experienced bank failure, and

D. Ognjenovic, *Deposit Insurance Schemes*,
DOI 10.1007/978-3-319-51143-6_2

therefore, such DISs have never been fully tested since their operational effectiveness could not be assessed.

This chapter explores the desirable features of an explicit DIS, based on international guidelines and best practices, to justify its establishment and cost-effectiveness of operation. It discusses policy considerations when deciding to establish or to restructure the existing DIS, ranging from legal and institutional arrangements to implementation issues. It also addresses issues of clarification and implementation of the respective Core Principles.

2.2 International Guidelines for an Effective Explicit DIS

When establishing or redesigning an established DIS, national authorities often look for the best solutions and role models established in the international standards of good practice. Policymakers often probe the best solution for a particular question.

In order to address the issue of a 'role model' for a successful DIS, IADI and BCBS during 2008 and 2009 developed Core Principles with the idea of creating an internationally agreed set of guiding principles and benchmarks for the best practice regarding deposit insurance.

A selected group of deposit insurance practitioners was a part of the established working group that jointly prepared the first drafts. Afterward, all IADI members (national DISs) were invited to provide comments prior to the final adoption of the document and its publication in June 2009.

Before Core Principles even existed, national jurisdictions were comparing existing practices in the neighboring countries or randomly chose DISs with features that seemed applicable, yet such approach was not focused on the best practice, nor was it guided by the best solutions for the respective deposit insurance issues. In other words, choices were not based on the standards of practices.

In addition to the use for internal purposes, international financial institutions such as the World Bank (WB) and the International

Monetary Fund (IMF) needed unbiased benchmarks when conducting the Financial Sector Assessment Programs (FSAP) and designing and conducting the technical assistance programs.

After the first years of implementation, it was clear that some principles were overlapping, which resulted in a full revision of the adopted document. Another reason for the revision was due to the constant changes and improvements in national legislations on the deposit insurance and banking resolution framework.

The Revised Core Principles were adopted and published in November 2014 (IADI 2014, 1–56). Two initial Core Principles (Mitigating Moral Hazard and Transition from a Blanket Guarantee) were deleted and one new principle was introduced (Deposit Insurer's Role in Contingency Planning and Crisis Management), while two separate principles (Mandate and Powers) were merged together into one principle, upon

Table 2.1 Initial and Revised Core Principles

No.	Core Principles 2009	Revised Core Principles 2014
1	Public policy objectives	Public policy objectives
2	Mitigating moral hazard	Mandate and powers
3	Mandate	Governance
4	Powers	Relationship with other safety-net participants
5	Governance	Cross-border issues
6	Relationship with other safety-net participants	Deposit insurer's role in contingency planning and crisis management
7	Cross-border issues	Membership
8	Compulsory membership	Coverage
9	Coverage	Sources and uses of funds
10	Transition from a blanket guarantee	Public awareness
11	Funding	Legal protection
12	Public awareness	Dealing with parties at fault in bank failure
13	Legal protection	Early detection and timely intervention
14	Dealing with parties at fault	Failure resolution
15	Early detection and timely intervention	Reimbursing depositors
16	Effective resolution process	Recoveries
17	Reimbursing depositors	
18	Recoveries	

the development of the Revised Core Principles. As a result, the number of Core Principles decreased from 18 to 16 (Table 2.1).

After the adoption and publication of the Core Principles, IADI organized a number of workshops to assist national jurisdictions with the implementation of the Core Principles in the self-assessment process and the developed Assessment Manual (IADI 2016, 1–87).

2.2.1 Public Policy Objectives for the DIS

Core Principle 1: Public Policy Objectives

> *The principal public policy objectives for the deposit insurance schemes are to protect depositors and contribute to financial stability. These objectives should be formally specified and publicly disclosed. The design of the deposit insurance scheme should reflect the system's public policy objectives.* (IADI 2014, 18)

Public policy objectives for the DIS are its ultimate goals and tasks established by the legislation. These objectives define the mandate of the deposit insurance authority and determine its powers. In the last decade, it has been advocated to clearly state the public policy objectives in the legislation to avoid assumptions and misunderstandings related to unrealistic expectations from a DIS.

If a DIS has a narrow mandate (as is the case with the paybox DIS) but a broad public policy objective (such as minimizing costs of bank failures), it is clear that the deposit insurance authority will not be able to meet the set broad public policy objectives and great public expectations. In the past, the legislation of many national jurisdictions did not clearly state public policy objectives. Such practice has been changing mostly due to a more proactive attitude of the deposit insurers. Inevitably, the gap between expectations and powers may lead to the failure of the DIS mandate. When the public policy objectives are clearly stated, then the public is also better informed of the mandate and the role of a country's DIS.

In general, public policy objectives of any DIS are to protect depositors and provide financial stability. These are two main objectives of any DIS and one cannot be achieved without the other.

By ensuring fast and efficient availability of insured deposits to eligible depositors, the DIS protects depositors from financial losses. The international standard for a fast payout becomes shorter over time and insured deposits are available to depositors in several days or weeks after the bank's failure. When depositors understand that their money will be at their disposal in the prescribed manner and within the prescribed time frame, they don't panic and preserve confidence in the system.

However, a DIS with an envisaged greater role in the financial safety net, such as, for example, minimizing the costs of bank resolution or minimizing the risks of bank resolution, should as well have a clear definition of such policy objectives. In the case of larger public policy objectives, the DIS authority should be given a broader mandate and role corresponding to public expectations.

Sometimes laws on deposit insurance even prescribe unrealistic public policy objectives, such as, for example, 'elimination of poverty' or 'increase of savings'. It is evidenced by many countries that savings increased after the introduction of the deposit insurance due to the enhanced public trust and good public awareness campaign that explained the benefits of the DIS to depositors and potential depositors, especially if, prior to the establishment of the DIS, substantial amounts of money were circulated outside the banking sector. Nevertheless, it is unrealistic to expect from a DIS to increase public savings or to decrease poverty as the DIS does not have tools for such goals. The DIS may have within its scope other objectives as well, but in such cases such objectives should not override the two main objectives.

The international best practice also advocates a periodic review of the public policy objectives. Such review should be conducted on a regular basis, within a predetermined timeline, for example over a period of three to five years. When reviewing the existing public policy objectives, national authorities should rethink and discuss whether the set public policy objectives are still valid and important or they should be changed, expanded or amended.

Public policy objectives may change over time naturally, due to the development and changes of the financial sector and challenges which the financial sector faces. Sometimes, a national DIS evolves over time and is ready to undertake a more serious role within the safety net.

The revision of the public policy objectives may also be initiated by external parties, such as, for example, the Parliament or other external body sufficiently empowered with the responsibility for the overall financial stability.

2.2.2 Mandate and Powers of a Deposit Insurance Authority

Core Principle 2: Mandate and Powers

> *The mandate and powers of the deposit insurer should support the public policy objectives and be clearly defined and formally specified in legislation.* (IADI 2014, 19)

The mandate of a DIS is interrelated to its role, responsibilities and the set public policy objectives. Any DIS may have narrow or broader scope of its mandate and responsibilities. Mandate is closely dependent on public policy objectives prescribed to the DIS. If the public policy objective of a national DIS is to only ensure a fast payout of the insured deposits, such a DIS has a narrow 'paybox' mandate and will not able to influence the method of bank resolution. The more diversified the public policy objectives are, the broader the mandate of the DIS should be.

Core Principles (IADI 2014, 8–9) categorize the mandate of the DIS into four groups:

(i) Narrow paybox DIS
(ii) Paybox plus DIS
(iii) Loss-minimizer DIS
(iv) Risk-minimizer DIS

A paybox DIS is the simplest DIS with the narrowest mandate, without any active role in the bank's resolution, except the one related to the payout of insured deposits. The role of paybox DIS is to repay, as fastest as possible and as efficiently as possible, insured deposits once the insurance event occurs. It does not participate in imposing supervisory measures of problem or failing banks, nor does it decide on the resolution model. A paybox DIS only pays the 'bill' in the amount of the total insured deposits in a failing bank. Out of a total of 113 established explicit DISs around the world, 48 are declared as paybox with the narrowest mandate (Demirguc-Kunt et al. 2014, 37–38).

Since the onset of the latest financial crisis, the most recent trend when establishing a DIS has been in favor of the paybox plus mandate. In addition to a fast payout, the paybox plus DISs assume more responsibilities, such as participating in the transfer of insured deposits and assets into another bank or participating in on-site inspection of banks and verifying the accuracy of the submitted reports, which is considered to be a 'plus' mandate, or in financing bank resolution methods.

Furthermore, DGSD (Directive 2014/49/EU 2014, L 173/151) advocates an enhanced paybox plus mandate. That is, the Directive was written for the paybox DIS, though such paybox DIS also uses its funds in bank resolution and may even undertake a more active role in the bank resolution process.

As a result of the ongoing reform, there will be fewer pure paybox DISs among the EU members and more different variations of paybox plus DISs.

Although the paybox plus DIS is not a sole decision-maker on bank resolution (it still has the paybox mandate), it can also assume other complementary tasks outside the narrow paybox mandate. Due to the fact that IADI introduced this new classification only recently, there are no clear details on how many DISs are actually paybox plus. It may be assumed that many DISs, which classified themselves as paybox in the latest database, have already transformed themselves into paybox plus DISs.

A loss-minimizing DIS is one which conducts the least cost test and chooses the least cost resolution method when making deposits available to depositors. The loss-minimizing DIS may opt for the transfer of insured deposits into another sound bank if there is an interest for such transaction and if such a transaction is less costly than the traditional payout. The loss-minimizing DIS is one which is actively involved in the bank resolution and chooses one of legally available resolution instruments and its decision is driven by overall resolution costs. For depositors, it is irrelevant which method is used as long as they have the option to use their funds freely and deposits become again available to them in a short period of time. The FDIC's historical development is significant for the implementation and popularization of the least cost calculation prior to making the final decision on the resolution method.

The paybox DIS executes a payout (reimbursement) of insured deposits, where depositors are free to withdraw cash or keep the money on the account, at their will. The total cost for a DIS is the sum of the total insured deposits increased for expenses occurring during the payout such as the fee to the payout agent, stationery and other costs, and at the same time decreased for the total recovery collected in the course of the insolvency proceedings, at net present value. If a DIS had an option to choose among the resolution instruments, some of them, if applied, could incur lesser final costs for the DIS. This is usually the case when the covered deposits are transferred along with the assets into another sound bank since at the time of the deposit payout the DIS faces a lower cash outflow. This transaction is known as the basic P&A and due to the fact that the assuming bank must accept an equal amount of assets and liabilities (covered deposits), the outflow of liquidity for the DIS equals the net difference between the amount of the transferred book value of covered deposits and the market value of assumed assets. The market value of assumed assets will not be the same as the book value of insured deposits, and the difference has to be provided by the deposit insurer. The scope of the assuming assets and its market value will differ from one failing bank to another, depending on the structure and composition of the assets, its collection value, collateral and many other aspects.

Mainly, the structure of the balance sheet, the primary business orientation of the bank and the performing value of loans determine the real value of the assuming assets. Banks fail due to high risk taking and excessive granting of loans with poor performance. Therefore, such loans result in low market value. The assuming bank usually performs its due diligence of the bank where the valuation of the offered assets is an important component, or asset valuation is executed independently by recognized valuers and offered at a minimum price. Eventually, the assuming bank has to accept the offered assets, and it usually insists on 'cherry-picking', that is, the selection of the best-performing assets with a higher market value. The difference in the values of the assuming assets and covered deposits has to be compensated by the deposit insurer. The smaller the difference between the market value of the assuming assets and the book value of insured deposits, the lower are the final costs for the deposit insurer, and vice versa.

The DISs prefer P&A transactions because they are, in general, 'less costly' than the traditional payout and less labor intensified. Instead of receiving a check, payment order or any other form of cash payout, depositors' money is available on the accounts of the assuming sound bank. Depositors may freely use their money as they wish. In order to be able to calculate costs prior to any decision whether or not to conduct a P&A transaction, a DIS needs to have an approximation of costs in a P&A transaction or other resolution method, with the letter of commitment from the assuming bank and valuation of the bank's assets that will be purchased, prior to making a decision.

The FDIC, for example, conducts the full bidding process prior to finalizing the selected best bid as well as the proposal on the resolution method which always has to be the least costly.

The risk-minimizing DIS is one which has supervisory powers and is able to conduct and impose prudential measures, withdraw banking license, make decisions related to bank resolution, execute the resolution process and so on, in order to minimize risks for the system and for the DIS funds. The risk-minimizing DIS may be authorized to provide financial support to a problem bank, prevent its failure if the bank is viable and actively participate in the bank's resolution. There are many different models of risk minimization, but the FDIC (FDIC 2016), Canadian DIS (CDIC 2016) and Korean DIS (KDIC 2016) are well-known examples of risk-minimizing DISs.

The mandate and powers of any DIS should be clearly defined and prescribed in the law. When consulting the legal act on DIS, it should be clear whether the DIS is paybox or it has a wider role and what is its role, if any, in the process of bank resolution. In addition, it should be clear how the DIS's role fits into the overall safety net of the financial system.

The deposit insurance authority should be empowered to assess and collect funding from its member banks and to receive information from banks in a timely manner. It must have sufficient powers to reimburse depositors either directly or via the transfer of deposits into another bank. It must be able to establish its budget independently through its governing body and enter into contracts. Its supreme governing body should approve its subordinate legislation and other internal acts.

There is some negative experience from certain countries where the deposit insurance authority is not empowered with the development or approval of its internal legislation, and such power is given to another entity, for example, to the Central Bank or the government. These practices are not in line with the international guidelines and principles on good governance.

2.2.3 Governance of the DIS

Core Principle 3: Governance

> *The deposit insurer should be operationally independent, well-governed, transparent, accountable, and insulated from external interference.* (IADI 2014, 21)

Some DISs have an one-tier board system and others a two-tier one. The number of board members differs among countries, depending on the overall governance structure and legislative framework. If the administration of the deposit insurance authority is public, board members are appointed among public servants, that is, among the representatives of the government and governmental agencies and/or representatives of a central bank or financial supervisor, depending on who 'sponsored' the establishment of the DIS or depending on the distribution of political powers.

The board usually appoints the management, although there are examples that the management may be appointed directly by the government or even by the Parliament. However, even when the government directly appoints the management and supervisory board members, the selection process should be transparent and based on clear criteria, including fit and proper tests, in order to ensure competence and independence in decision making.

In countries where administration is jointly divided between the government and the private sector, there are representatives of industry (banking association) and academia at the board, as well.

If the administration of a DIS is private, member institutions appoint board members and the management of the deposit insurance authority.

When deciding on institutional arrangements, there are no 'good', 'bad' or 'best' solutions. The available published literature on deposit insurance doesn't research the topic of institutional arrangements in respect of recommendations. However, the rationale for the selection of an appropriate model is mainly based on advantages and disadvantages of institutional arrangements experienced by other DISs.

International guidelines further prescribe what a good governance of DIS is, such as use of the powers and mandate without interference from the government, industry, central bank or supervisor; accountability of the management and staff; sufficient capacity to support operational independence (budget, decision making, human resources); established internal controls; transparency and disclosure; internal and external audit; avoidance of conflict of interests and so on (IADI 2014, 21).

The IADI advocates establishing the DIS as a separate legal entity, arguing that when the DIS is administered by another legal entity, it would have limited capabilities, dependence on the resources and difficulties to separate responsibilities and conflicts of interest (IADI 2009, 7).

Therefore, when deciding on institutional arrangements for a DIS, the following should be taken into consideration: cost effectiveness (budget projections), operational independence and separation of responsibilities in order to avoid conflict of interest, establishment of key functions necessary for the fulfillment of duties (sufficient capabilities), independent decision making as well as accountability, transparency, integrity and disclosure.

The management is responsible for everyday operations of the deposit insurer, while the board (or the supervisory board in two-tier systems) is responsible for the oversight of managerial decisions and for strategic decisions related to the DIS, as well as for the adoption of key bylaws, instructions and guidelines.

The management should be selected based on transparent criteria in a transparent selection procedure. It should have prescribed key competences with a clear accountability. Members of the board should be clearly appointed or selected, providing a good balance of the stakeholders. The size of board (number of members) should be odd, and clear rules should define the process of decision making and meetings.

Legislation should not prescribe too many details on governance because the detailed law is often restrictive and difficult to modify and adjust to circumstances. However, the legal act should be sufficiently clear in prescribing the main features so as to provide sufficient assurance that neither party is misusing the law.

Legislation should at minimum prescribe governance structure (governing bodies) of the deposit insurers, their main tasks, selection criteria, terms and accountability. Full details of each topic should be prescribed in the statute (charter) or a similar bylaw adopted by the board of the deposit insurer.

The deposit insurance authority should be sufficiently transparent to provide information on its operation, publishing an annual report and ensuring its availability.

2.2.4 Membership

Core Principle 7: Membership

> *Membership in a deposit insurance scheme should be compulsory for all banks.* (IADI 2014, 26)

When establishing a DIS, national authorities face numerous policy decisions related to membership, such as whether the membership should be obligatory or voluntary, whether all or selected types of deposit-taking institutions should become members of a DIS and lastly whether the membership should be granted automatically with the enactment of the law or it should be conditional based on meeting the prescribed criteria.

Before deciding on these important questions, authorities should analyze the financial sector in order to understand the importance and significance of all types of deposit-taking institutions, their licensing, supervision, regulatory framework, types of products and consequences, if any, of their potential exclusion from a DIS membership.

In principle, all licensed and supervised deposit-taking institutions should become members of a DIS. If some types of deposit-taking institutions are not properly or strategically supervised, due to the fact that not all types of deposit-taking institutions are equally important for the future development of the financial sector, authorities may decide not to grant membership in a DIS to those types of financial institutions.

In addition, there are different options how to establish a DIS for different types of financial institutions. Authorities may decide to establish several DISs, one for each type of the deposit-taking institution. These separate DISs may be jointly administered or each could have its own governance and administration, separate from other existing DISs. Another option is to establish one DIS for all deposit-taking institutions.

Decisions should be based on a thorough analysis of the financial sector and existing financial institutions. Whichever option is chosen, it is a strategic decision related to the public policy objectives and national circumstances.

In some countries, one deposit insurance authority may easily manage several deposit insurance schemes and funds through joint management under the same governing structure, with or without separate funding and financial management. In other countries, such arrangements don't work and different deposit insurance schemes are better managed if different separate deposit insurance entities are established.

However, once it is decided which types of deposit-taking institutions will be members of the DIS, it is recommended to prescribe compulsory membership. Voluntary membership in a DIS may work only in very advanced financial markets where banks are aware of the significance of market discipline and of all financial safety-net pillars.

In underdeveloped and developing financial markets, where banks see deposit insurance only as a cost, not as a benefit, their membership should be prescribed as compulsory.

If the banking sector is sound at the time of the DIS introduction, membership for banks should be automatic. Some countries opted for a different approach where banks had to qualify for a membership in a

DIS, based on meeting a number of prudential criteria and thresholds. As evidenced, that was a good option to motivate banks to improve their financial conditions and stabilize operation prior to enjoying benefits of a DIS membership.

A delayed (not automatically granted) membership may be considered for problem banks (banks in a special supervisory regime) at the time of introduction of a DIS, unless such conditional membership would decrease public confidence. Supervisors should provide a strong opinion and recommendation on how to proceed with problem banks at the time of introduction of a DIS. In addition, if there is a bank that does not comply with the membership criteria (in case that membership criteria are established), there should be a credible plan and a reasonable time frame established for such a bank in order to provide sufficient elements for its compliance.

It is, nevertheless, recommended to introduce a DIS at a time when the banking sector is sound, not in the middle of restructuring or bank resolution. Wrong timing for the DIS introduction may jeopardize its effectiveness because neither would the deposit insurance authority be properly established, nor would its staff be trained, and most importantly, the DIS would be financially weak.

Banks are often reluctant, and sometimes even oppose, to introduce the DIS as it creates costs for them, which bankers consider unnecessary.

This is especially the case with large banks whose managers argue that they don't need deposit insurance because they are systemically large enough so that the authorities would not allow their failure and deposit payout. Such attitude was evidenced in many countries at the time of the introduction of a DIS.

Authorities will use the arguments of overall financial stability and benefits that large and systemically important banks enjoy when the banking sector is safe and sound. In addition, large banks argue that most likely the DIS would not be able to provide full deposit insurance to their clients. This argument is partially true. All banks, regardless of their size and soundness, benefit from deposit insurance and enhanced public confidence.

In the financial sector without an established DIS, failure of a small bank may affect all depositors, who can fear for their savings and withdraw money from other banks, since depositors may feel vulnerable and unprotected and realize that they don't enjoy sufficient legal protection.

Even the largest bank in the world may fail as well. Public confidence may be destroyed even by innocent rumors. Banks don't keep deposits as cash in vaults and ready at all times. Banks finance approved loans and long-term credits from savings and other long-term financial resources.

Therefore, depositors' money is safe as much as the granted loans and credits are prudent. Even if all granted credits are a hundred per cent prudent and collectible, they will be fully collected over a longer period of time, some of them even over a 20-year period, in accordance with the granted loans schedules. For all these reasons, banks don't have an available and ready liquidity for all depositors. At times of distress, many depositors request their money simultaneously and put liquidity pressure on healthy banks, too.

Asset liability management in banks has become more and more of a science, since banks finance their liquidity needs (among others the repayment of sight deposits) from current repayment of loans and credits and from other liquidity reserves (in a larger portion), such as cash at hand, investments in liquid instruments and so on.

At the time of the lack of public confidence, all banks, healthy or problem ones, need more liquidity than usual, in order to comfort the disturbed depositors and provide assurance that their money is safe and available if needed.

Legislation on the DIS should clearly prescribe that the membership is compulsory and whether it is granted automatically or conditionally. If the membership is gained after meeting the established conditions, these conditions should be transparently prescribed in the legislation.

The membership may also be canceled by the deposit insurance authority and the cancellation may be a consequence of the license withdrawal or breach of liabilities related to deposit insurance. If such case is established by the legislation, then depositors should be notified that their deposits would still be insured for a specified envisaged time frame (e.g. for a year from the moment of termination or cancellation of the membership).

2.2.5 Payout

Core Principle 15: Reimbursing Depositors

> *The DIS should reimburse depositors' insured funds promptly, in order to contribute to financial stability. There should be a clear and unequivocal trigger for insured depositor reimbursement.* (IADI 2014, 39)

Payout is the most important task of any deposit insurance authority, regardless of its mandate or other features. It is the main duty and a crucial test for every established DIS. If the deposit insurance authority fails in fulfilling this task, everything else is irrelevant.

Compensation of the depositors should be fast and simple, conducted in a similar manner to the existing general banking practice. The deposit insurance authority should not 'invent' uncommon methods of payout as depositors may be confused in their attempt to obtain money. For example, if checks or ATMs are not widely used in the country, the deposit insurance authority should avoid such payout methods as depositors would not be familiar with them.

In order to achieve fast and efficient payout, the deposit insurance authority should have sufficient financial resources, as well as organizational and technical capacities. The process should be supported by information technology (IT) and tailor-made software solution.

DISs tend to shorten the payout time. The FDIC and other more developed deposit insurance schemes established the benchmark of fast payout since they introduced the practice of closing the bank over the weekend and commencing the payout on the first day of the week so that the depositors don't even notice that the bank was in trouble.

This effect of a fast payout decreased the risk of losing public confidence and the domino effect. In the past, only the most developed countries successfully repaid depositors in a few days.

The Directive 2004/19/EC prescribed the payout of depositors within three months (i.e. 90 days), and many European countries had complied with this rule until recently. Since the adoption of the DGSD, the payout time frame has shortened as countries are required to comply with the imposed rules on payout within seven working days by mid-2024 and phased transition (Directive 2014/49/EU 2014, L 173/163).

The FDIC is often a role model for the fast deposit payout. It must be emphasized that the FDIC is also responsible for bank resolution and access to the bank's data much before the formal bank's closure.

Most of paybox DISs have never had such privilege and struggle to gain access to the data prior to the occurrence of the insurance event. When the DIS is paybox or paybox plus, the national supervisor is the one that withdraws the banking license and triggers the moment for payout. Many deposit insurance authorities around the world often complain about the delayed access to information and data which may delay their preparation for the payout. Upon the occurrence of the insurance event, it is of utmost importance for the deposit insurance authority to receive sufficient information from the failing bank as soon as possible and in a ready-made electronic form.

The deposit insurance authority may mitigate problems related to the payout by prescribing processes and procedures of payout in subordinate laws within the prescribed legal framework.

In addition, IT and the software for payout must be set up. The deposit insurance authority must test its software and procedures regularly in order to prepare for the payout event.

2.2.6 Relationship with Other Safety Net Players

Core Principle 4: Relationship with Other Safety-Net Participants

> *In order to protect depositors and contribute to financial stability, there should be a formal and comprehensive framework in place for the close coordination of activities and information sharing, on an ongoing basis, between the deposit insurer and other financial safety-net participants.* (IADI 2014, 23)

The best practice of deposit insurers advocates a formal and comprehensive coordination among the safety-net players, that is, deposit insurance authority, banking supervisor, authority responsible for bank resolution and lender of last resort (this is usually the Ministry of Finance). Such coordination should be regular, on a predetermined basis, through meetings arranged in advance and information sharing as well as through established coordinated activities and actions. Cooperation may be formalized by a decree, decision or a signed contract with definitions on cooperation and mutual rights and liabilities toward each other.

Due to the same goal of preserving financial stability, the deposit insurance authority should closely cooperate with the national banking supervisor and there is a need for formalization of their cooperation and regular exchange of information. The deposit insurance authority must understand and monitor the developments in the banking sector, whether banks are safe and sound and what the riskiest banks are from the supervisory point of view. All this information is confidential, and the main purpose of sharing them is to ensure that the DIS is ready for the fulfillment of its tasks if needed and when needed without disruptions.

The deposit insurance authority must fully understand banking regulation, issues related to databases and deposits' register. If banking supervision prescribes prudential measures against an individual bank, the deposit insurance authority should be aware of them. If the banking supervisor intends to withdraw the banking license, the deposit insurance authority should be informed prior to the making of the decision in order to ensure sufficient time for the preparation of the deposit payout. It is important that the public knows that the deposit insurance and bank resolution authorities closely cooperate and support each other.

When the deposit insurance authority develops a risk-based premium methodology, it should consult the bank supervisor and request an official opinion. If the deposit insurance authority is preparing for the deposit payout, the timing and the method of payout will be shared with the bank supervisor and the central bank (if banking supervision is not placed within the central bank) in order to maintain monetary stability.

All safety-net players share a common goal and must ensure that each entity has sufficient information submitted by other entities in order to do their respective share of work efficiently.

2.2.7 Public Awareness in DIS

Core Principle 10: Public Awareness

> *In order to protect depositors and contribute to financial stability, it is essential that the public be informed on an ongoing basis about the benefits and limitations of the deposit insurance scheme.* (IADI 2014, 32–33)

Deposit insurers pay more and more attention to public awareness. In the past, it was usually argued that deposit insurance, similar to banking supervision, dealt with banking secrecy and consequently no issues whatsoever should be discussed publicly; that is, less publicity was a better option.

Over time, it was evidenced that informed depositors would react better. Therefore, deposit insurers invest more time and money on public relations and provide more information to the public, educate target groups, regularly conduct surveys and minimize risks which may trigger panic and concern among depositors.

There are DISs which do not provide sufficient or detailed information on their activities, or publish annual reports or communicate with the public in a transparent way. Thus their activities are covered by a veil of secrecy. Such approach is not considered best practice.

The deposit insurance authority should regularly inform the public about the benefits and limitations of deposit insurance At the time of introduction of a DIS, it is important to ensure a public awareness campaign focused on educating the general public (existing and potential depositors) about the role of the DIS in the safety net and what the DIS brings to depositors and non-depositors.

By default, depositors are not over-excited about the deposit insurance as long as their deposits are safe. Deposit insurance is not a topic of much interest in general, as long as the banking sector is safe and sound. There are always many opponents to deposit insurance and any public discussion, if the national DIS is weak, may go in a wrong direction and create counter-effects.

Depositors, as other banking service users, are generally reluctant and passive and accept the information as it is. A very small number of depositors or non-depositors are interested in learning more about deposit insurance features. However, depositors are usually interested in whether their savings are safe and at their disposal.

Nowadays, the public is generally more financially educated than in the past. The deposit insurance authority should develop its policy and guidelines related to the public awareness in subordinate laws. On an annual basis, a public awareness plan should be developed with a list and description of activities that are planned in the forthcoming period in order to provide more information on deposit insurance.

The public is informed of the deposit insurance in banks and from banks' employees, when opening the account or conducting any services in bank premises. For that reason, front offices of banks are first and direct contact points with depositors and potential depositors where they can learn about deposit insurance and specifics of the national DIS. It is important to educate depositors in order to avoid their disappointment later as a result of unrealistic expectations.

Deposit insurers should regularly educate banks' front office employees in order to make sure that the information provided to depositors is accurate and of good quality. In order to ensure precise information, deposit insurers can 'control' the information content either by preparing and publishing leaflets which are then given to depositors in banks or by prescribing the exact content of information and wording that the banks must provide to their clients about the deposit insurance. It is common practice to develop and print an information leaflet containing basic information on deposit insurance, written in simple language which any reader of an average level of education may understand. Sentences should be simple and with examples of calculation of covered deposits. Leaflets are often written in 'Questions and Answers' form in order to provide as much as possible of key important information on deposit insurance.

Deposit insurers don't support aggressive advertising by banks on deposit insurance membership in order to attract new clients.

In order to enhance depositors' protection, many deposit insurers prescribe that depositors, when opening accounts in banks, must be informed by banks whether that particular account is under the deposit insurance coverage scope and must be provided with general information on the DIS. Depositors should sign acknowledgement of such information.

Deposit contract, as well as depositors' regular statement reports, should additionally provide standardized wording on the information on deposit insurance.

Deposit insurer should use different distribution channels, other than banks, when approaching depositors. These distribution channels are newspapers, direct mailing, and popular media such as television, the Internet and, of course, the social media such as Facebook or Twitter and other social networks. Many deposit insurers argue that it is hard to control information in the social media; however, it may also be dangerous to avoid the social media, especially due to the growth of financial awareness among the public and because of young generations of depositors that are used to communicating mostly via the social media.

Deposit insurers should establish public awareness goals which they desire to achieve and determine their focused groups. In its annual public awareness plan and in accordance with the general public awareness policy, the deposit insurance authority should prepare a list of activities in order to enhance the level of public knowledge on the deposit insurer and DIS or on specific issues related to deposit insurance.

Before and during the payout, deposit insurers should pay special attention to providing timely information at places where depositors would receive the compensation. The main purpose is to provide information on depositors' rights and to regain the public's confidence.

At the time of a bank failure, public eyes are focused on the deposit insurance authority and from the first day, without delay, depositors must be informed how and when their deposits will become available to them.

Many deposit insurance authorities engage professionals to assist them with regular and occasional public awareness activities in order to be sure that the right messages are supplied in the best possible way.

From time to time (every 3–5 years), deposit insurers should conduct public awareness survey with a questionnaire in order to learn which areas should be improved and how to respond to the results. The results of surveys should be subject to a thorough analysis and the deposit insurance authority should design responses to critical issues to ensure improvement within the envisaged time frame.

Studies on the level of awareness on deposit insurance (Bartiloro 2011, 8) suggest that only 29 per cent of Italian depositors are aware of the existence of the Italian DIS (although it was established in 1987), while 40 per cent of German depositors are aware of the German DIS and 67 per cent of American depositors are aware of the FDIC and the American DIS. Such low level of awareness on the DIS should not be a surprise due to the fact that the deposit insurers have only recently started a proactive public awareness program but also because depositors, in general, do not care as long as they don't experience bank failure and unavailability of deposits.

2.2.8 International Cooperation

Core Principle 5: Cross-Border Issues

> *Where there is a material presence of foreign banks in a jurisdiction, formal information sharing and coordination arrangements should be in place among deposit insurers in relevant jurisdictions* (IADI 2014, 24).

Due to the globalization of banking, large banks operate in many jurisdictions, in different forms, under different banking laws and prudential norms. Sometimes, within specific regions, due to similar historical or political environment, national jurisdictions are strongly affected by economic developments in the neighboring countries.

Inevitably, efforts of authorities to create a single market on the territory of EU, where it is not necessary anymore to obtain a banking license from the host country supervisor for operation in another member country and where banks can establish branches and operate in compliance with home supervisory rules, create complicated rather than simple 'playground fields' because banks are supervised by different supervisory authorities.

Some regions and territories, although divided by national borders, have strong common historical roots or their economies depend on each other. In such circumstances, banking supervisory authorities cooperate closely not only to enhance information sharing but to jointly build the safety net and minimize the spread of negative effects from one country to another.

Public confidence is driven by depositors' emotions and it is hard to prevent the spread of ex post contagious effects. Similarly, deposit insurers must establish close cooperation with each other and such cooperation should be established in a formal manner with countries where interests are shared. Specifically, if the home DIS covers deposits in branches of home banks operating abroad or if branches of foreign banks operate on the territory of host countries, deposit insurance authorities of both countries should establish a formal cooperation between each other and with home and host supervisors.

There are many examples of good and bad relationships among the authorities of different countries. The case of Icelandic banks' failures is probably a typical case study on how cooperation did not work in practice, although it was formally established.

2.2.9 Contingency Planning

Core Principle 6: Deposit Insurer's Role in Contingency Planning and Crisis Management

> *The deposit insurer should have in place effective contingency planning and crisis management policies and procedures, to ensure that it is able to effectively respond to the risk of, and actual, bank failures and other events. The development of system-wide crisis preparedness strategies and management policies should be the joint responsibility of all safety-net participants. The deposit insurer should be a member of any institutional framework for ongoing communication and coordination involving financial safety-net participants related to system-wide crisis preparedness and management.* (IADI 2014, 25)

There is no unique model how the deposit insurance authority should properly prepare for its main function, that is, the payout of insured depositors. Payout of depositors during a bank failure is a key task of any deposit insurer regardless of its mandate. When the DIS is given only the paybox mandate, the payout function becomes even more important as it is the only function of the DIS that is in the public eye.

Preparation for smooth and effective payout is important for success of any DIS. The deposit insurance authority is prepared for the payout if it has all procedures in place, if its human and financial resources are sufficient and if it has appropriate MIS which may effectively support the payout process.

The deposit insurance authority must have a working plan in place for bank failure. It must be equally ready to execute the payout under any circumstances. The deposit insurance authority may face the situation of a failure of a small bank or a failure of several banks at the same time. In case of large systemic bank failures, if not properly prepared, a DIS may face significant technical and financial challenges paying out large sums of money to large number of depositors.

The deposit insurance authority should, at all times, be aware of the developments in the banking sector, especially of risks and financial stability issues which may trigger a deposit run. It must not ignore the fact that a particular bank is under severe supervisory regime of the competent authorities.

The deposit insurance authority should regularly conduct testing of its MIS (both hardware and software for deposit payout) and simulate the payout. If the plan is to use the services of the payout agent bank, procedures and guidelines on the compensation process should be regularly updated to reflect the legislation and to ensure readiness of the payout agent for the work during the compensation process. The deposit insurance authority employees should be educated for the payout process and aware of their individual tasks in order to avoid any panic and overlapping of work.

The deposit insurance authority should regularly meet with the supervisory authority and other safety-net representatives within the established financial stability framework and discuss the recent issues reflecting national financial stability (e.g. whether to increase deposit insurance coverage or not, how to prevent panic in case of a large bank failure, what kind of measures are in place and how to smoothly coordinate issues related to a bank failure). Financial authorities should develop a crisis management plan with a clear role for each entity and activities that should be executed jointly and which are within their respective jurisdictions.

In case of a large bank failure, if the only possible resolution is regular insolvency proceeding, the deposit insurance authority should ensure sufficient financial resources and coordinate its activities with other safety-net authorities.

2.2.10 Legal Protection of Deposit Insurance Authority and Its Staff

Core Principle 11: Legal Protection

> *The deposit insurer and individuals working both currently and formerly for the deposit insurer in the discharge of its mandate must be protected from liability arising from actions, claims, lawsuits or other proceedings for their decisions, actions or omissions taken in good faith in the normal course of their duties. Legal protection should be defined in legislation.* (IADI 2014, 34)

By executing its mandate, the deposit insurance authority and its staff are exposed to dealing with individuals affected by bank failure. When under stress of not being able to use their money, depositors are often angry and look for someone to blame. Many affected don't care or don't understand the legal language and how the legislation affects them specifically. Sometimes depositors look for legal solutions and initiate legal proceedings against the deposit insurance authority and its employees. It is therefore important to ensure legal protection for those affected by such possible legal actions while conducting regular work and legal mandate that was entrusted to them.

The law on DIS and the deposit insurance authority's charter should prescribe that employees enjoy legal protection and are awarded damages for the costs incurred in the legal proceedings if any such activity happens.

2.2.11 Legal Redress against Parties at Fault in Bank Failure

Core Principle 12: Dealing with Parties at Fault in a Bank Failure

> *The deposit insurer, or other relevant authority, should be provided with the power to seek legal redress against those parties at fault in a bank failure.* (IADI 2014, 35)

Banks often fail due to the human factor, that is, due to the negligence of management and owners, weak governance structure and high-risk-taking policy (soft lending policy). Bank managers and owners are responsible on their part for causing problems or not preventing problems and failures. In some cases, management and owners directly cause failure of a bank due to criminal activities. Whatever the role of those individuals was, the safety-net players should be able to initiate investigation over their involvement and, if findings prove their faults, initiate legal actions against them.

The deposit insurance authority should have a procedure in place related to investigation and actions against the bank's management, insiders, owners and others possible agents involved in the bank's failure. Sometimes actions can be initiated even against the bank's auditors who issued a qualified opinion and failed to detect (or help management to deceive) problems in banks prior to the failure. Every case of a bank failure is specific and financial authorities, especially deposit insurance and supervisory authority, should be empowered to initiate legal proceedings against those parties at fault in a bank failure.

2.2.12 Timing Is Crucial

Core Principle 13: Early Detection and Timely Intervention

> *The deposit insurer should be part of a framework within the financial safety-net that provides for the early detection of, and timely intervention in, troubled banks. The framework should provide for intervention before the bank becomes non-viable. Such actions should protect depositors and contribute to financial stability.* (IADI 2014, 36)

Robust supervision and bank failure regime, efficient deposit insurance and consumer protection and an established lender of last resort are pillars of the safety net around a failing bank. The stronger each pillar is, the stronger the whole net will be. Each pillar ensures its share of responsibility within the given legal mandate but also shares joint responsibility for the overall financial stability. The public doesn't know and doesn't need to know the details on whose responsibility it is to ensure financial stability. The public is interested in the overall financial security.

The deposit insurance authority must be an equal partner within the safety net. It must share and receive timely information on the possible failure of a bank and overall financial stability of the whole banking and financial sector. If authorities disagree on some issues, the public should not be aware of such a relationship and arguing in public as well as and mutual blaming may decrease public confidence instead of increasing it. Nevertheless, by the definition of its mandate, the national supervisory authority holds the most important role in the early detection and timely intervention of problems and failures of the individual bank.

2.2.13 Efficiency of DIS and Bank Resolution Framework

Core Principle 14: Failure Resolution

> *An effective failure resolution regime should enable the deposit insurer to provide for protection of depositors and contribute to financial stability. The legal framework should include a special resolution regime.* (IADI 2014, 37–38)

The resolution process of a failing bank should be as effective as possible in order to ensure the main public policy objective of deposit insurance which is the protection of depositors and financial stability. When a bank fails, the most common failure mechanism is liquidation of the bank, that is, insolvency proceedings with the deposit payout.

Over time, other resolution mechanisms evolved with a purpose of more efficient and less expensive procedures. Such resolution mechanisms are alternative or additions to insolvency proceedings and ensure transfer of a part or all assets and liabilities into another bank, creation of a bridge bank with a purpose to overcome a time gap between initiation and finalization of the resolution process and other mechanisms which combine several activities.

The goal is always the same: to protect the most vulnerable general public and to ensure that the financial stability is not jeopardized. The only way by which this goal can be achieved is to have a legal framework in place that allows all possible resolution mechanisms to be implemented. Resolution and deposit insurance authorities must have a clear division of responsibilities in the resolution process.

The decision on the choice of the resolution mechanism would depend on many factors such as the size and development of the banking sector, the size of the losses and any potential remaining value of assets and attractiveness of liabilities of a failing bank, length of the resolution process and cost comparison, complexity of legal proceedings and so on. The resolution authority should have several resolution options at its disposal as well as a clear procedure on how to choose among them. Similarly, the deposit insurance authority should have at its disposal the option to choose the usage of DIFs for other resolution methods only if they are less costly than the deposit payout in insolvency proceedings.

2.2.14 DIS Recovery in Insolvency Proceedings

Core Principle 16: Recoveries

> *The deposit insurer should have, by law, the right to recover its claim in accordance with the statutory creditor hierarchy.* (IADI 2014, 41)

Whenever the deposit insurance authority conducts a payout of insured deposits to eligible depositors, it is entitled to recover the paid money from the bank's assets during the insolvency proceedings. A simple saying is used to describe the deposit insurance authority's recovery right: 'deposit insurance steps into the shoes of depositors'.

In the past, the time frame for the deposit payout was longer (e.g. up to 90 days in the EU), while the time frame for registering the claim in insolvency proceedings was shorter (e.g. up to 30 days), which could create a problem for the deposit insurance authority in determining the precise amount of its claim and in registering it on time.

Deposit insurance authorities had problems in registering the claim within the prescribed time frame since in many cases they did not even start the compensation process and thus did not have the proof for their claim.

Therefore, it is important to prescribe in the law creditors' hierarchy rights and DIS's automatic subrogation right for the total amount of insured deposits that must be compensated to depositors.

In many countries there is a prescribed statute of limitations in the course of which depositors have the legal right to claim compensation from the deposit insurance authority. The deposit insurance authority should recover the maximum amount of the paid insured deposits from the insolvency proceedings.

Insolvency proceedings are usually slow and inefficient. The recovery rate varies among countries and jurisdictions depending on many factors. In countries where legal systems are generally inefficient and slow, recovery rates are lower. It is important for any deposit insurer to maximize the recovery rate in order to preserve DIFs. Otherwise, any payout of insured deposits would deplete financial resources of the DIS and it would never be recovered.

2.3 Coverage Scope and the Coverage Amount Level

Core Principle 8: Coverage

> *Policymakers should define clearly the level and scope of deposit coverage. Coverage should be limited, credible and cover the large majority of depositors but leave a substantial amount of deposits exposed to market discipline. Deposit insurance coverage should be consistent with the deposit insurance scheme's public policy objectives and related design features.* (IADI 2014, 27)

Coverage scope refers to those types of deposits which are covered by the deposit insurance scheme. When designing the scheme, national authorities may decide to cover all types of deposits or to exclude from coverage certain types of deposits. Usually, anonymous deposits are excluded from coverage. Depositors should not be discriminated based on the currency of held deposits, nationality or residence.

In addition, coverage scope refers to the type of depositors who are covered by DIS. Although depositors should not be discriminated based on their nationality or residence, some DISs cover only resident depositors (Demirguc-Kunt et al. 2014, 37–38). Public policy objectives usually determine the coverage scope of a DIS. When reading public policy objectives, it should be clear whether the DIS is granted to all types of depositors or it is limited to a certain group and type of depositors. For example, many countries insure only household deposits, which are usually stated in public policy objectives.

At present, due to the harmonization of deposit insurance within the EU, the coverage scope and coverage amount are harmonized and prescribed for EU members. Certain categories of depositors are excluded from coverage, such as financial institutions and insurance companies, collective investment undertakings (investment funds), pension funds, public authorities, deposits arising from money laundering and so on. However, non-EU members and other national DISs are not obliged to follow EU rules on deposit insurance.

Database researched only two features related to coverage scope: coverage of foreign exchange (FX) deposits and coverage of interbank deposits. Based on the data at the end of 2013 (Demirguc-Kunt et al. 2014, 37–38), 70 DISs cover FX deposits and 35 DISs cover interbank deposits. As a rule of thumb, a DIS should not be discriminative, and therefore, national currency deposits and FX deposits should be treated equally, especially if FX deposits are widely used and represent a significant share in the total deposit base.

It is recommended to create a catalog of types of deposits which are covered by a national DIS and to update it regularly for the purpose of clarification whether all types of deposits are covered or not. Member banks develop new savings products and sometimes these products are not clearly classified as an atypical deposit or a savings account. Modern banking offers modern, non-standard savings and investment products.

Legislation usually provides only general definition of banking products that are covered by the DIS. Subordinate laws should provide a more detailed list of protected banking products. Member banks can, whenever developing and offering a new product to the public, inform the deposit insurance authority about the new product and ask for clarification whether or not such product is covered by the DIS.

In addition, depositors should know if their deposit is insured or not and acknowledge that they are familiar with the type of the product and its status related to the DIS, in order to avoid false expectations in case of bank failure.

Co-insurance was a popular measure combating moral hazard issue for a certain period of time, but its real value and contribution in the combat against moral hazard has never been proved. The idea of co-insurance is that depositors should bear a certain percentage of costs regardless of the prescribed coverage amount. If co-insurance is, for example, 10 per cent and the coverage amount is €100,000, for depositors with a deposit balance of €100,000, compensation would be only €90,000 as he (she) bears the remaining 10 per cent, that is, €10,000 of the co-insured cost.

Countries which at a certain point of time implemented co-insurance abandoned the same measure as it delayed calculations and created a number of complications related to the payout without proven positive effects. Depositors may be disappointed upon learning that deposits were not covered in the full amount, which, regardless of the fast and efficient reimbursement process, may result in their mistrust and shaken public confidence.

Deposit insurers who opted for co-insurance additionally state that it is not worth from the cost savings point of view. DGSD also abandoned the principle of co-insurance which was advocated as a recommendation (not obligation) in the first EU Directive on Deposit Guarantee Schemes (Directive 1994, No L 135/10), valid from 1994 until 2014.

Determining the optimal or most appropriate coverage amount level is one of the most challenging tasks for any jurisdiction at the time of introduction of the DIS and whenever a national authority intends to increase the coverage amount. In order to ensure public confidence and financial stability, coverage should provide adequate protection (guarantee) to the public to prevent mistrust and the domino effect in the case of market disruption.

But how to determine what is an 'adequate' and optimal coverage level?

The coverage level represents the maximum amount to be compensated to insured depositors in case of bank failure and insurance event occurrence. If the coverage amount is set too low, it does not provide sufficient assurance to depositors that they are protected and, regardless of the existence of a DIS, depositors may continue to feel unprotected and fear for the loss of their deposits. Such feeling may trigger their actions and withdrawal of deposits. If the coverage amount is set too high, the incremental costs are higher than the incremental benefits. The DIS will experience a higher potential liability and overall higher costs of funding.

Some authors (Demirguc-Kunt and Detragiache 2000, 13) argue that the higher coverage amount leads to moral hazard and more excessive risk taking by member banks and extra safe feeling of depositors and thus their less careful watching over the quality of the bank.

The main question related to determining an appropriate coverage amount for the system is, what methodology should be used in order to come to a figure that would make sense?

If the main public policy objective and the goal of deposit insurance scheme is to protect small and unsophisticated depositors, then such category of depositors and deposits should be 'defined' as precisely as possible in order to determine what is considered to be a 'small deposit'. In addition, a line between the 'majority of small deposits' and 'fewer large deposits' should be set in order to avoid the tendency to protect every depositor, especially those who have large sums of money.

Authorities often tend to protect as many as possible, offering higher than optimal coverage amount. In addition, at the time of introduction of the DIS, national authorities often tend to disregard the statistics and analytics relying on 'personal perception'. Therefore, as a consequence, many countries prescribed 'larger coverage rather than optimal and affordable' as setting higher coverage was a matter of 'national pride' rather than a realistic analysis. Sometimes, authorities 'feel' that a larger coverage is more appropriate, although the evidence on average savings figures doesn't support it.

Historically, the coverage amount was determined as a 1:2 ratio of the GDP per capita. The idea emerged in early papers on best practices of deposit insurance schemes and it was copied as a 'good example' for many years. GDP per capita benchmark was mainly used before the crisis in 2008 (Garcia 1999, 40–41). Since the onset of the financial crisis and a significant increase of the coverage amount, this measure 'lost' on its importance and usage.

Other benchmarks that were occasionally used in some countries were consumer price indices and average salaries.

The most recent rule of thumb for determining the coverage amount is called the '80:20' rule, with the idea that the coverage amount should protect a minimum of 80 per cent of the total number of depositors and a minimum of 20 per cent of the total amount of their deposits.

Before any decision is made on the coverage amount, authorities should analyze the deposits' size breakdown (with amounts of deposits and number of depositors in each size category) in all banks, in order to determine how many depositors and deposits would be affected with the proposed coverage amount and what the potential liability exposure for DIS would be.

However, when proposing the amount of coverage, a number of other issues should be taken into account, such as the size and the structure of the banking sector, the growth of insured deposits and sources and the adequacy of funding.

Every increase of coverage increases the total exposure of DIFs and exposure to individual member banks in a different way, depending on the breakdown of the deposit size in each bank. Therefore, the market share of each bank in insured deposits should be taken into the account as it represents the exposure of DI funds toward each bank, assuming that all banks bear the same level of risk for the deposit insurer.

2.3.1 Example: Decision on Coverage Scope and Coverage Amount Level

The following example shows minimum analytical steps that authorities should take in order to gather sufficient information prior to determining the appropriate level of the coverage scope and amount.

In our example, there are ten banks operating in the banking system. All banks collect deposits from households and legal entities.

Before making any decision, national authorities would like to study and analyze the data on the types of depositors, their numbers and amount of deposits. It is necessary to obtain the minimum basic information on the number and value of deposits held by retail and legal entities depositors in banks as well as useful to understand the structure of deposits and depositors.

Additional analysis on the currency structure of deposits may also be useful if the authorities wish to understand the impact of FX deposits in the deposit insurance. Best practice showed that there should not be any discrimination based on the currency of deposits. However, some jurisdictions insure deposits only in the local currency and exclude savings in foreign currencies from the deposit insurance. Information on the currency structure of total deposits and insured deposits in the banking system is important for funding, financial management and FX risk management.

Data on bank-by-bank basis would provide sufficient information on the distribution of deposits among banks and concentration of deposits in each bank. If authorities wish to make better quality-based decisions, they need to analyze more detailed information. For example, authorities may wish to understand details on deposits held by the government or financial institutions, because those types of deposits could be excluded from the deposit insurance. It is advisable not to make any policy decision prior to understanding the full impact of decisions as well as not to skip the data analysis.

Data from banks are as follows:

- There are 2.9 million depositors, out of which 2.6 million are individuals (retail depositors) while 310,000 depositors are legal entities. In relative terms, 89.35 per cent are individuals and the remaining 10.65 per cent are legal entities' depositors.
- Individual depositors hold 58.17 per cent of the total amount of deposits' value.

Based on the information from our example, at the time of the introduction of the DIS, authorities may decide to protect only retail depositors and such decision can be justified by the significance of retail deposits in the total deposits. In a later phase of the DIS development and after the DIS is sufficiently funded, all remaining depositors (legal entities' deposits) may be included in the DIS coverage.

In the next step, the focus is shifted on the data on individual (retail) depositors and total depositors.

Although information on the simple average deposit amount for the system may give an idea of the 'size' of the deposit for the banking sector, it is advisable to conduct a detailed analysis on the distribution amount ranges of deposits and depositors for all banks.

The deposit amount ranges may, at first, be determined by 'rule of thumb' of the supervisors or could be based on prior data analysis, if such exists.

In our example, as a rule of thumb and for simplicity, initial deposit ranges breakdown was determined at €10.000. Each bank would be asked to provide detailed information on the number of depositors and the value of deposits in accordance with the predetermined deposit amount range.

For example, if a depositor X has placed in a bank deposits worth €15,000 (regardless of whether that amount is held on one or more deposit accounts), he would fall into the category from €10,001 to 20,000. This approach is more accurate and corresponds to the deposit insurance coverage amount principle which is determined per depositors' base and a single customer view (SCV) of depositors within the bank.

Banks may also provide data on deposit basis instead on depositor basis. In such case, data are less precise but even as such authorities can use them in order to determine the coverage amount. If data are provided on the deposit basis, all deposits falling within a certain range would be categorized within that specific range regardless of whether one depositor holds only one or more deposits.

It is important to understand the distribution of deposits in order to apply the '80:20' rule of thumb, which says that the deposit coverage amount should cover a minimum of 80 per cent of depositors holding a minimum of 20 per cent of the total deposit amounts.

Therefore, we go one step further in order to determine within which deposit range the '80:20' rule is ensured. In the following step, we are more interested in the total data for the whole banking sector and not in

Table 2.2 Calculation of possible coverage amount levels

Amount scales (in €)	Number of depositors	Amount, in €	Per cent in total number	Per cent in total amount
Up to 10,000	2,631,370	21,726,036,500	90.36	19.79
From 10,001 to 20,000	54,010	985,960,000	1.85	0.90
From 20,001 to 30,000	33,820	845,143,500	1.16	0.77
From 30,001 to 40,000	16,300	617,300,000	0.56	0.56
From 40,001 to 50,000	11,100	543,900,000	0.38	0.50
From 50,001 to 60,000	13,200	765,600,000	0.45	0.70
From 60,001 to 70,000	11,900	773,100,000	0.41	0.70
From 70,001 to 80,000	9,600	746,900,000	0.33	0.68
From 80,001 to 90,000	14,200	1,219,600,000	0.49	1.11
From 90,001 to 100,000	13,500	1,293,500,000	0.46	1.18
More than 100,000	103,000	80,276,000,000	3.54	73.12
Total	**2,912,000**	**109,793,040,000**	**100.00**	**100.00**

the data on individual banks. In this step, we use the data as presented in the Table 2.2, arranged and presented in such order to be able to calculate the total number of depositors and the total amount of deposits within the given amount ranges, for all banks, and to express them as percentages.

The data in Table 2.2 are presented on depositors' basis (not on deposit accounts' basis). The number of depositors and the total amount of their deposits by each deposit amount distribution range are aggregated on the level of the banking sector. The last two columns represent the relative values of each absolute value figure.

In our example, out of a total of 2.9 million depositors, 2.6 million (i.e. 90.36 per cent of the total number of depositors) hold deposits lower than €10,000, in the amount of €21.7 billion (i.e. 19.79 per cent of total deposits).

We can interpret these figures as follows: 90.36 per cent of total depositors hold deposits which are less than €10,000. The figures suggest that with the coverage level of €10,000, authorities are close to complying with the '80:20' rule.

Further analysis suggests that 92.22 per cent (90.36 + 1.85) of total depositors hold deposits which are less than €20,000, in the amount of 20.69 per cent (19.79 + 0.9) of total deposits.

Based on the analysis at this stage, authorities may decide to establish a coverage amount at either €10,000 or €20,000. If authorities decide to set the coverage amount at €20,000, '80:20' rule will be fully complied with.

When the DIS is based on per depositor per bank deposit insurance, when calculating the total amount of insured deposits, the attributable amount of €10,000 from the deposits that are higher than €10,000 must be taken into calculation by interpolation. With the coverage level set at €10,000, the total covered deposits would amount to more than €21.7 billion. However, with the coverage level at €20,000, the total covered deposits would amount to €27.2 billion.

This calculation suggests that by increasing the coverage amount from €10,000 to €20,000, full coverage expands onto 1.86 per cent of additional depositors and insures additional 2.47 per cent of deposits' amount, which would increase the total exposure of deposit insurance toward banks by €2.7 billion in absolute terms (from €24.5 to 27.2 billion).

Authorities now must decide between €10,000 and €20,000. Any decision would be in compliance with the '80:20' rule. If the coverage amount is set at €10,000, the total exposure of DIS is lower. Such decision could be justified because the DIS would protect 90.36 per cent of total depositors and 22.34 per cent of the total deposit amount in the banking system.

However, this conclusion, for the time being, would be made without taking into consideration funding options and without considering individual bank's risk profile. The DIS with a higher coverage amount must ensure more funding.

2.4 Sources and Uses of Deposit Insurance Funds

Core Principle 9: Sources and Uses of Funds

> *The deposit insurer should have readily available funds and all funding mechanisms necessary to ensure prompt reimbursement of depositors' claims, including assured liquidity funding arrangements. Responsibility for paying the cost of deposit insurance should be borne by banks.* (IADI 2014, 29)

Deposit insurance scope and coverage amount will influence the amount of the required DIS funding. The wider the scope and the higher the amount of coverage, the bigger the need for more financial resources and more robust funding for a deposit insurance authority.

Legislation should at minimum prescribe, in a clear manner, sources of initial, regular (ongoing) and extraordinary (backup, emergency) funding.

The purpose of initial funding is to ensure financial resources at the beginning of the DIS establishment, both for the operation of the DIS and for building public confidence through collecting DIFs. Usually a DIS becomes effective at the time of the enactment of the law or within the short period (up to one year) following the enactment, leaving a short grace period of time for the capitalization of funds.

There are different sources of initial funding at disposal; however, the major provider is usually the government or another major sponsor (central bank) and founder of the DIS.

In addition to the government, initial funding is also provided by member institutions as an 'entry fee' or a membership fee. When legislation prescribes sources, and even projects the amount of initial funds, it ensures certain legal commitment on initial funding. Lately there have been many discussions on whether governments should provide initial funds at all. Many support the idea that DIS funding should solely rely on funding by member banks. In cases where the government provided initial funds, the premium should not be lowered or stopped; otherwise, money provided by public sponsors should be returned first.

Regular funding should be provided by member institutions. This is one of the main rules in funding deposit insurances since banks enjoy benefits from an established DIS and thus should also pay for those benefits. Deposit insurance is not cost-free; it is not a gift from the government, and therefore, regular funding should be ensured by member banks.

Legislation should prescribe the main elements of regular funding formula such as the basis for calculation (total, eligible or covered deposits) and the formula for premium calculation. If the law prescribes the exact percentage of the annual premium, any attempt of funding optimization over a longer period of time would be limited, if not impossible.

It is therefore a much better option to prescribe only the maximum upper limit of annual premium or percentage ranges for the premium. The deposit insurance authority must be able to propose an annual premium level based on its projected needs.

If the risk-based premium is envisaged, it is sufficient to prescribe only basic information on the methodology, while details on formulas, ranges and exact pricing can be further prescribed by subordinate laws.

Legislation should also prescribe sources of extraordinary funding and when and how this type of funding will be triggered. Details on the procedure of extraordinary funding should be prescribed by subordinate laws.

As a consequence of the recent financial crisis, there is a pressure from international financial institutions on governments to institutionalize extraordinary funding arrangements for the DIS, meaning that such arrangements should be explicitly stated in the legislation and subordinate laws should provide detailed information on how such arrangements should be activated if necessary.

If a DIS is a paybox, it should have an option whether and how to use the funds for resolution methods other than for the payout of insured deposits. For example, a DIS should decide on its own (decision should be made by its governing body) whether to use the DIFs for financing the transfer of assets and insured deposits into another sound bank (P&A) or to participate in the establishment of a bridge bank if such resolution options are conducted by the resolution authority. Core Principles prescribe a number of conditions that should be met prior to using the paybox DIS funds for resolution purposes.

When resolving banks, the resolution authority may be tempted to request funding, in the form of financial assistance, from a DIS (even if the DIS has only a paybox mandate) in order to prevent consequences of bank failure. Supervisory authorities sometimes argue that 'higher interests' of financial stability of the whole system are important. If paybox DIS funds are used for the purposes other than envisaged by the law on DIS, transparent rules and procedures should be in place, in order to avoid financial losses and politically motivated decisions.

Deposit insurers, in general, advocate obligatory ex ante funding and establishment of a target size fund which should be determined on the basis of clear, consistent and transparent criteria and subject to a periodic review. If a DIS is regularly financed and collects ex ante premium in predetermined intervals (quarterly, semiannually or annually), the deposit insurance authority manages substantial amounts of financial resources. In order to preserve the capital substance, funds should be invested to generate additional funds. Specifics of DIFs' investments are that profit is not the primary investment goal.

A deposit insurance authority is similar to any large investment company, pension fund or asset management company because it manages funds collected for a specific purpose (deposit payout) where the risk of bank failure is not always known and where liquidity must be readily available at short notice.

It is important to develop and approve internal procedures on funds' investment and management, as well as to establish internal controlling function. Appropriate fund's management procedures and practices help to ensure sufficient liquidity of a DIS. During the periods without bank failures, most of the collected funds can be freely invested in low-risk securities in order to earn a yield on investments. Preserving the substance of collected funds and ensuring sufficient liquidity at all times are two main goals of any good investment policy of a DIS.

There are some practical questions that the deposit insurance authority must answer when establishing an ex ante DIF. The first question is related to opening a business account. It is advisable that the collected ex ante DIF is kept on a special-purpose account in the central bank or another entity (depending on the structure of the payment system in the country), but not within one or more member banks. If DIFs are kept within member banks, that would be a conflict of interest for the deposit insurance authority and such policy can jeopardize the purpose of establishment of DIF.

A deposit insurance authority's regular business account, where money for operating expenses is kept, can be opened in one or several commercial banks. Ex ante DIF should not be subject to enforcement and the deposit insurance authority should establish strict rules on who can issue payment orders. Legislation should prescribe uses of DIFs.

Every deposit insurance authority should develop and adopt an investment policy. Investment policy, as the underlying document on investment principles, should prescribe minimum elements on investment objectives, rules and practices in order to provide sufficient grounds for preparation of annual investment plans and actual investments in line with the approved plan.

Investment policy should prescribe key objectives for the investment of DIF, which are based on liquidity and safety principles. Deposit insurance authorities usually invest in short-term liquid governmental and central bank securities such as treasury bills, government notes and bonds. In addition, DISs make deposits within the central bank.

Many DISs operate in less developed capital markets where investing is even more challenging. In some countries, secondary markets for securities do not exist, making it almost impossible for a deposit insurance authority to liquidate its investments prior to their maturity. Sometimes there are no sufficient security issues and a deposit insurance authority must compete for the same papers with other institutional investors such as banks, investment funds and pension funds to invest the excess of its liquidity. Some jurisdictions experience a rigid regulatory framework which prohibits investments abroad and promotes only investments within national jurisdictions, thus making the diversification of investments 'mission impossible'. Some small DISs experience challenges because their DIFs are small in size and expenses related to investments are high in comparison to the invested amount.

A deposit insurance authority must decide whether to manage its investments internally or it is more appropriate to outsource the investment function for a professional asset management company. Both options have pros and cons. If possible, it is always a better option to hire professional asset management that will propose an annual investment plan and manage funds within the prescribed benchmarks.

When deciding on investments, a deposit insurance authority must develop a liquidity reserve policy and decide how much cash liquidity is required. Some DISs tend to keep substantial amounts of cash on the account. Such policy is based on safety principles, although the money which is not invested when not needed does not earn yield. How much cash liquidity is appropriate to keep on the account as a reserve? The answer is easy and difficult at the same time. If a deposit insurance authority conducts a projection of cash flow on a regular basis, it is easy to understand when the annual regular premium is going to be collected and how much money is necessary on a monthly basis to cover operating expenses such as rent, salary and other miscellaneous expenses. A deposit insurance authority wishes to have sufficient liquid funds at least to cover its budgeted expenses for a period ranging from few months to a year.

In addition to keeping a minimum cash reserve sufficient to ensure the smooth operation of a deposit insurance authority, a close look will be given to the situation in the banking sector and whether the liquidity will be needed for deposit payout.

If the DIS is a paybox mandate, close cooperation with the supervisory authority will enable better financial management. If the deposit insurance authority learns that a particular member bank might fail in the next few months, such information is important when making investment decisions. If the secondary market is developed and invested securities can be liquidated without problems and losses, investment can be made even when knowing that in a few months securities must be sold. However, if the secondary market does not exist and/or is shallow and securities can be sold prior to their maturity only at a large discount, in such cases it is not wise to invest funds knowing that liquidity would be required in a short time. Inappropriate investment decisions may turn to be costly.

A deposit insurance authority should, on a regular basis, once per year, develop and propose for approval its annual investment plan, in line with the approved investment policy. Annual investment plan is more specific and more detailed than the investment policy. It should list all types of securities for investments, benchmarks, expected yields, maturity, time frame, responsible persons and so on. After the approval, a deposit insurance authority should inform on a regular basis its governing body about the investment results and, if necessary, adjust the investment plan to specific market circumstances.

A deposit insurance authority should manage market risks, and if covered deposits are placed in foreign currencies in a significant amount, its investment policy should reflect the management of FX risk.

Investments should be made professionally and safely, taking into account the adopted investment principles, and they should be based on the adopted investment plan.

The safety of investments is ensured if investments are not frozen, devalued or otherwise restricted for the investor to use and paid out on demand. Safe investments are those with the highest credit rating assigned by credit rating agencies, such as Moody's, Fitch Ratings and Standard & Poor's.

Liquid investments are those which can be converted into cash without losses, at a minimum purchased price, and in a short period of time (not longer than seven days). The price of securities depends on the supply and demand and is affected by key interest rates. Government securities are typical 'safe and liquid' investment options, at least in theory. Financial markets in some countries are small and can be driven by different notions such as, for example, political or economic instability when the liquidity is squeezed. When experiencing such conditions, cashing in investments may be a painful and uneasy task.

Ideally, investments should be sufficiently diversified to achieve an optimal level of safety, liquidity and profitability. Investments should be diversified, at minimum, by issuers, types of securities, duration of investments and currency of investment. DISs which are exposed to a high foreign currency risk due to the high portion of foreign currency deposits in banks, should ideally hedge their currency risk with investments in securities denominated in those currencies. For example, if most deposits in banks are denominated in Euro, which is the case of many western Balkan countries (such as Croatia, Serbia, Bosnia, Montenegro, Slovenia), but also of many countries outside Euro area, DISs operating in those countries should protect some of its financial resources by investing in securities denominated in Euro. Otherwise, any devaluation of the local currency toward Euro would create losses for the DIS without hedging.

Legislation should prescribe minimum rules related to financial management and investments of DIFs, in order to prevent negligence and investments in risky financial instruments.

Conservatively, deposit insurance authorities invest collected financial resources in different, predominantly short-term government securities. In addition to government securities, deposits with central banks are options for safe deposit insurance investments. Some governments issue securities denominated in foreign currency and a DIS does not necessarily need to invest in foreign governments' issues to diversify its portfolio by currency. Investments in central banks' deposits have low profitability and such investments may be limited by central bank laws and monetary policy rules.

When the domestic market is underdeveloped and limited, instead of safety, a DIS is exposed to liquidity risks facing problems such as limited securities offers, shallow market turnover, non-existence of the secondary market, high public debt and inability of the government to buyback securities before the due date if required and other problems.

2.4.1 Case of Lithuanian Deposit and Investment Insurance Liquidity Issues in 2011

The Lithuanian Deposit and Investment Insurance authority invested more than €493 million of DIFs into diversified portfolio of government bills and bonds issued by the Lithuanian government (62 per cent of total investments), the Republic of Italy bonds, the Republic of Hungary bonds, the Belgium Kingdom bonds, the German Federal Republic bonds, the France government bonds, the Republic of Austria bonds, the Netherlands government bonds and the US Treasuries (Zilinskas and Gazauskas 2015, 137–138). In addition, some €28 million were placed as deposits with the Bank of Lithuania.

In general, the investment portfolio was diversified (32 per cent of total investments were placed in 31 issues of issuers), but the concentration of securities in the Lithuanian government papers was very high.

On 16 November 2011, the license of the bank Snoras was revoked and the DIS faced an obligation to pay out €1,159 billion of covered deposits. The solvency gap was approximately €666 million, for which it was agreed to borrow money from the Lithuanian Ministry of Finance.

All foreign-invested government bonds were successfully liquidated without losses within one to five days, except domestic securities, where it took more than 200 days to liquidate (sell) the Lithuanian government bonds.

As a result of the long inability to cash in domestic bonds in a timely manner, the Lithuanian DIS had to borrow the total amount of €945.61 million from the Ministry of Finance. The ex post analysis showed that if all investments were made in the securities of German, Dutch or French governments, those investments would have been liquidated within one to two days.

2.5 Legal Structure and Legal Form of the Explicit DIS

Deposit insurance authority may be established as a public or private entity, although in the practice of some countries it is hard to clearly define the criteria for this classification. Therefore, the DISs often define themselves as a combination of public and private.

Some jurisdictions choose to place the deposit insurance within the existing legal entity that is not a separate legal entity solely responsible for the deposit insurance which may create challenges in a DIS daily operation and the decision-making process (IADI 2009, 7). Such practice is not in line with the international guidelines as it fails to ensure operational and financial independence of DIS which is necessary for the fulfillment of the mandate (IADI 2014, 21).

There are several criteria how we can differentiate the public from the private DIS, based on administration, governance and financing. However, these criteria are not equally defined on the international level.

Public DIS is usually classified and defined as the 'governmental' DIS, where the deposit insurance is 'sponsored' by the government or where governmental officials are members of the board or the government appoints the majority of members of the board and/or management of the deposit insurance authority. In addition, the government may provide initial funds for the DIS. However, regular funding is always provided by member banks.

Private DIS is also established by the legislation and its establishment may be sponsored by the government, but administration and management as well as funding are provided by the banks themselves.

Combined administration and governance are more and more evidenced in practice, where market representatives participate at the board level, ensuring transparency and a better dialogue with member banks. The representative of member banks at the board of the deposit insurer should avoid conflict of interest and participation of active bankers at the board of the deposit insurance entity should be avoided.

Why should the government be involved in the deposit insurance in the first place? It is generally considered that banks collect deposits from depositors who don't have a deep understanding of the bank's risk profile and therefore should be protected from the consequences of excessive risk taking. Some even consider that banks, although being in private ownership, actually do 'public good' and therefore their existence is in the public interest. Consequently, deposit insurance does 'public good' and also contributes to an overall financial stability, so the government should have a role and interest in the DIS, too.

In some countries, the initiative for the establishment of the DIS came from the private sector and the DIS was established without the government's sponsorship (e.g. in Italy, Germany, Switzerland).

The government's involvement may also have negative effects on the DIS, if politics is more important than expertise, in cases when board members are appointed according to their political preferences and activities, and if the political influence is prevailing, which all may lead to the underdevelopment of DIS.

When the government decides to establish a DIS, the process is usually formally initiated by some sort of the government decree or a decision as an official declaration and determination to implement the reform and introduce the DIS.

In some countries, governments create entities with a specific aim to promote specialized governmental goals such as, for example, promoting export or entrepreneurship or protecting some key industries. Such entities are established as 'agencies' or 'institutes' or as 'public companies'. Similarly, if the government establishes and sponsors a DIS, it may be established as a 'government (state) agency'.

It is always a question what is the most appropriate legal form or format for a deposit insurance authority. Countries look for solutions with their neighbors and sometimes 'copy-paste' those solutions that could fit into their own legal framework or 'invent' new legal solutions if appropriate.

The legal form of a deposit insurance authority will determine its legal status, tax status, governance, accountability and reporting, accounting and many other details. It is always recommended to understand the global practice but to be aware that whenever legislators copy solutions from other countries such action may create practical problems as the legal and corporate frameworks of two countries are rarely identical.

Deposit insurance authority should be established not for profit and should be exempt from the profit tax liability.

DISs are, therefore, often established as 'specialized not-for-profit' authorities in the form of a specialized financial organization (agency, fund, corporation, etc.).

In addition, the business account of the DIS, where collected funds from member banks are kept, should not be placed in any of the member banks. As an exemption, the business account for regular business transactions (except those related to deposit insurance) may be placed in one of the member banks.

The prevailing idea is that the deposit insurance authority should be fully operationally and legally independent and independence can be exercised only if the DIS is established as a separate legal entity with its own management and governance structures. The independence of the DIS is ensured with the ability to make independent decisions and by financial independence from external interests.

If the deposit insurance is a part of another legal entity, it may not exercise its full independence on a daily basis and its operation and financing would be subject to the authority within which the DIS is established.

In order to devote to the work and implement the best practices of deposit insurance, staff should be fully dedicated only to deposit insurance. If deposit insurance is only a 'part-time job' where experts devote their professional work to other tasks (which is the case when the deposit insurance is not established as an independent entity), results are always at the expense of the deposit insurance.

As is the case with the work of a fire brigade, the successful operation of the DIS largely depends on the preparation and only to a minor extent on the execution. Deposit insurers must prepare themselves for the tasks which are highly volatile.

If a DIS is established as part of another legal entity, there are risks that deposit insurance will not develop its functions properly, and consequently it will not be able to fulfill its mandate when required. The cyclicality of the deposit insurance payout function (banks do not fail on a regular basis) often creates the illusion that deposit insurance is redundant and not necessary.

Out of a total of 113 DISs, 96 are established as independent legal entities (Demirguc-Kunt et al. 2014, 37–38). The remaining 17 DISs are placed within the Ministry of Finance, the central bank, association of banks or independent financial sector supervisor as an internal organizational unit (such as a department, division, unit).

As of 2014, 73 DISs have been publicly administered, 25 have established a joint public and private administration, and the remaining 15 have set up private administration.

2.6 Internal Organization of Deposit Insurance Authority

There is no universal model of internal organization structure for the deposit insurer, nor is there an optimal number of permanent staff. The more complex the mandate, the more diversified the internal organization will be, though there are some universal minimum functions in every DIS, especially when the DIS has the simplest paybox mandate, that is, a legal obligation to pay out insured deposits in case of insurance event occurrence.

In addition, the number of permanent staff (employees) does not depend on the number of banks in the country or on the size of the country (JRC 2010, 1–453), as there is plenty of evidence where the DIS with a small number of employees is responsible for the deposit insurance in several hundred credit institutions (e.g. DISs in France and Italy for years operated with a small number of full-time employees, while there are several hundreds of banks who are members of DIS). There are other DIS examples where the ratio of full-time employees in comparison to member banks is 2:1.

A large number of DIS staff doesn't guarantee efficiency, nor does a small number of employees guarantee cost efficiency. It is therefore important to ensure efficiency and effectiveness.

The main functions of any DIS are deriving from legally prescribed tasks and the mandate of DIS (i.e. from the approved national legal act).

However, these tasks may be organized in several different ways, on different organizational levels such as, for example, establishing units, departments, divisions or simple line functions. Some smaller DISs don't establish separate organizational units (due to the rationalization of staff). Instead, they are organized through line functions and have one or more employees dedicated to each function.

When designing organizational structure, authorities should have in mind what are the mandate and functions prescribed by the legal act (paybox has the simplest mandate and a few functions only); what is the desirable size of the DIS and optimal number of employees (which is in relation with budgeting issues and expenses), what would be the strategic development of the DIS and what is the established corporate practice in the country.

Details on internal organization of functions, organizational chart and responsibilities of each organizational unit or function are usually prescribed by an internal regulation (statute or charter and other bylaws).

The simple paybox DIS has common tasks related to regular collection and analysis of the data on deposits and insured deposits in credit institutions, premium calculation and collection, financial management of DIFs (financial planning, investments), timely payout of insured deposits, providing information to depositors and development of internal regulation. In addition, there are some supporting functions like accounting, legal support, IT, internal audit and human resources.

The above-listed core tasks may be accomplished with a minimal number of permanent staff and with support from external parties (e.g. some tasks may be outsourced), regardless of whether the DIS is established as a separate legal entity or as an organizational part within another legal entity. However, a small number of staff also creates some operating risks (e.g. in the case of staff absence from work, change of job).

Deposit payout is the core function of any DIS. The tasks of the deposit payout include all activities related to the period of pre-occurrence of the insured event (preparation for deposit payout), period after the withdrawal of the banking license and all preparatory steps that must be taken in order to organize a timely, effective and efficient payout of depositors in a legally prescribed manner. The reimbursement process is not possible without IT infrastructure, hardware, database platform and tailor-made payout software.

Every DIS is responsible for the control of data accuracy and reimbursement procedures. Although in the case of bank failure and deposit payout, DISs use payout agents (other credit institutions), deposit payout function can't be fully outsourced and transferred to others. A minimum of one full-time employee is needed to coordinate and control all tasks related to the deposit payout. In addition, a special software for the deposit payout should be designed. The software enables import of data from the bank when the insurance event occurs, aggregation of deposit amounts according to the rules prescribed by the legal act, calculation of the covered amount for each eligible depositor, preparation for the payout, payout itself, control, bookkeeping of the process and all necessary reporting forms.

The deposit payout is a pro-cyclical function, depending on whether and how many banks may be liquidated, and it is hard to predict how many staff would be required for this function.

The deposit payout software, as part of the MIS, may be developed internally or procured externally (many DISs opt for this solution), where

IT function may be fully outsourced to external partners. The deposit payout software is necessary to ensure the correct calculation of the covered amount that is a SCV.

The analytical function is responsible for the regular collection and analysis of reports on deposits received directly from banks as well as collected from audited reports, financial statements, financial indicators and other relevant information on the bank's financial position, profitability and stability, which the DIS wants to monitor. The main purpose of this function is to monitor trends in deposits, their structure, size, eligible and insured deposits, project financial resources and its potential liabilities, but also to create a reliable database on banks, their profiles and deposits. DISs use collected data for regular premium calculations, for financial planning and financial management and for the preparation for the deposit payout.

Financial management function is responsible for calculation, charging and collection of premium and deposit insurance funding in general, development of investment plans and investments of funds, as well as for the budgeting of the DIS. Many DISs outsource asset management of funds (investment function) to professional asset managers. The remaining tasks of financial management may be organized within a separate treasury department or jointly with an accounting function.

Accounting function may be organized internally or outsourced to external partners. However, DIS's accounting should be timely, accurate and according to International Financial Reporting Standards (IFRS). The DIS shall produce and publish its financial statements and annual report. Financial statements should be audited by external auditors.

The DIS is responsible for providing correct and timely information to depositors and general public, regular communication with credit institutions and other stakeholders and for ensuring smooth crisis communication during the insurance event. At minimum, communication strategy should be developed and information leaflet printed. Usually, this function is outsourced to specialized PR companies, but at least some tasks related to communication with stakeholders will be performed internally.

Internal control and internal audit are becoming a standard for a sound DIS; therefore, the internal auditor should work according to the approved plan, but specifically pay attention to the investments of funds, use of financial resources, budgeting issues, compliance with the law and internal regulation and so on.

At the beginning of the establishment of a DIS, especially in the first years of the DIS operations, there would be a need for the development and drafting of a number of internal regulations (of general and technical nature). It is always recommended to hire a local legal expert with some experience in drafting legislation as well as with experience and knowledge of the national legal framework.

2.6.1 Budgeting, Internal Controls, External Audit

A well-governed and well-managed deposit insurance authority establishes and develops the budgeting rules, establishes internal controls and is subject to annual external audit.

A DIS's annual budget should be subject to approval of a higher governing body, which depends on good governance practice in each jurisdiction and on the type of legal entity responsible for the DIS.

When preparing the annual operating budget, a deposit insurance authority should list all types of revenues, such as operating, financial and extraordinary, and all types of expenses, based on the approved budgeting rules. If, throughout the business year, operating revenues and expenses exceed the budgeted figures, it is common practice to propose amendments and adjust the operating budget to be in line with real figures. In addition, budgeting rules should envisage regular reporting on the budget execution.

Establishment of internal controls is important for the DIS due to the specific nature of public objectives entrusted with the deposit insurance authority and large sums of financial resources which are collected on a regular basis. Therefore, similarly to any other financial institution, all rules and procedures should be in place to minimize operating risks, mismanagement and fraud. A clear division of responsibilities and duties among the staff should be established to prevent unauthorized use and manipulation of the DIF.

Annual financial statements of the deposit insurance authority should be subject to external audit where a higher governing body should select an external auditor and enable its rotation every three to five years to ensure objectivity and professionalism.

2.6.2 Accounting for Deposit Insurance

Many jurisdictions establish a deposit insurance authority as a not-for-profit entity, where the main goal is to build and preserve sufficient funds and not to generate profit, and where premium contributions paid by banks are not taxable.

Premiums are collected either directly charging banks for the exact amount or a deposit insurance authority issues an invoice with the due amount and due payment date.

Regardless of the method of charging and payment, for a deposit insurance authority the premium paid by member banks are revenues from operation (premium income). When investing surplus funds into securities, yield on investments is revenue from financial transactions (investment income). Operating expenses and other general administrative expenses are deductible items, as per approved and executed budget. If there is a bank failure, on the day the insurance event occurs, the deposit insurance authority should recognize the liability in its statement of financial position and expenses for deposit insurance in a profit and loss account.

A typical simplified profit and loss account and balance sheet of a deposit insurance authority used in examples in this book would be as presented in Tables 2.3 and 2.4, respectively.

Table 2.3 Sample of profit and loss account of a deposit insurance authority

Profit and loss account, in €000	Year 1	Year 2	Year 3
Revenues from premium			
Initial premium	100	0	0
Regular premium	49,000	51,000	53,000
Income from investments	1,739	5,809	3,826
Operating expenses	−210	−210	−210
Covered deposit payout			−75,000
Net result for the year	**50,629**	**56,599**	**−18,384**

Table 2.4 Sample of balance sheet of a deposit insurance authority

Balance sheet, in €000	At end Year 1	At end Year 2	At end Year 3
Assets			
Cash and cash equivalents	3,704	7,774	5,791
Available-for-sale securities	46,825	99,354	82,953
Non-current assets	100	100	100
Total assets	**50,629**	**107,228**	**88,844**
Liabilities and equity			
Equity/deposit insurance fund			
Fund reserve	50,629	50,629	107,228
Net result for the year		56,599	−18,384
Total DIF	**50,629**	**107,228**	**88,844**
Liabilities	0	0	0
Total liabilities and equity	**50,629**	**107,228**	**88,844**

As for the profit and loss account, in year 1 and year 2, the deposit insurance authority presented a net result for the year as a difference between revenues and expenses. Operating expenses are planned and budgeted according to the approved annual budget.

A deposit payout of covered deposits as a consequence of a failure of a Bank number 8 results in a negative result for year 3, in the amount of €18 million. A deposit insurance authority is not profit oriented and the negative financial result decreases its overall DIF. However, although the amount paid to eligible depositors is high, it does not jeopardize the overall solvency of the DIS, nor does it impact the liquidity. The deposit insurance authority, due to its financial management, sold an appropriate portion of previously invested securities and ensured sufficient liquidity on time for a deposit payout.

If and when a deposit insurance authority recovers financial resources in insolvency proceedings from Bank number 8 estate, recovery will represent the extraordinary income in the year when it would be gained.

The balance sheet represents the assets and equity and liabilities of the deposit insurance authority. A DIF is presented as part of item equity, either called fund or reserves or even capital (in line with IFRS and or national accounting standards and legislation). Regardless of the formal title of the item, it is presented in a balance sheet as part of long-term financial resources, that is, under the title 'Equity'. At the end of Year 3, a DIF amounted to almost €89 million.

2.7 Conclusion

Core Principles advocate that the DIS's mandate and powers must be clearly stated in the legislation and the accompanying laws and that its governance structure must be of the highest ethical standards ensuring operational and financial independence, accountability and transparency. A DIS must ensure formal and comprehensive cooperation framework with other financial safety-net authorities, especially on the exchange of information with the national supervisor, but protecting banking secrets and ensuring professional confidentiality, even in case of cross-border failing banks. A DIS should participate in national contingency planning and crisis management preparation. All licensed banks should be members of a DIS, with no exceptions. Coverage should be clearly defined where scope and coverage level should provide credible protection to majority of depositors at lower costs for the system as a whole and without jeopardizing the market discipline. Depositors must be informed and be aware of the DIS features and their own rights and liabilities. Deposits must be made available to them in a fast and efficient manner in order to prevent panic and instability. Above all and in order to be able to fulfill all given tasks, a DIS must have all funding mechanisms in place. A DIS should create and build an optimal and credible DIF where banks contribute in a regular manner and based on their risk profiles. A deposit insurance authority must manage a DIF with due professional care and responsible financial management, setting the target fund size within a reasonable time frame and establishing arrangements in case of extraordinary funding needs and large bank failures. If a DIS has all functions and features established in compliance with international guidelines and standards, but fails to build a credible DIF, it achieved nothing and failed in everything.

Bibliography

Bartiloro, Laura. 2011. Is Your Money Safe? What Italians Know About Deposit Insurance. Occassional Paper, Banca d'Italia, Occassional Papers no 104.

CDIC. 2016. http://www.cdic.ca/en/about-cdic/Pages/default.aspx. Accessed 2016.

Demirguc-Kunt, Asli, and Enrica Detragiache. 2000. Does Deposit Insurance Increase Banking System Stability? An Empirical Investigation. *The World Bank.*

Demirguc-Kunt, Asli, Edward Kane, and Luc Laeven. 2014. Deposit Insurance Database. http://siteresources.worldbank.org/INTRES/Resources/469232-1107449512766/Deposit_insurance_database_preWP.pdf. Accessed 2016.

Directive. 1994. Directive 94/19/EC on Deposit Guarantee Schemes. *Official Journal* L 135: 0005–0014. 31/05/1994.

Directive 2014/49/EU. 2014. Directive 2014/49/EU of the European Parliament and of the Council of 16 April 2014 on Deposit Guarantee Schemes. http://eur-lex.europa.eu/legal-content/EN/TXT/?uri=CELEX:32014L0049. Accessed 2016.

FDIC. 2016. https://www.fdic.gov/about/learn/symbol/index.html. Accessed 2016.

FSB. 2012. *Thematic Review on Deposit Insurance Systems, Peer Review Report.* Financial Stability Board.

Garcia, Gillian G.H. 1999. Deposit Insurance: A Survey of Actual and Best Practices. *WP/99/54.* Washington, DC: IMF.

IADI. 2009. *Guidance Paper: Governance of Deposit Insurance Systems.* Basel. IADI.

———. 2014. *The Revised Core Principles for Effective Deposit Insurance Systems.* Basel. IADI.

———. 2016. *A Handbook for the Assessment of Compliance with the Core Principles for Effective Deposit Insurance Systems.* Basel. IADI.

JRC. 2010. *JRC Report under Article 12 of Directive 94/19/EC as Amended by Directive 2009/14/EC; Annex 1.* European Commission.

KDIC. 2016. http://www.kdic.or.kr/english/major/sub1.jsp. Accessed 2016.

Zilinskas, R., and L. Gazauskas. 2015. The Investment Policy of Deposit Guarantee Funds under Conditions of Limited Domestic Securities Markets. *Ekonomika* Vol. 94(1): 137–138.

3

Challenges of Funding a DIS

3.1 Introduction

Building and maintaining a credible DIF is a prerequisite for any DIS, regardless of its mandate or policy objectives. Authorities choose among many options when deciding on funding options, that is, when prescribing the level and sources for the initial, regular and emergency funding, and when addressing funding issues in legislation. Given the enhanced role of the DIS, higher public expectations and shorter payout time frame, policy makers and deposit insurers are shifting their focus to the establishment of a robust but efficient ex ante DIF. Deposit insurers manage large sums of money which are necessary in case of unforeseeable events of bank failures. Simple or more advanced financial planning enables deposit insurers to project their cash flows, retain adequate liquidity reserves, invest excess of liquidity in accordance with approved investment policies, determine appropriate annual regular premium, assess and anticipate its exposure toward individual member banks.

This chapter clarifies important definitions such as the deposit insurance funds (DIFs) and introduces the concept of coverage ratio and the

D. Ognjenovic, *Deposit Insurance Schemes*,
DOI 10.1007/978-3-319-51143-6_3

DIS' payout capacity. It provides classifications of DIFs and funding options, and explains concepts of initial, regular and emergency funding. It discusses advantages of implementing a risk-based premium. Examples are given on how to choose an appropriate level of annual regular premium under different circumstances of deposit growth and banking sector concentration, how to apply a risk-based methodology for premium calculation, how to project a cash flow over a three-year period and manage liquidity in case of an envisaged deposit payout.

3.2 Understanding the Deposit Insurance Fund

Although it is one of the key terms related to deposit insurance, there is no definition of the deposit insurance fund(s) in the existing literature. Usually, the terms 'fund' and 'funds' create confusion because they are not synonymous yet are often used as synonyms. When it comes to deposit insurance, both terms are widely interpreted as:

(i) long-term sources of funding (presented on the liabilities and equity side of the balance sheet of the deposit insurance authority as 'capital', equity' or 'fund reserve') and
(ii) financial assets (in the form of cash and financial investments) arising from the collection of premium from banks and other sources.

DGSD (Directive 2014/49/EU 2014, L 173/157) uses the term 'available financial means' and defines it as 'cash, deposits and low-risk assets which can be liquidated within a period not exceeding that referred to in Article 8(1) and payment commitments up to the limit set out in Article 10(3).'

Article 8(1) of DGSD prescribes a 7-day time frame for the payout of insured deposits upon the occurrence of the insurance event. Therefore, according to the definition, available financial means are cash and most liquid financial assets which can be turned into cash within 7 days (Directive 2014/49/EU 2014, L 173/162).

Article 10(3) of DGSD prescribes payment commitments in amount up to 30 per cent of available financial means (Directive 2014/49/EU 2014, L 173/165). This means that, in general, 70 per cent of total DIFs must be collected in cash (ex ante funds) and up to 30 per cent may be in the form of payment commitments (collected ex post).

In other words, the term 'available financial means' refers to:

- cash, deposits and low-risk assets which can be liquidated within 7 days and
- payment commitments (ex post banks' contribution) which can be collected from member banks within 7 days.

IADI in its Core Principles does not define deposit insurance fund (or funds) either, but defines the terms 'target fund size' and 'ex ante funding' (IADI 2014, 9–10). Ex ante funding is defined as 'the regular collection of premiums, with the aim of accumulating a fund to meet future obligations (e.g. reimbursing depositors) and cover the operational and related costs of the deposit insurer.'

When referring to the target size funding, Core Principles refer to the 'size of the ex-ante deposit insurance fund, typically measured as a proportion of the assessment base (e.g. total or insured deposits), sufficient to meet the expected future obligations and cover the operational and related costs of the deposit insurer.'

Therefore, indirectly, we may assume from these two definitions that there is 'a deposit insurance fund' and that it is formed on an 'ex ante' basis. In addition, Core Principles also indirectly indicate that the purpose of ex ante funds is to meet the expected future obligations and to cover the operational expenses of the deposit insurer.

In the main text of Core Principle 9 (Sources and Uses of Funds), under the point five (5), the following phrase is used 'after establishing an ex ante deposit insurance fund…' indicating again that there is 'an ex ante deposit insurance fund' created and managed by the DIS (IADI 2014, 29).

In its original Guidance Paper on DIS' funding, IADI uses the phrase 'a deposit insurance reserve fund', but does not provide the definition of it (IADI 2009, 4). The same paper provided the definition of 'a target reserve ratio' as 'the ratio of fund reserves to total deposits or insured deposits' (IADI 2009, 3). Clearly, IADI used the term 'reserve fund' for the DIF. As it is evident from this example, IADI does not use its definitions and terms consistently. Even an updated Guidance Paper on ex ante funding uses the term 'reserve funds' several times, although the definition of the term is not provided (IADI 2015, 6–7).

In a post-financial crisis period, when DISs tended to rebuild confidence by building robust ex ante funds, it became more and more important to understand the basic terms and definitions and focus on funding planning and projections with a much more serious approach.

There are still jurisdictions around the world where DISs are financed ex post or with hybrid (combined ex post and ex ante) funding and not all those jurisdictions prescribe the target size of their funds.

For simplicity and for better understanding of the real meaning and importance of DIFs, let's assume, unless stated differently, that DIFs refer to *all funds available to deposit insurer on either ex ante basis or ex post basis, including backup funding.*

DIF refers *only to ex ante fund,* that is, *financial resources already at disposal to the deposit insurance authority, collected on a regular basis with main purpose to build up the 'fund' of significant size for the purpose of deposit payout.*

3.2.1 Is the DIF a Synonym for the Capital of the DIS?

The original idea of the DIS was to build an ex ante fund with the purpose to ensure long-term protection of insured depositors. Ex ante DIF, thus, can be treated as the 'capital' of the deposit insurance authority.

In some jurisdictions, regardless of whether the deposit insurance authority is established in accordance with the legislation, the terms 'capital' or 'equity' are used as a 'synonym' for the DIF and presented on the liabilities' side of the balance sheet of the DIS authority, while in some other jurisdictions, they are interchangeable with the terms 'reserve fund' or the 'fund'.

The legislative framework of each country defines whether the deposit insurance authority must provide a 'statutory (paid-in) capital'. If that is so, then the statutory capital requirement is ensured from the initial DIS funding.

Core Principles use the term 'fund capital' (IADI 2014, 9–10). The term 'fund capital' is somewhat an awkward formulation as the term 'fund' does not refer to the authority responsible for the DIS. Literally, the 'fund capital' would read as 'capital capital'. It seems that Core Principles' definition suggests that the DIFs are indeed the capital of DIS, but the term lacks precise definition.

Regardless of similarities and differences in terms, it is conclusive that the DIF is in its substance the capital of DIS.

Financial resources, when collected through ex ante funding arrangements, are in the form of cash (liquid financial assets). Over time, those financial resources are invested in liquid and safe investments in order to provide a yield for the deposit insurer, at least to cover the expenses of running the DIS, but also, if possible, to increase the size of the total funds for the deposit payout.

Deposit insurance *coverage ratio* is a measure for the DIS's 'compensation power' or its 'payout capacity'. It is, somewhat, similar to the concept of bank's capital adequacy ratio (CAR).

At the same time, DIS' coverage ratio and bank's CAR are different measures. The coverage ratio is the proportion of DIS' collected funds in relation to the potential liabilities. CAR represents the level of capital in relation to bank's risky assets (already disbursed funds), expressed as an accounting figure, which banks tend to maintain as a minimum reserve cushion.

DIF is preserved for the purpose of ensuring safety but it is also realistic to expect that sometime in the future those funds will be disbursed (consumed) for deposit payout, resulting in the decrease of coverage ratio.

If a bank consummates its 'capital' through offsetting risky assets (bad loans that will not be repaid), that is the signal that the bank was not sufficiently conservative when approving loans. As a result of its risky appetite, the bank must 'spend' its capital to cover the losses.

By default, the DIS invests its financial assets in non-risky and liquid short-term investments. However, also by default banks invest their 'capital' (as well as financial assets from collected deposits) in all forms of liquid or less liquid assets, with a different gradation of risk.

Therefore, capital adequacy is rather figurative than a real 'cushion' against risk-weighted assets.

The difference between coverage ratio and CAR is in the denominators used in two formulas. Namely, DIFs are compared to total covered deposits which represent a potential liability for the DIS through an outflow of funds in case of bank failure, but bank capital is compared to risk-weighted assets, which represent the risk of being unable to collect previously disbursed money.

There is additionally another significant difference between the bank's CAR and the coverage ratio of the DIS. While the bank business has evolved to the state-of-the-art assessment of clients' risks, calculating the capital adequacy on a daily basis, many deposit insurance authorities still don't take into account (on a regular basis) risk profiles of individual banks when assessing the sufficiency of their funds or when calculating coverage ratio and target size funds. When calculating the coverage ratio there is no prescribed rule regarding risk assessment of the failure of individual banks. Therefore, the coverage ratio does not reflect the risk for the DIF. The coverage ratio only measures the DIS exposure to total covered deposits in all member banks.

More advanced DISs analyze and assess the sufficiency of their funds based on the risk assessment of their member banks and the possible failure of each of them. Although many DISs apply a risk-based premium system, they don't use the same risk assessment methodology for the purpose of financial management and optimization of funds.

3.3 Classification of the Deposit Insurance Funding

There are at least three broad classifications of the deposit insurance funding which are widely accepted by deposit insurers, and two classifications are based on regularity and timing of the collection of funds (Garcia 1999, 9–13).

One classification differentiates funding as:

- initial,
- regular (ongoing) and
- extraordinary (backup, alternative) funding.

Another classification differentiates:

- ex ante and
- ex post funding.

If the funds are collected prior to the insurance event, that is ex ante DIS. On the contrary, when only surviving member banks provide funding after the insurance event, this is ex post DIS. Over time, many jurisdictions have combined ex ante and ex post funding, in order to retain and preserve some ex ante funds for running the DIS, where the majority of funds can be collected if and when required. There are many variations of combined (mixed, hybrid) funding.

There is one more classification of the deposit insurance funding, based on the applied premium rate, that is, whether the applied rate is flat or it differs according to the risk profile of member institutions and therefore we distinguish between:

- linear (flat) and
- differential premium funding.

IADI (IADI 2015, 6–8) uses the following classification of sources of funds:

- internal funds (premium collection),
- external funds (liquidity funding) and
- alternative funding mechanisms.

Such classification may be criticized due to unclear classification rationale. Deposit insurance authority collects all funds from external resources. Banks may provide funds as regular premium (which IADI classified as internal funding) and as additional premium (which IADI classified as external funding), so it is not quite clear why the regular premium is classified as internal funding and additional premium as external funding.

3.3.1 Initial Funding

The purpose of initial funding is to ensure sufficient funds for the establishment of DIS and operation of the deposit insurance authority and to create sufficient public trust on deposit insurance at the time of its introduction.

Common questions which are often raised at the time of introduction of the DIS are:

- how would the DIS be funded and
- is the DIS cost effective?

In other words, will there be sufficient financial resources if a bank fails and how much the system costs?

These are legitimate questions but answers are not always straightforward and depend on the policy objectives of a DIS.

Or, we can provide an answer by asking the authorities another question: Do you want to establish a credible DIS?

If the answer is – *we want to establish a credible DIS* – then the answer to the first question is – *we need as much funding (including initial funding) as possible to ensure fast payout to depositors of failed banks in the future.*

Someone may argue that both questions and answers are rather philosophical and not precise enough in financial terms. This is partially true as we can approximate the future credibility of a DIS only by assessing the risk factors of the banking sector and by ensuring that they match.

At the time of DIS introduction, authorities must decide on initial funding as the first step in building a credible DIS.

There is no formula for determination of optimal initial funding, assuming that the DIS is introduced at the time of stability of the banking sector. Authorities should use their common sense and simple financial planning reasoning.

If assuming that deposit insurance is introduced in stable conditions when the banking sector is safe and sound, the midterm institutional development plan of deposit insurance authority should be taken into consideration (predicting all expected operational and development expenses) and, based on realistic cash flow projections for the same period, initial funding should be determined up to the amount that provides sufficient public confidence. Usually, sufficient confidence can be expressed in the amount sufficient to cover the DIS's operating expenses and a potential payout of the covered deposits in a few smaller banks in the system, without alluding to a particular bank. In order to determine a specific amount, policy makers should look at the distribution of covered (insured) deposits in member banks and consult with banking supervision on the financial soundness of the banking sector.

In general, initial funding must be sufficient and credible to provide enough assurance at the initial stage of building a desirable DIF (capital) over time.

It is not realistic to expect that immediately upon establishment, the DIS can effectively cover all deposits in all banks in the system or that a big DIF can be created in a few years.

If more funds are ensured through initial funding, the pressure on regular funding will be lower, assuming that there is no immediate risk of bank failure.

Initial funding, ideally, is provided parallel to the establishment of the deposit insurance authority.

Sources of initial funding vary.

If deposit insurance is established as a public DIS, then most likely the government is a possible source of funding. The government, in most cases, promotes the project of establishment and implementation of a DIS and sets public policy objectives.

Many DISs (among them FDIC and CDIC) repaid the governmental initial contribution over time. Core Principles also advocate repayment of the initial government contribution prior to any premium reduction (IADI 2014, 29). Such guiding principle is based on the assumption that the funding of a DIS should be borne solely by member banks.

If member institutions contribute to initial funding, these collections are usually referred to as initial (membership) fees or contributions.

In addition to member banks and governments, initial funding may be provided by the central bank or donors (e.g. international financial institutions).

Regardless of the source of initial funding, it is usually a one-time contribution or a lump-sum amount.

3.3.2 Regular Funding

The concept of deposit insurance is built and based on the assumption that regular funding should always be provided by member banks for the purpose of creation of the DIF. Banks benefit from the DIS and thus must bear the costs.

Funding is closely related to policy objectives and mandate and powers of the DIS.

If the DIS's mandate is paybox plus where the DIS is liable in terms of financing the prescribed resolution methods, the funding options should comply with the given paybox plus mandate. A paybox DIS is responsible for the protection of depositors in the event of an individual bank's failure. Not a single paybox DIS is able to provide full protection of depositors in case of a systemic bank failure or during a systemic crisis, where overall financial safety net must have at disposal a set of resolution tools. Even if the total covered deposits in a bank are much higher than the total available DIF, deposit insurance may be used as a tool when resolving that bank and its funds may be used in combination with other funding sources and other resolution tools.

Systemically important banks benefit from the DIS as much as smaller banks and thus it is in their interest that the banking sector is safe and sound and that the DIS has sufficient resources for the payout of covered deposits, even if their deposit base is too big to be paid out through deposit insurance in case of distress.

Within the legislation, authorities have many options related to prescribing the DIS funding. For example, they must decide whether to prescribe the exact percentage of the annual regular premium or only the upper limit or the range of values, the basis of assessment of the premium, the most appropriate target fund size level and other important elements. The level of details would depend on national legal practice and on the advanced level of governance.

Some countries prescribe in their legislation the exact level of annual premium. By doing so, their legislation limits adjustments of premium according to the funding needs and prevents any flexibility of funding because the level of premium can be changed only if and when the legislation is changed (amended). The rationale for such an option is often justified by weak governance and used as a preventive measure of a potential abuse of power of the DIS's governing bodies.

More advanced deposit insurance schemes opt for the flexibility and optimization of funds where the board (the decision-making governing body) decides on the level of the premium to be paid by banks annually, taking into account the projection of funding needs, current level of DIFs and established target fund size level.

Before making the final decision on annual premium level, authorities should additionally take into the account the overall situation in the banking sector, in order to assess whether and how the proposed annual level of premium could affect banks' liquidity and profitability.

It is important that the DIS is independent and makes decisions professionally, without external influences. Banks always tend to decrease their expenses and always argue against the deposit insurance premium level.

In order to calculate the annual premium amount to be paid by individual banks, the premium level is multiplied by the assessment base. There are four most commonly used assessment bases for determining annual premium:

- covered (insured) deposits,
- insurable (eligible) deposits,
- total deposits and
- total banks' liabilities (total deposits and other liabilities).

According to IADI's survey, 58.8 per cent of respondents use insurable (eligible) deposits and 27.5 per cent of them covered (insured) deposits as the assessment base for premium calculation, respectively (IADI 2015, 13).

In order to be able to determine the due amounts of banks' contribution to the DIF and to assess its potential liabilities, any DIS must have accurate and updated information on deposits, at an aggregate level, for the sake of its financing purposes. On the other hand, the DIS must be prepared for the payout case in advance, in which case the detailed data on individual depositors and their covered deposits are needed occasionally in order to be sure that the precise scope and format of data would be delivered in case of payout.

In order to do so, deposit insurance authorities must instruct member banks to provide information on insured deposits on a regular basis, create databases, continually analyze deposits and adjust financial management functions in line with information on liabilities.

Therefore, the deposit insurance authorities should develop and adopt a sufficiently detailed subordinate law on banks' regular reporting or otherwise prescribe submission of one or more reports by banks on a regular basis.

The scope of data on deposits that are of interest to the deposit insurance authority varies and would depend on many factors. For example, if foreign currency deposits are significant in size, the deposit insurance authority would be interested to learn of the structure and trend of these types of deposits. If banks use deposits as prime collateral, the deposit insurance authority would like to learn of the size of the collateralized deposits. Therefore, the deposit insurance authorities should carefully design regular reporting forms and explain their purpose to banks with clear instructions for the presentation and submission of data. More detailed data are useful source of information for different analysis. The DIS must find a balance between the quantity of the requested data and information and benefits for the system of the analyzed data and avoid overburdening member banks with less important data.

In general, it is important that the deposit insurance authorities have access to updated data, on a regular basis, in order to create a reliable database. Regularity may differ, but it is generally considered that banks should report on a monthly basis; otherwise, the data would be obsolete.

More specifically, banks' regular reporting enables the deposit insurance authority to determine each bank's liability to pay the regular premium and to precisely assess its potential liability toward each bank, in case of bank failure.

Decision on the annual level of the regular premium can be done with or without taking into account the target fund size that is the desired (target) coverage ratio.

3.3.2.1 Deciding on the Annual Regular Premium Without Determining the Target Fund Size Level

There are two decisions that authorities must make when determining the annual regular premium. One decision relates to the assessment basis and another relates to the annual premium level.

If the target fund size is not already determined or if the existing target fund size is not used as a tool for calculating the annual regular premium and if no advanced risk assessment of member banks is applied, the only reference point or a benchmark for determining the annual premium is the level of annual premium which is applied in other countries.

Countries usually compare themselves with the neighboring countries which may be logical due to economic and geographical connections between them and general similarities of their financial sectors.

Another approach is to look at the countries with a similar size and structure of the banking sector regardless of their geographical position. It is worth to conduct extra analysis and learn as much as possible about the practice applied in other countries and then decide what could be applicable to the national DIS.

In addition, an average level of the annual regular premium applied in other countries can be a starting reference point. For example, research on annual regular premium can suggest that the annual regular premium applied in a number of countries is on average 0.5 per cent.

Thus, the initial idea of an annual regular premium set at 1 per cent should be reconsidered, not to burden the banks too much compared to other countries' experience, unless having a specific reason for a higher than average annual premium.

Research and comparative analysis on the applied annual regular premium can provide sufficient details for the initial projection of a possible level of annual premium calculations.

3.3.2.2 Example: Deciding on an Annual Regular Premium Without Determining the Target Fund Size Level

This example shows interactive steps in order to determine the annual regular premium level without previously setting the target fund size and desirable level of funds in a projected time frame.

Many DISs don't determine the target fund size or even if they do, it is not used in the adjustment of funding through active financial management. This example suggests analytical steps for the decision-making process in such cases.

In the first step, simple analytical calculations are conducted starting with an arbitrary assumption of different levels of annual premium and decision on the applied assessment basis.

In this example, authorities considered the range of annual regular premium level between 0.2 per cent and 0.5 per cent and decided that the premium would be calculated based on the amount of covered deposits (assessment base). By doing so, authorities would calculate the total amount of annual regular premium for each premium level option and the amount of annual regular premium that each bank would need to pay.

Calculation presented in Table 3.1 suggests the following:

- if the annual premium is set at 0.2 per cent, deposit insurance authority would collect a total amount of €49 million, while individual bank's liability for the premium (direct annual expense affecting the bank's operating profitability) would range from only €5,073 in the smallest bank to €17 mil in the largest bank.
- if the annual premium is set at 0.3 per cent, the total collected annual premium would amount to €73 million, while individual bank's liability would rise to a range from €7,610 to almost €26 mil.
- if annual premium is set at 0.4 per cent, the total collected funds from all banks would amount to €98 million and finally,
- if annual premium is set at 0.5 per cent, the total collected funds from banks would amount to €122 million, in which case the smallest bank would pay only €12,683, but the largest bank would pay €43 million on an annual basis.

Table 3.1 Consideration of possible annual premium level, coverage level is €10,000

Banks	Covered deposits, in €	Annual premium, in percentage	Annual premium, in percentage	Annual premium, in percentage	Annual premium, in percentage
		0.2	0.3	0.4	0.5
10	2,536,500	5,073	7,610	10,146	12,683
9	65,800,000	131,600	197,400	263,200	329,000
8	70,000,000	140,000	210,000	280,000	350,000
6	273,000,000	546,000	819,000	1,092,000	1,365,000
7	535,500,000	1,071,000	1,606,500	2,142,000	2,677,500
5	955,500,000	1,911,000	2,866,500	3,822,000	4,777,500
4	2,195,000,000	4,390,000	6,585,000	8,780,000	10,975,000
3	4,255,000,000	8,510,000	12,765,000	17,020,000	21,275,000
2	7,550,000,000	15,100,000	22,650,000	30,200,000	37,750,000
1	8,630,000,000	17,260,000	25,890,000	34,520,000	43,150,000
Total	**24,532,336,500**	**49,064,673**	**73,597,010**	**98,129,346**	**122,661,683**

Authorities should also assess the impact of the annual premium expense on the banks' profitability and the potential consequences for the banks' liquidity, looking at individual banks, in order to find the balance between the benefit for the DIS from the collected premium and the costs of the premium for the banking sector.

In the next step, before making any decisions, authorities should compare the impact of the projected annual premium options with the resulting 'payout capacity' of the DIF for each premium option. In other words, the amount of the collected annual premium should be compared with individual bank's covered deposits (exposure of the DIS toward individual banks) in order to understand the financial impact of the collected premium.

Table 3.2 compares the payout capacity of the collected annual premium (in one year) with individual and cumulative exposure of the DIF toward banks, using a bottom-up (cumulative) approach.

The payout capacity options for the DIS are as follows:

- annual premium of €49 million (when the premium is 0.2 per cent) enables the DIS to compensate only depositors in the smallest bank (bank number 10), individually and cumulatively.

Table 3.2 DIS' individual and cumulative (bottom-up) covered deposits' exposure

Banks	Covered deposits, in €	
	Individual	Bottom-up cumulative
10	2,536,500	2,536,500
9	65,800,000	68,336,500
8	70,000,000	138,336,500
6	273,000,000	411,336,500
7	535,500,000	946,836,500
5	955,500,000	1,902,336,500
4	2,195,000,000	4,097,336,500
3	4,255,000,000	8,352,336,500
2	7,550,000,000	15,902,336,500
1	8,630,000,000	**24,532,336,500**
Total	**24,532,336,500**	

- annual premium of €73 million (when the premium is 0.3 per cent) increases the DIS's payout capacity to any of three smallest banks if they fail individually or two smallest banks (bank numbers 10 and 9) if they fail simultaneously.
- annual premium of €98 million (when the premium is 0.4 per cent) does not increase DIS's payout capacity further, because the fourth-smallest bank in the system has covered deposits in the amount of €273 million and the annual premium represents only one-third of the required money.
- annual premium of €122 million does not increase DIS's payout capacity either, because the funds are still insufficient for the payout of the covered deposits of the fourth-smallest bank.

Looking only at the potential exposure toward the failure of individual banks, the payout capacity (measured by the amount of covered deposits in any of three smallest banks in the system) does not improve with the premium level being higher than 0.3 per cent annually.

Similarly, the cumulative payout capacity of the DIS remains the same in case when 0.3 per cent, 0.4 per cent or 0.5 per cent annual premiums are applied.

If a decision has to be made at this point, irrespective of the dynamic growth of deposits and the projected desired size of DIFs, then setting the annual premium at a 0.3 per cent level and applying it to the amount of covered deposits is the most logical decision, due to the fact that with a 0.3 per cent annual regular premium benefits for the DIS would be the highest compared to banks' costs for the premium.

Many DISs decide on an annual regular premium in the manner similar to the provided example. However, when deciding on an annual regular premium, at least two other factors must be taken into consideration and analyzed, and they are namely annual growth of covered deposits and the banking sector concentration (distribution of covered deposits in banks). Both factors influence (increase or decrease) the payout capacity of the DIS.

If covered (insured) deposits are used as a basis for the calculation of annual premium level, the growth of covered deposits will impact the total collected funds. In other words, the bigger the basis is, the more funds will be collected if the same level of premium is applied.

At the same time, the growth of covered deposits impacts the exposure of the DIS to each member bank as well. In other words, the bigger the basis, the larger the DIS exposure (and potential liability) to each bank is.

A mathematical exercise will show that the impact of the growth of covered deposits is higher on the exposure of DIS to each bank than on the total DIF.

When conducting a forecast analysis, assumptions on the future deposit growth should be made based on historical statistics of growth of deposits in the past. In addition, assumptions on the future deposit growth should be realistic. It is recommended to conduct several projections (scenarios) based on different levels of growth of covered deposits.

3.3.2.3 Example: Growth of Covered Deposits by 3, 4 and 10 Per cent

Our example is expanded with a projection of annual growth of covered deposits over a five-year period by 3 per cent, 4 per cent and 10 per cent in order to explore how different levels of annual growth of covered deposits affect the DIF and its capacity in case the annual premium level at 3 per cent is applied (Table 3.3).

Table 3.3 Comparison of annual growth of covered deposits by 3, 4 and 10 per cent

Banks	Year 0	Year 1	Year 2	Year 3	Year 4	Year 5
Covered deposits annual growth 3 per cent, in €	24,532,336,500	25,268,306,595	26,026,355,793	26,807,146,467	27,611,360,861	28,439,701,686
Annual premium 0.3 per cent, in €		75,804,920	78,079,067	80,421,439	82,834,083	85,319,105
Total DIFs, in €		75,804,920	153,883,987	234,305,427	317,139,509	402,458,614
Coverage ratio, in percentage		0.30	0.59	0.87	1.15	1.42
Covered deposits annual growth 4 per cent, in €	24,532,336,500	25,513,629,960	26,534,175,158	27,595,542,165	28,699,363,851	29,847,338,405
Annual premium 0.3 per cent, in €		76,540,890	79,602,525	82,786,626	86,098,092	89,542,015
Total DIFs, in €		76,540,890	156,143,415	238,930,042	325,028,133	414,570,149
Coverage ratio, in percentage		0.30	0.59	0.87	1.13	1.39
Covered deposits annual growth 10 per cent, in €	24,532,336,500	26,985,570,150	29,684,127,165	32,652,539,882	35,917,793,870	39,509,573,257
Annual premium 0.3 per cent, in €		80,956,710	89,052,381	97,957,620	107,753,382	118,528,720
Total DIFs, in €		80,956,710	170,009,092	267,966,712	375,720,093	494,248,813
Coverage ratio, in percentage		0.30	0.57	0.82	1.05	1.25

Results are the following:

- Covered deposits would amount to €28 billion, more than €29 billion and more than €39 billion by the end of Year 5 at annual growth of covered deposits by 3, 4 and 10 per cent respectively.
- Total DIFs would amount to more than €402 million, €414 million and €494 million by the end of Year 5 at annual growth of covered deposits by 3, 4 and 10 per cent respectively.
- The coverage ratio at the end of Year 5 is the highest at annual growth of covered deposits by 3 per cent (1.42 per cent) and smallest at annual growth of covered deposits by 10 per cent (1.25 per cent).

Impact of growth of deposits onto the DIS's funds and its payout capacity are as follows – the payout capacity is always larger at lower covered deposits' annual growth rate. Authorities should take into account the growth of deposits' impact when deciding on an annual premium level, especially if the country experienced a significant growth of deposits (Fig. 3.1).

One must understand though the limitations of a coverage ratio. Coverage ratio is a measure of a payout capacity of a DIS expressed by a simple figure. It compares the total ex ante collected DIFs with the

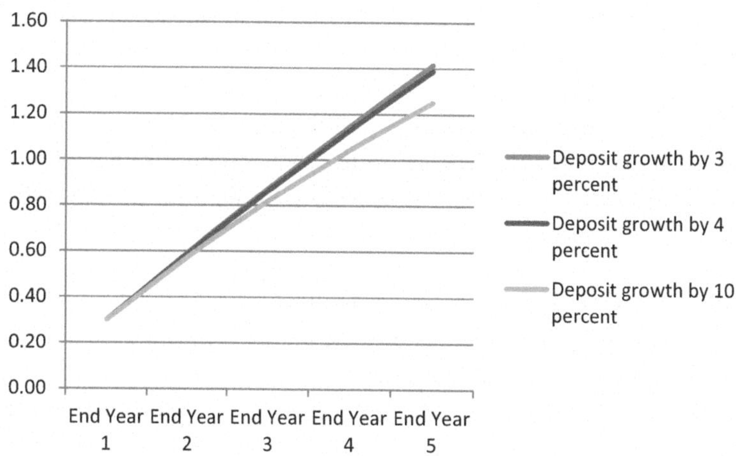

Fig. 3.1 Coverage ratios under different deposits growth rates

potential liability of the DIS that is the total covered deposits in all member banks at certain point of time.

For example, the coverage ratio of 5 per cent reads that the DIS collected DIFs in the amount of 5 per cent of the total covered deposits in the system. It does not provide details on the banks whose deposits would be fully covered.

For many years, deposit insurance authorities used the coverage ratio as a symbol of the strength of the DIF.

However, the coverage ratio does not specify details on the DIS's payout capacity. Therefore, the total DIFs must be compared with the total DIS's liabilities in individual banks.

If the bottom-up analysis is used, at the end of Year 5 the DIS would be able to compensate depositors in any of the four smallest banks individually or cumulatively if the covered deposits grew by 3 per cent annually and if the annual premium of 0.3 per cent was applied. If a DIS would like to accumulate a more robust DIF, authorities should consider applying a higher annual regular premium.

3.3.2.4 Concentration of the Banking Sector and Coverage Ratio

Another factor that must be taken into account when deciding on the coverage ratio and target fund size is the distribution of covered deposits among banks and concentration of the banking sector.

Table 3.4 presents three different banking sectors, all consisting of ten banks, with total covered deposits in the same amount of €24.5 billion, but with different distribution of covered deposits that is with different banking sector concentration:

- Variant I shows an example of the banking sector already used in this book where four largest banks present 92 per cent of the market share measured by total covered deposits,
- Variant II is a possible theoretical example of equal distribution of covered deposits among all banks in the system and
- Variant III is a less concentrated banking sector than the one in Variant I but a more concentrated banking sector than in Variant II.

Table 3.4 Coverage ratio at 5 per cent and different banking sector concentrations

Banks	Banking sector concentrations, in €		
	Variant I	Variant II	Variant III
10	2,536,500	2,453,233,650	50,000,000
9	65,800,000	2,453,233,650	100,000,000
8	70,000,000	2,453,233,650	500,000,000
6	273,000,000	2,453,233,650	800,000,000
7	535,500,000	2,453,233,650	1,000,000,000
5	955,500,000	2,453,233,650	2,000,000,000
4	2,195,000,000	2,453,233,650	3,000,000,000
3	4,255,000,000	2,453,233,650	4,000,000,000
2	7,550,000,000	2,453,233,650	5,000,000,000
1	8,630,000,000	2,453,233,650	8,082,336,500
Total covered deposits	**24,532,336,500**	**24,532,336,500**	**24,532,336,500**
Total DIFs	1,226,616,825	1,226,616,825	1,226,616,825

For illustration, we have decided that the desirable coverage ratio should be 5 per cent or €1,226 billion in absolute figures.

The total DIFs measured by a coverage ratio of 5 per cent result in a different payout capacity in three differently concentrated banking sectors as follows:

- Variant I banking sector DIS is able to compensate six smallest banks individually;
- Variant II banking sector DIS is unable to compensate any of the banks because each bank represents 10 per cent of the market share;
- Variant III banking sector DIS is able to compensate five smallest banks individually.

As is evident from the example, the same coverage ratio of 5 per cent would have a larger payout capacity, measured by the bottom-up approach, in case of a banking sector with higher banking concentration.

3.3.3 Extraordinary Funding

Extraordinary funding (backup, emergency funding) is a type of funding which is required when a DIS experiences insufficient regular funds, such as, for example, for bridging liquidity or insolvency gaps.

As a concept, deposit insurance is often criticized because banks consider the DIS expensive and ineffective. It is often argued that the DIS should provide 'full coverage to all covered deposits in all banks', otherwise it does not make sense. This is not possible because a DIS can't provide full coverage to all banks with ex ante DIFs.

There will always be some (larger) banks out of the scope of the DIS umbrella due to their (systemic) size. For such banks, other resolution tools must be in place, in addition to the DIS.

The DIS may face liquidity shortages if several (medium-sized) banks fail at the same time or if a large number of small banks fail simultaneously. The DIS may face liquidity gaps even if it is solvent (has sufficient funds) but money is not at disposal when needed (e.g. if invested securities can't be cashed fast).

Such liquidity gaps may be financed with extraordinary funding options. Any DIS should have a legal framework for extraordinary funding and procedures ready for real case scenarios in order to avoid improvisation and ad hoc solutions which are costly and time consuming.

Sources of extraordinary funding are:

- additional premium charged to banks and
- borrowings from the private sector (national or international) in the form of loans or issued debentures with or without a government guarantee, treasury (government) and from the central bank (if the legal framework allows such a funding option)
- state budget transfers
- international financial institutions.

When a DIS faces liquidity gap, the Treasury (Ministry of Finance) is the most likely source of extraordinary funding, although transfers from the Treasury (state budget) are regulated by the budgetary legislation and national rules on budgetary spending.

Based on national legislation, pre-arrangements should be made between the DIS authority and the Treasury, if the law allows such a funding option. Pre-arranged details should provide details on terms and conditions, procedures such as the maximum amount, financial conditions (costs) and other details.

In many jurisdictions, transfer or borrowings from the Treasury must be approved by the parliament. In order to ensure that extraordinary funding is executed when needed, the DIS should take preparatory steps in advance.

Some DISs experienced difficulties in arranging extraordinary funding options from the Treasury although the legislation allowed such a possibility. Difficulties arose due to legal obstacles that were not taken into account and were not envisaged in advance. Some jurisdictions request from the DIS to follow a strict procedure, some can provide funding if the request is submitted until a certain date or if the announcement for the borrowing requirement is provide a year in advance and so on. All these peculiarities should be taken into account and regulated in the subordinate laws in order to avoid delays in payout.

Several countries issued bonds in order to collect extraordinary DIS funding. In 1999, the Croatian State Agency for Deposit Insurance and Bank Rehabilitation issued two tranches of bonds in the total amount of €550 mil on the national stock exchange, under the state guarantee. Buyers were local banks. However, issuing bonds is a lengthy procedure (may last up to several months), cumbersome due to capital markets' regulations (approval of the prospectus by the regulatory agency) and costly. In addition, bond issuance is successful as long as the buyers trust the issuer. Therefore, it is realistic to expect that in many cases the government guarantee would be required by the issuer

The idea behind extraordinary funding is to ensure fast access to cover liquidity gaps when DIFs are insufficient. If the financial gap is smaller and collectable from the remaining member banks, then the most realistic option is to collect additional funding from member banks in the form of extraordinary premium. However, if the amount required is higher than the annual limit on the premium from banks, if the remaining banks are already in distress and if the liquidity of the banking sector is jeopardized, in such circumstances it is not recommendable to collect additional (ex post) funds from banks.

Some countries established a legal cap (upper limit) on the DIS's borrowing facility. The borrowing capacity of the DIS is determined (limited) by several factors, such as whether the government guarantees for the DIS's borrowing (collateral) and what the repayment sources of borrowing are.

In other words, how would deposit insurance authority repay an emergency loan? If the DIS repaid the loan from funds collected on a regular basis, what would be the loan time frame? Would the lender be willing to accept future annual regular premium as a collateral? If yes, the DIS must adjust its financial planning and target future funding. Credibility of the borrower, like in any other standard borrowing contract, is at stake when borrowing from the market.

Therefore, it is more likely to borrow funds directly from the Treasury, assuming that there are no legal obstacles and that there is an established procedure which the DIS must follow to obtain funds. The Treasury is not a bank that must operate on a profit basis rules and thus may afford a longer payout time frame or softer lending criteria.

3.3.4 Ex Ante versus Ex Post Funding

DIFs may be collected on a regular basis, prior to (ex ante) the occurrence of the insurance event in a prescribed manner and timing or after (ex post) the bank failure. In case of ex post funding, the deposit insurance authority collects only a smaller amount of money for covering failure and operational expenses and does not collect regular funding from banks unless there is a failure and payout case. The combination of ex ante and ex post funding is defined as a hybrid (mixed) funding.

Early papers on deposit insurance explored the benefits and deficiency of these types of funding systems. In the 1980s and 1990s, the question whether to establish ex ante or ex post funding was the key question for any DIS.

By 2003, as stated by IADI (IADI 2009, 9–10), only 14 out of 88 DISs had ex post funding. At the end of 2013, 91 DISs (more than 88 per cent of all established DISs) were ex ante funded, whereas only 12 DISs were ex post funded (Demirguc-Kunt et al. 2014, 37–38).

In times of financial stability, prior to the latest financial crisis, many jurisdictions opted for ex post funding or hybrid (combined) funding with a minimum portion of funds collected in advance and the rest of the required money to be collected after the occurrence of the insurance event. Over time, some jurisdictions even ceased to collect funds introducing a premium break.

However, the financial crisis in 2007–2008 emphasized the importance of the deposit insurance and thus the importance of sufficient funding available for the deposit payout. Many jurisdictions almost bankrupted their DISs in an attempt to compensate insured deposits in failing banks because they did not have the sufficient amount of readily available financial resources. Therefore, it became important to build and rebuild ex ante financial resources in order to enhance the DIS.

Regularity of collection of ex ante funds may vary from quarterly payments to annual payments (one-time payment). Due to the potential impact on liquidity, but also for the purpose of efficient financial management, it is more favorable to collect funds on a regular basis in predetermined periods rather than to collect funds once a year, especially if deposits are growing at higher annual growth rate. The amount due for each individual bank is calculated by applying the prescribed (assessment) rate to the prescribed (assessment) basis.

Ex post funds are collected upon occurrence of the insured event, in a less predictable manner and timing than with ex ante funding. The amount to be repaid to insured depositors is divided among the remaining banks on a linear basis or distributed in accordance with their risk profiles when applying the differential premium system.

Member banks traditionally favored ex post funding for obvious reasons such as no immediate outflow of the premium and no direct expenses reported, as long as there is no deposit payout. It may be argued that ex post premium collection is unfair as the premium is collected only from 'surviving' banks and not from all member banks, especially not from those banks that failed and created costs for the system.

In addition, the collection of premium ex post premium upon the occurrence of the insurance event may impose a liquidity burden to banks because they did not plan such cash outflow or the cash outflow is sudden and large (pro-cyclical effect is strong).

At the same time, the conversion of the payment commitment into an actual premium contribution also affects the profitability of banks. Payment commitments are presented in banks' balance sheets (as bank's assets) until the moment of actual payment of the contribution to the DIS entity when the amount due becomes expense.

No doubt, with ex ante collection of funds on a regular basis, the DIS is more liquid and more solvent than the DIS which does not collect funds prior to the occurrence of the insurance event and pay-out of covered deposits. Such regular collection of funds enables the DIS to conduct better financial planning and financial management in general

With ex ante DIF, payout can start quickly after the bank's failure. Although banks argue that the premium is expense which decreases their profitability, with ex ante funding both liquidity and profitability impacts are spread over time on a regular basis, compared to ex post funding when the banks must provide a bigger amount of liquidity at once (at the time which is not known at all times). Banks can budget the costs related to deposit insurance on time and project their liquidity needs better with ex ante funding.

Ex ante funding is more fair because all banks contribute to the established DIF, not only 'survived' (non-failed) banks.

Ex ante funding is countercyclical and funds are collected at all times (good and bad), while ex post funded DIS may have a negative impact at the time of an economic downturn.

Ex post funding is characterized by funding provided by banks after a failure. Thus, banks don't report 'deposit insurance expense' on an annual basis. However, many DISs with ex post funding prescribed that banks had to ensure a certain amount of their liquidity in the form of obligatory investments in liquid securities issued by the central bank or government (as form of payment commitments).

Countries with a relatively developed bank supervision and stable banking sector favored ex post funding of the DIS, but the trend has been changing after the 2008 financial crisis and the implementation of the DGSD in the EU.

Hybrid funding is a combination of ex ante and ex post funding allowing a certain percentage of funding to be funded ex post while a greater share of funds is provided on a regular basis. In other words, almost all ex ante funding schemes are de facto hybrid because almost all of them have the ability to collect additional premium (levy, contribution) ex post if needed.

3.3.5 Linear (Flat) versus Differential Premium Funding

If the premium rate is set flat (linear), the same percentage is applied to the assessment base for all banks. As a result, the only difference in the premium amount that each bank pays would depend on the assessment base to which the premium is applied. Most often, the total covered deposits or total eligible deposits are used as the assessment base.

Therefore, banks that have a larger deposit base will pay a higher regular premium. Such pricing is not related to the risk exposure of the DIS to each individual bank, and thus, many argue that it is not fair. Consequently, banks don't have incentives to improve their risk profiles because of deposit insurance.

However, it may be argued whether banks are willing to improve their risk profiles only because of risk-based methodology at all. Banks establish their credit policies and risk profiles regardless of the deposit insurance pricing. Moreover, the assessment base that is the amount of deposits on a particular date contributes much more to the amount of the premium payment than the premium level percentage.

If authorities opt for the flat premium, the level of linear premium may be prescribed in the legislation for a longer period of time. Such an option limits an active adjustment of funding, because the DIS is not able to change the premium level without changing the law.

Another and more flexible option is to give to the board, as the highest governing body, the power to prescribe the level of annual premium once per year. Such practice would allow more optimal funding over time adjusted to the funding needs by an increased or decreased annual premium level, ideally, in accordance with the established target fund size.

Some jurisdictions prescribe in their legislation only the upper limit of the premium or the premium range allowing the board to prescribe the annual premium level but within legally prescribed values.

The premium level should be smoothed over the years, and any sharp differences in the premium level should be avoided.

The differential premium system could provide better financial incentives for good banks and minimize cross-subsidization among banks, but there are some preconditions that must be met in order to apply the differential premium system.

Many argue that applying the differential premium system is complex and that is the reason why the differential premium funding is not spread among the DISs on a wider base.

In 1995, the FDIC was the only DIS in the world applying the differential premium system. It was introduced in 1993, after nearly 60 years of DIS's existence. At that time, it was an 'innovative' idea. The premium level was prescribed in the legislation (the minimum premium level was 0.23 per cent) (FDIC 1998, 54), and only the US Congress could change it.

The FDIC's subordinate law prescribes the risk-based premium methodology, as a combination of objective and subjective criteria. The objective criteria used by the FDIC were focused on capital ratios where the subjective criteria were based on CAMELS ratings derived from on-site examinations. The introduced risk-based premium system had several goals, such as to be fair and easily understand, to produce sufficient income to recapitalize the DIF within a 15-year time frame, to increase incentives for banks' less risky operation and to provide a transition from flat (linear) premiums to permanent risk-based premiums. As a result, the rating matrix contained nine cells.

Since then, the FDIC has significantly improved its risk-based premium system with many refinements and changes. As a result, there is a separate risk-based system for small banks (those with assets below USD 10 billion) and large banks, including very complex large banks. Nine risk categories consolidated into four risk categories for small banks. In case of large banks, the FDIC still combines CAMELS rating with some forward-looking financial measures; the base premium level can be adjusted (credited or levied).

At the end of 2013, only 34 DISs implemented the risk-based premium system (Demirguc-Kunt et al. 2014, 37–38). The number of countries applying the risk-based methodology nowadays is increasing, significantly. This is partly so because the DISs have started developing their analytical skills only recently and paying much more attention to assessing the risks in individual member banks. Another reason is obligatory implementation of the new EU rules for all EU member countries, after the DGSD approval in 2014. Although only EU member countries must comply with the DGSD, many countries in transition, with or without aspiration to join the EU, look at the DGSD as a benchmark and implement many features prescribed by the DGSD in their national legal framework.

3.3.5.1 Methodologies for the Differential Premium System

There are several minimum conditions to be met in order to develop and implement the differential premium system:

- the methodology for the differential premium system must capture the main banking risks and must be transparent,
- the deposit insurance authority should have access to data on a regular basis in order to calculate banks' risk profiles and update them,
- the bank supervisor must not have reservations toward the methodology; that is, the bank supervisor should either participate in its development or approve it if the methodology is developed solely by the deposit insurance authority.

Bank supervisors have all the necessary information and data on banks which usually serve as inputs when calculating differential premiums, since, within their scope of work, they are responsible for assessing banks' risk profiles.

Thus, by default and based on their legal mandate, bank supervisors should be able to assess the risk profiles of individual member banks. In general, bank supervisors sometimes hesitate to share data on individual bank's risks with the deposit insurance authority and are often limited by regulation on bank secrecy. The concept of financial stability is sufficiently important to overcome issues of bank secrecy and confidentiality when sharing information and data among safety net entities.

If there is no other solution, and the cooperation between the deposit insurance authority and the bank supervisor is weak, the deposit insurance authority may build its database only from publicly available information sources and via a direct access to member banks in order to be able to assess individual member banks' risk and apply the differential premium system.

There is a general misunderstanding that risk assessment, for the purpose of premium collection, must coincide in full with the supervisory risk assessment of banks. Ideally, yes, although the deposit insurance authority may use a simplified and adjusted risk assessment methodology for its own purpose. Therefore, bank secrecy regulation or lack of institutional cooperation should not be a limiting factor for the development and implementation of the risk-based methodology for deposit insurance.

Criteria which are used in the methodology for assessing bank risks must be transparent to all member banks and banks must understand how their risk profile is generated and updated. At the same time, results on risk ratings of individual banks should be kept confidential and not shared publicly or to other member banks. Each bank should be informed of its own risk rating, but not of the risk rating of other banks.

The deposit insurance authority should update calculations on risks on a regular and prescribed basis in order to update the methodology calculations with fresh data and the latest developments in banks which reflect and change their risk profiles.

There are three general types of different risk-based premium approaches (models) (IADI 2011b, 8–14), based on:

(i) quantitative data,
(ii) qualitative data or
(iii) combination of quantitative and qualitative data.

Quantitative risk-based premium methodology models are relatively unbiased, objective (less subjective) and more transparent. However, the main deficiency is that the quality of quantitative model depends on the quality, consistency and reliability of the used inputs (financial ratios). Nowadays, supervisors use many qualitative indicators and rarely rank banks based solely on financial ratios. Therefore, the DISs must be aware of shortcomings of financial ratios when developing the methodology for the differential premium based on historical financial ratios.

Qualitative models are based on regulatory and supervisory judgment and qualitative information such as, for example, the banks' compliance with guidelines and prudential norms. A commonly used qualitative model is CAMELS. The main problem with using CAMELS is that often full ratings (scores) can't be updated in predictable short intervals. In some jurisdictions, CAMELS ratings are updated every few years. Many supervisors still don't apply CAMELS as their recognized methodology for assessing bank risks.

Many jurisdictions develop the risk-based methodology combining selective quantitative and qualitative data and adjust them to specific risks, depending on the banking sector specifics and on the level of its development.

In addition, the methodology for the differential premium may apply a single risk indicator or multiple risk indicators. In general, multiple risk indicators may capture risks better, although too many indicators should be avoided.

The deposit insurance authority may use the following sources of information and data for the risk-based premium methodology:

(i) banks as the direct source,
(ii) supervisor
(iii) publicly available sources or
(iv) combination of any of the sources (i) to (iii).

A detailed methodology on risk assessment for premium collection should be prescribed in the subordinate laws of the deposit insurance authority with the description of the procedure, sources of information and data, risk criteria, risk scoring and weights given to each criterion, premium level assigned to each risk rating and how the methodology is going to be updated on a regular basis.

The key objectives of the differential premium systems are to calculate and collect the premium, on a fairer basis, in accordance with the risk exposure to each individual bank so that banks that are riskier contribute more to the DIS (pay higher premium) and banks that are less risky are rewarded with a lower premium.

One of the main prerequisites of the risk-based methodology is that it should be simple for understanding, but accurate for capturing the overall risks of the member banks.

When designing the differential methodology for premium calculation, authorities should first determine the risk indicators for the banking sector. Not all risks are equally important and not all risks can induce a bank's failure. Some risks have a higher importance in a particular banking sector than in another banking sector.

Most common risk indicators used in the risk-based premium methodology are those related to:

(i) capital adequacy
(ii) asset quality
(iii) profitability
(iv) liquidity of banks.

One or more measures for each indicator may be used. Authorities should decide which indicators are more important and which are less important at the time of the introduction or revision of the risk-based premium system.

After determining the risk indicators, risk measures for each indicator and risk categories should be developed. The number of risk categories may vary, but in general the number should not be too low or too high.

The risk-based methodology should be transparent and simple enough that all member banks understand it. The methodology itself should be disclosed to the public, but not the risk profiles of the banks, nor the premium level which is paid by each bank.

International guidelines and best practice related to the differential premium system presented in Core Principles (IADI 2014, 30–31) state that if the deposit insurance authority uses the differential premium system:

- it shall be transparent to all participating banks,
- the scoring and premium categories shall be significantly differentiated and
- the ratings and ranking results of individual banks shall be confidential.

3.3.5.2 Example: Application of the Risk-Based Premium Methodology

The DIS developed a simple differential premium model based on three risk categories (normal, watch and risky banks) and one measure for each risk category.

Table 3.5 presents the chosen risk indicators and risk measures with established thresholds for risk categories.

In the following step, scores are assigned to each risk category. In other words, the DIS should assess how important each risk category is for the overall risk profile of a bank. Does each of these risk indicators contribute to the risk profile of the bank equally? Is capital adequacy 'more relevant' than 'asset quality' or 'profitability' and 'liquidity'?

The DIS should assign the highest weight to the most relevant risk indicator. Each banking sector has its own specifics, in specific periods of time. The DIS should analyze bank risks and risk indicators on a regular basis in order to capture the most important risk indicators at particular time. Therefore, not all risk indicators are equally important in every country.

In our example, all risk indicators would be assigned with an equal weight; that is, each risk indicator would have a 25 per cent of the total score, as presented in Table 3.6.

Table 3.5 Risk indicators, risk measures, risk categories and risk thresholds

Risk indicator	Measure	Normal	Watch	Risky
Capital adequacy	Total capital ratio	>14	≤8 ≤14	<8
Asset quality	Non-performing loans ratio	<5	≤5 ≤15	>15
Profitability	Cost to income ratio	<60	≤60 ≤90	>90
Liquidity	Loans to deposit ratio	<80	≤80 ≤100	>100

Table 3.6 Selected scores for risk categories if each risk indicator has equal weight

Risk categories	Capital adequacy	Asset quality	Profitability	Liquidity
Normal	1	1	1	1
Watch	2	2	2	2
Risky	3	3	3	3

As a result, banks would be classified as normal risk banks, watch risk banks and risky banks.

Under the proposed model, banks with normal risk profiles can get a maximum of 4 scores; watch risks banks are scored from 5 to 8 and high risky banks are scored from 9 above.

If authorities wanted to use some qualitative factors, then the methodology should be adjusted for the qualitative indicators. Authorities could, for example, decide which qualitative indicators are important for determining the risk profile of banks and how much weight should be placed on quantitative and qualitative risk indicators respectively.

After determining the scores, the scores need to be reflected in the premium levels. The DIS tested different premium levels and approved the methodology where:

- banks within the normal risk category pay 0.2 per cent annual premium,
- banks within watch risk category pay 0.3 per cent annual premium and
- banks with risky overall profile pay 0.4 per cent annual premium.

The deposit insurance authority receives quarterly and annual financial statements on banks as well as a separate set of compliance reports with prudential norms, directly from the banks. In addition, the deposit insurance authority confirms the calculated ratios values with the bank supervisor in order to check the accuracy of the received data. Table 3.7 presents a list of banks and their quantitative risk indicators at a given moment.

In the following step, the deposit insurance authority converts the risk indicators into risk categories, in compliance with its approved methodology, as normal, watch and risky category, and each risk category is assigned the risk scores respectively in order to calculate the total risk score for each bank.

In compliance with the earlier approved risk-based methodology, normal risk banks have score 4, watch risk banks are those with the total score of 5–8 and risky banks are the ones with the total score of 9. The risk-based premium ranges from 0.2 per cent to 0.4 per cent, applied to covered deposits as presented in Table 3.8.

Table 3.7 Selected risk indicators for banks, adjusted on a quarterly basis

Banks	CAR	NPL	Cost to income	Loans to deposit
1	16	10	55	70
2	15	6	50	90
3	12	12	55	90
4	11	18	60	70
5	13	12	70	90
6	12	8	110	90
7	12	23	78	100
8	8	12	90	130
9	10	20	80	120
10	8	12	65	110

Table 3.8 Calculated risk-based premium

Banks	Total score	Risk category	Annual premium, per cent	Covered deposits, in €	Annual premium, in €
1	5	Watch	0.3	8,630,000,000	25,890,000
2	6	Watch	0.3	7,550,000,000	22,650,000
3	7	Watch	0.3	4,255,000,000	12,765,000
4	8	Watch	0.3	2,195,000,000	6,585,000
5	8	Watch	0.3	955,500,000	2,866,500
6	9	Risky	0.4	273,000,000	1,092,000
7	9	Risky	0.4	535,500,000	2,142,000
8	9	Risky	0.4	70,000,000	280,000
9	10	Risky	0.4	65,800,000	263,200
10	9	Risky	0.4	2,536,500	10,146
Total				**24,532,336,500**	**74,543,846**

As a result of the conversion of total scores into risk categories for each member bank, the deposit insurance authority is able to assign an annual premium level to each bank's risk category. As presented, there is no bank categorized as 'normal risky bank'. All banks are categorized as either 'watch' or 'risky'.

Banks in the 'watch' group pay a 0.3 per cent annual premium, while risky banks pay 0.4 per cent annually. When the annual premium level is applied to covered deposits' amount, the deposit insurance authority calculates the exact amount of the annual premium that each individual member bank is obliged to pay.

Banks number 6, 7, 8, 9 and 10 pay a higher premium level as 'punishment' for their 'risk profile'. However, these banks still pay a lower annual premium in the absolute amount than banks that are less risky, due to smaller covered deposits' base to which the annual premium level is applied.

The deposit insurance authority should send to each bank its own risk profile and calculation, but should keep confidential other banks' risk profiles and calculations.

3.4 Financial Management of the DIF

All deposit insurance authorities manage large sums of money, collected within a relatively predictable time frame, aiming to ensure sufficient liquidity in case of unforeseeable events, such as bank failures.

Can appropriate financial management ensure sufficient and optimal funding to the deposit insurance authority?

The main task of deposit insurance is to compensate depositors in case of insurance event occurrence. This simple task is equally true and valid for paybox and for advanced risk-minimizing DIS. The only difference is in the range of tools at disposal to the deposit insurance authority and the range of powers at hand which comes with the broadened mandate. In both cases, the protected depositors should have fast access to their funds and sufficient assurance that the financial system is robust despite the failure of a particular bank or banks.

Legislation should clearly provide the definition of the insurance event occurrence in order to avoid misinterpretation and false expectations, as it is the trigger for the deposit insurance payout.

It is also important to have a clear understanding when, on a specific date, the deposit insurance authority is legally obliged to commence the process of compensation payout to depositors. Insurance event occurrence is usually triggered by bank failure; however, some jurisdictions may prescribe the 'trigger' of deposit insurance even if the bank has not formally failed (e.g. even when the bank is still open for business but it is in some form of the resolution regime) but depositors don't have access to their deposits. For the purpose of this book, we will assume, unless indicated differently, that the insurance event occurrence is the date of a bank's legal failure (revoking the banking license and initiating formal insolvency legal proceedings).

In simple terms, in order to be able to fulfill its main task and repay insured depositors upon bank failure, every DIS must have sufficient financial resources available for fast and efficient deposits' payout in order to provide the needed assurance to depositors and prevent panic and deposit run. If it is the paybox plus DIS or even a DIS with a broader mandate, the main principles of financial management are the same, although there are differences in the applied practice of funds' usage.

How many financial resources are sufficient and how much is needed for the DIS to be credible and efficient? These are crucial questions for any DIS, and deposit insurers should focus on finding the answers.

Answers are never simple, though, since the DIS must be ready for the possibility that any bank in the system may fail or that even several banks may fail at the same time. In many jurisdictions the DISs do not have supervisory powers or cooperation with the bank supervisor is poorly established, resulting in insufficient information on the problem or failing bank. In such circumstances, is it then possible to optimize the funds at all?!

However, there is no magic crystal ball to help understand the funding issues better. The path toward finding the right answers always lies in the thorough preparation of the deposit insurance authority.

Among others, sufficient financial resources should be at hand or readily collectible when necessary, preferably in the form of liquid assets (cash collected from premiums paid by member banks, short-term liquid investments or as a part of some agreed financial arrangements). The DISs that operate in less liquid markets, or where the secondary market is not developed, face the issue of inability to convert their securities' investments into cash. In such cases, the DIS might face liquidity challenges, although being de facto solvent.

Due to numerous uncertainties which are interrelated to possible banks' failure, the DIS should be prepared and understand all threats it faces and all risks that can jeopardize the successful execution of its mandate.

In order to conduct the planning properly as well as to test its readiness, the DIS must have a minimum set of timely information on individual banks' risks. The main risk for the DIS is bank failure and consumption and depletion of the DIFs.

The best way to be informed of risks of a bank failure is proactive cooperation with bank supervisor at all times, especially if there are some problem or failing banks. If the deposit insurance authority does not have any supervisory powers, it should agree with the supervisor to share information on a regular basis and to develop a credible methodology for assessing bank risks and probability of default of its member banks.

In addition, the DIS may gather some information directly from the banks and from publicly available information. In many jurisdictions, the deposit insurance authorities don't rely only on the exchange of information with the supervisors or such cooperation is symbolic and insufficient, so the DISs rely on building their own analytical database from the information gathered through banks' annual reports, supervisor's statistics and development of their own criteria for risk awareness.

3.4.1 Financial Planning in the DIS with Ex Ante Funding

Any deposit insurance authority with a prescribed ex ante funding collects on a regular basis the premium from its member banks in order to build, over time, a sufficiently large ex ante fund to fulfill its legal mandate.

The deposit insurance authority is concerned with a number of questions, such as:

- Are there enough resources in the DIF?
- Should there be a target and how should it be set?
- What is the optimal size of the DIF?
- What are the optimal premiums for banks?

Proper financial planning helps in finding answers to all of these questions.

Like in any other financial institution, every DIS should establish a financial planning function in order to be better prepared, especially when the successful execution of the mandate depends on many uncertain events and risks.

In practice, there is no unique way how to organize the financial planning function, nor is the scope of the financial planning activities standardized. Some DISs don't even set up the financial planning function at all, or the financial planning is very simple and focuses on understanding the future cash inflows of regular banking premiums. However, some DISs use sophisticated modern analytical tools to assess possible risks of the outflow of funds.

The purpose of financial planning also determines the scope and the planning process. If the DIS uses financial planning for budgeting purposes only, the scope of financial planning will not be the same as when the DIS optimizes its funds with a defined target and makes strategic decisions based on midterm projections.

It is, however, of great importance that, regardless of the approach used, the DIS should focus its financial planning activities in order to understand its risk exposure and the potential outflow of financial resources for the deposit payout.

When assessing individual bank's risks and the financial consequences of these risks, the deposit insurance authority has choices, observing them in the short term, that is, focusing on its liquidity needs in case of a bank's failure, or observing it in the long term, that is, understanding its expected final loss over time. If the DIS chooses the long-term approach, it may use financial planning and financial management tools for optimization of its DIF.

The first step in the overall financial management of the DIF with ex ante funding is financial planning. There are three levels of financial planning in the ex ante DIS, regardless of the DIS mandate:

- Projection of cash flow for 3 years ('balancing future cash flows'),
- Strategic planning (e.g. target funding) and, ideally,
- Optimization of the DIF size.

All DISs should project cash flows regularly. In practice, more advanced DISs use strategic planning for determining target funding but the most advanced DISs use financial planning for optimizing the size of the DIFs.

Although the mandate of the paybox DIS seems simple compared to the risk-minimizing DIS with complex functions, there should be no difference in the scope of financial planning between them. Every pay-box DIS may optimize the size of its financial resources using advanced financial planning within the scope of its mandate.

The level of financial planning in ex ante DIS depends on the level of awareness on the importance of financial management and the level of development of the analytical function and analytical tools.

When planning annual budgeting of funds, the DIS should at least forecast its overall future cash flows, that is, plan all identified inflows and outflows for the following year.

Strategic planning for deposit insurance relates to preparing mid- and long-term financial plans which serve for targeting the size of the fund and, ideally, defining the optimal size of the fund.

DISs that ignore financial planning and risk exposure when setting the target fund size are either underfunded or overfunded, since the actual size of their DIF does not reflect or correspond to the real financial needs.

Figure 3.2 illustrates the planning cycle and its individual steps in the DIS. However, many jurisdictions conduct only the first of the planned steps or omit some steps (such as risk analysis of banks).

Every DIS conducts some sort of financial planning, at least in the form of a simple cash flow projection of its operating budget and its DIFs. The financial planning cycle starts with a simple cash flow projection for a minimum of one year, with the initial presumption that there will be no new deposit payouts in that period.

If the deposit insurance authority already conducted the payout of failed banks, the cash flow transactions related to the payout events should be reflected in the cash flow projection for the upcoming period based on expert assessment and historical data. Cash flow should be presented on a monthly basis.

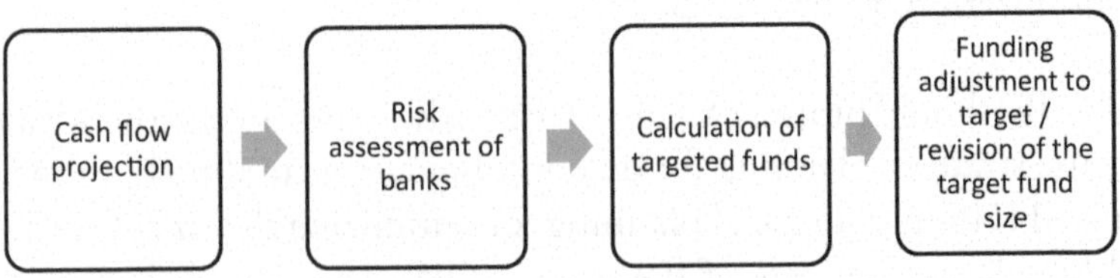

Fig. 3.2 Methodological steps in financial planning

In the following iteration, ideally, the risk assessment of individual member banks should be conducted in order to assess the probability of failure of member banks and to project the potential outflow for the payout of covered deposits as well as the liquidity needs for the payout. Information on risk analysis should be reflected in the updated version of the cash flow projection.

By doing so, the deposit insurance authority is able to adjust its financial management to its financial needs. If funds are invested in securities, the deposit insurance authority must liquidate a sufficient amount of investments on time to collect as much cash as needed at the time when needed.

If necessary, several alternative projections may be made, based on different risk scenarios.

With cash flow projections (projections of cash inflows and outflows) for the following business year, the DIS balances its cash inflows and cash outflows and plans a potential need for additional funding (or planned investments).

Ideally, the cash flow projected results are used for target funding and management of target fund size in order to adjust the annual regular premium, if necessary, in order to comply with the targeted funds within the targeted time frame.

3.4.2 Cash Flow Projections in the DIS

The quality of the cash flow exercise depends on the quality of the input data. Therefore, the deposit insurance authority must understand all variables and inputs that are used in its cash flow forecast.

Cash flow projections should be conducted on a regular basis, as a part of a routine financial exercise in order to understand the potential future inflows and outflows of cash and to make an investment plan for the upcoming budget year.

Cash flow projections list all cash flows related to the DIFs, that is, all cash inflows and all payments from the account, as prescribed by the legislation. Cash flow projection does not contain accrued accounting categories such as receivables, foreign exchange differences or depreciation.

The DIS should use a simple formula to calculate its available resources at the end of each period.

Iterations in forecasting cash flows are:

- Every cash flow projection starts with available resources at the beginning of the period;
- Funds are increased by all projected cash inflow such as initial and regular premium collection, yield on investments, recoveries from payout, borrowing and others;
- Cash is decreased by all cash outflow such as the budgeted level of operating expenses, existing and expected payout cases, fees, investments of funds;
- The DIS usually determines the minimum liquidity reserve (cash that is available on the account for operating expenses and upcoming bank failures);
- Excess of available funds is available for investments and
- The deficiency of funds should be funded from other available resources such as: additional premium collected, borrowing, budget (as prescribed by the legislation).

The dynamic balance equation of the DIF (IADI 2011a, 14) can be represented as:

$\boldsymbol{B}\,t = \boldsymbol{B}\,t - 1 - \boldsymbol{D}\,t + \boldsymbol{I}\,t + \boldsymbol{P}\,t + \boldsymbol{R}\,t,$

where.

B *t* denotes DIF's balance at the end of period *t*,

D *t* denotes the total payout to depositors over period *t*,

I *t* denotes the investment income of the fund over period *t*,

P *t* denotes the insurance premiums received over period *t*,

R *t* denotes the recoveries received over period *t*.

Even if the DIS does not take into account the risk, the cash flow projection helps to minimize 'unpleasant surprises'. However, a realistic projection of the DIS's outflow may be completed only when a potential liability is taken into account, that is, when the sum of all covered deposits in banks is identified as risky. If the DIS does not include its potential liability on the covered deposits in risky banks when projecting the cash outflow for the period, the projected DIF is overstated.

In the first step of the financial planning process the DIS ignores assessment of banks' risk profiles and assumes that the banking sector is sufficiently sound without the possibility of covered deposits' payout in the near future, that is, during the year for which the cash flow is projected, unless there is a knowledge on a possible bank failure (which should have been taken into account when projecting the cash flow).

In the next iteration, the DIS should go further and analyze member banks at the time of financial planning. Results of the individual bank's risk assessment should be taken into account after which the DIS should calculate its total resources' requirement as the sum of insured deposits in banks that are assessed as risky and which could bankrupt during that year.

The deposit insurance authority may assess its risks directly or through cooperation with the banking supervisory authority. Risk analysis of banks may be based on (historical) statistical models or on the use of early warning signals' methodology.

Some DISs apply qualitative measures, for example, CAMELS; others rely more on rating-grades models (Vaziri et al. 2012, 122–125). The DISs have been increasingly developing their own methodology use of combined measures. Some countries use peer group analysis or models based on financial ratios. Different credit risk modeling may be used for assessing banking risks of the DIS (Smirnov et al. 2005, 46–70).

Whatever methodology is used, the main goal is to assess the credit risk for the DIS.

3.4.2.1 Example of a Cash Flow Projection in the DIS

The deposit insurance authority projects its cash flow for Year 1 of its operation based on the following:

- Initial premium is set at €10,000 per each bank, paid by the end of January
- Regular premium is set at 0.2 per cent annually that is €49 mil in total, paid in quarterly installments in January, April, July and October in the amount of €12,250 mil
- Minimum liquidity reserve is set at €2 mil

- Available cash above the minimum liquidity reserve will be invested in government bonds with the maturity of 365 days and the projected yield on investments of 8 per cent annually (based on the statistics of government securities' issuance)
- Investments in non-current assets will be made in January in the amount of €100,000
- Monthly operating expenses are budgeted at €17,500.

As evident from Table 3.9, during the first month of its operation the DIS collected €12,350 mil of initial and regular premium. The monthly budgeted expenses and investments in non-current assets such as furniture and IT equipment were only cash outflow, resulting in €12,233 mil cash balance at the end of the month. If the deposit insurance authority wants to retain minimum cash liquidity in the amount of €2 million, the remaining €10,233 mil is available for investments. The DIS will invest its excess of funds the following month.

During the first year of operation, the DIS projected only operating expenses, resulting in the DIF in the amount of €50,529 mil by the end of the year, out of which €46,825 mil was invested and 3,704 were liquid reserves.

The deposit insurance authority continues its operation with similar projections of the cash flow in Year 2 of its operation, assuming that there is an annual increase of covered deposits of 3 per cent, resulting in an increase of the basis for the annual premium calculation by 3 per cent and resulting in the annual collected premium in the amount of €51 mil (instead of €49 mil as it was collected in Year 1 of the DIS operation), although the annual premium level is the same (0.2 per cent). The analysis shows that all banks are safe and sound, and the deposit insurance authority does not envisage any deposit payout during Year 2 of its operation. As a result, the DIS continues building the DIF throughout the two years of its operation to €107 million, out of which more than €99 million are invested in government securities, under the same investment conditions and there is more than €7 mil of cash reserves at the end of Year 2 of the operation.

The deposit insurance authority improved its cash flow projection using a simple risk assessment methodology developed in cooperation with the supervisory authority, applied in Year 3.

Table 3.9 Projection of a cash flow, Year 1, in €000

Cash flow projections	Jan	Feb	March	April	May	June	July	August	Sept	October	Nov	Dec
DIF at the beginning, in the account		**12,233**	**1,983**	**1,965**	**14,198**	**1,983**	**1,965**	**14,198**	**1,983**	**1,965**	**14,198**	**1,983**
Cash inflows												
Initial premium (10,000)	100											
Annual premium 0,2 per cent annually	12,250	0	0	12,250	0	0	12,250	0	0	12,250	0	0
Yields on investments (8 per cent)												1,739
Recoveries for earlier payouts (10 per cent)												
Other receipts (penalties)												
Additional funding – borrowing												
Transfer from budget												
Total inflows (receipts)	**12,350**	**0**	**0**	**12,250**	**0**	**0**	**12,250**	**0**	**0**	**12,250**	**0**	**1,739**

(continued)

Table 3.9 (continued)

Cash flow projections	Jan	Feb	March	April	May	June	July	August	Sept	October	Nov	Dec
Cash outflows												
Operating expenses	18	18	18	18	18	18	18	18	18	18	18	18
Interest payments, fees												
Deposit payout – existing cases												
Deposit payout – expecting failures												
Investments in long-term assets	100											
Investments in securities		**10,233**			**12,198**			**12,198**			**12,198**	
Total outflows	**118**	**10,250**	**18**	**18**	**12,215**	**18**	**18**	**12,215**	**18**	**18**	**12,215**	**18**
Total DIF at the end	**12,233**	**12,215**	**12,198**	**24,430**	**24,413**	**24,395**	**36,628**	**36,610**	**36,593**	**48,825**	**48,808**	**50,529**
DIF at the account	12,233	1,983	1,965	14,198	1,983	1,965	14,198	1,983	1,965	14,198	1,983	3,704
Available for investments next month	**10,233**	**–18**	**–35**	**12,198**	**–18**	**–35**	**12,198**	**–18**	**–35**	**12,198**	**–18**	**1,704**
Desired cash reserves	2,000	2,000	2,000	2,000	2,000	2,000	2,000	2,000	2,000	2,000	2,000	2,000

As a result of individual bank's risk assessment, the deposit insurance authority envisaged a 90 per cent probability of failure of the Bank number 8, whose covered deposits amounted to €75 mil. The supervisory authority informed the DIS that the failure may be expected in May of Year 3. Table 3.10 presents a cash flow projection prepared by the DIS in anticipation of the bank failure in Year 3.

The deposit insurance authority had already collected more than €107 mil at the end of Year 2 of its operation. However, at the beginning of Year 3 of the operation, more than €99 mil were invested in government securities.

After the first annual regular premium collected in January, the DIS continued with the same investment policy (investing available funds into liquid securities) and with the desired cash reserve policy (holding a minimum of €2 mil as cash reserves).

Therefore, in order to have sufficient liquidity for the deposit payout, the deposit insurance authority cashed a portion of its investments during May, in the amount of €61 mil and adjusted its investment pattern in the months that followed.

As a result of the deposit payout, the total DIF decreased to €88 mil, but proper financial planning helped with a smooth liquidity management and prevented unpleasant surprises.

If the DIS was not aware of the possibility of the bank's failure during the upcoming year, it could find itself in a situation where investment could not be cashed on time. Careful financial planning can assist in liquidity management and overall financial management of the DIF.

Table 3.11 presents a summary of the projected cash flow for the DIS over three years of operation with details on the size of the DIF and liquidity reserves in the DIS account. Due to the failure of a bank during Year 3 in the amount of €75 million, the total DIF decreased to €88.7 mil. As it is evident, the DIF was built on regular premiums and, in accordance with it, the DIS's investment policy funds were invested in short-term government securities whereas retaining minimum cash reserves in the account.

Using the 'risk-aware' approach, the DIS has the power to establish a relation between its resources and the risks posed by individual banks. In everyday practice many DISs use risk assessment on individual banks

Table 3.10 Projection of a cash flow, Year 3, in €000

Cash flow projections	Jan	Feb	March	April	May	June	July	August	Sept	October	Nov	Dec
DIF at the beginning, in the account	**7,774**	**21,006**	**1,983**	**1,965**	**15,198**	**1,941**	**1,924**	**15,156**	**1,983**	**1,965**	**15,198**	**1,983**
Cash inflows												
Initial premium (10,000)												
Annual premium 0.2 per cent annually	13,250	0	0	13,250	0	0	13,250	0	0	13,250	0	0
Yield on investments (8 per cent)												3,826
Recoveries for earlier payouts (10 per cent)												
Cash in investments					**61,761**							
Additional funding – borrowing												
Transfer from budget												
Total inflows (receipts)	**13,250**	**0**	**0**	**13,250**	**61,761**	**0**	**13,250**	**0**	**0**	**13,250**	**0**	**3,826**
Cash outflows												

Operating expenses	18	18	18	18	18	18	18	18	18	18	18	18
Interest payments, fees												
Deposit payout – existing cases					**75,000**							
Deposit payout – expecting failures												
Investments in long-term assets												
Investments in securities		**19,006**						**13,156**			**13,198**	
Total outflows	**18**	**19,024**	**18**	**18**	**75,018**	**18**	**18**	**13,174**	**18**	**18**	**13,215**	**18**
Total DIF at the end	**120,360**	**120,343**	**120,325**	**133,558**	**58,540**	**58,523**	**71,755**	**71,738**	**71,720**	**84,953**	**84,935**	**88,744**
DIF in the account	21,006	1,983	1,965	15,198	1,941	1,924	15,156	1,983	1,965	15,198	1,983	5,791
Available for investments next month	**19,006**	**−18**	**−35**	**13,198**	**−59**	**−76**	**13,156**	**−18**	**−35**	**13,198**	**−18**	**3791**
Desired cash reserves	2,000	2,000	2,000	2,000	2,000	2,000	2,000	2,000	2,000	2,000	2,000	2,000

Table 3.11 DIF over 3 years of operation

DIF, in €000	Year 1	Year 2	Year 3
DIF at the end of previous year	0	50,529	107,128
Initial premium	100	0	0
Regular premium	49,000	51,000	53,000
Yield on investments	1,739	5,808	3,826
Operating expenses	210	210	210
Non-current assets	100	0	0
Deposit payout	0	0	75,000
DIF at end of the year	**50,529**	**107,128**	**88,744**
out of which:			
Invested in securities	46,825	99,354	82,953
Cash reserves (liquidity)	3,704	7,773	5,791
Total	**50,529**	**107,128**	**88,744**

only for determining differential premiums (where premiums paid by individual banks are in relation to their individual risk), but rarely use information on risk profiles of their member banks for the adjustment of target funds and overall optimization of funding.

3.5 Conclusion

Every DIS must ensure a clear prescribing of its funding options, especially for regular and extraordinary purposes. If the annual regular premium level is prescribed in the legislation, the deposit insurer does not have many options to adjust its regular funding in accordance with its payout requirements. In such circumstances, the DIS authority should establish clear emergency funding arrangements. When the deposit insurer has the authority to determine the annual regular premium level, it must understand and anticipate developments in the banking sector, its risk exposure toward individual banks, the probability of banks' failure, deposit growth, investment framework and other elements that may affect its funding choices. In order to be able to project its funding requirements, the deposit insurer should establish a regular financial planning model and manage its overall and liquid funds in accordance with the projected requirements and established guidelines. When implementing simple risk assessment techniques, the deposit insurer is able to understand its risk exposure and charge the premium in accordance with the banks' risk profiles.

Bibliography

Demirguc-Kunt, Asli, Edward Kane, and Luc Laeven. 2014. Deposit Insurance Database. http://siteresources.worldbank.org/INTRES/Resources/469232-1107449512766/Deposit_insurance_database_preWP.pdf. Accessed 2016.

Directive 2014/49/EU. 2014. Directive 2014/49/EU of the European Parliament and of the Council of 16 April 2014 on deposit guarantee schemes. http://eur-lex.europa.eu/legal-content/EN/TXT/?uri=CELEX:32014L0049. Accessed 2016.

FDIC. 1998. *A Brief History of Deposit Insurance in the United States*. Washington, DC: FDIC.

FSB. 2012. *Thematic Review on Deposit Insurance Systems, Peer Review Report*. Basel. Financial Stability Board.

Garcia, Gillian G.H. 1999. Deposit Insurance: A Survey of Actual and Best Practices. *WP/99/54*. Washington: IMF.

IADI. 2009. *Guidance Paper: Funding of Deposit Insurance Systems*. Basel. IADI.

———. 2011a. *Evaluation of Deposit Insurance Fund Sufficiency on the Basis of Risk Analysis*. Basel. IADI.

———. 2011b. *General Guidance for Developing Differential Premiium System*. Basel. IADI.

———. 2014. *The Revised Core Principles for Effective Deposit Insurance Systems*. Basel. IADI.

———. 2015. *Enhanced Guidance for Effective Deposit Insurance Systems: Ex-ante Funding*. Basel. IADI.

Smirnov, Sergey, Alexander Daryin, Roman Rachkov, Alexey Buzdalin, Vladimir Zdorovenin, and Alexey Goncharov. 2005. Credit Risk Modelling for Assessing Deposit Insurance Fund Adquacy: The Case of Russia.

Vaziri, Mo, Rafiqul Bhuyan, and Ponkala Anand Vaseekhar Manuel. 2012. Comparative Predictability of Failure of Financial Institutions Using Multiple Models. *Investment Management and Financial Inovations* 9: 120–127.

4

Target Funding

4.1 Introduction

Most deposit insurers wish to establish and maintain sufficient financial resources in an ex ante DIF at all times. In order to do so, they regularly re-examine the adequacy of funding and compare the available funds with the potential liability. The establishment of an adequate target fund size over a reasonable time frame is based on a more advanced financial planning focused on a short- and medium-term time horizon. Different methodologies are used for setting the target fund size level, based on an expert opinion or risk analysis for predicting bank failures. Regardless of the chosen model, deposit insurers should compare planned, desired and actually collected funds and decide whether to adjust the annual premium levels to the established target fund size level.

This chapter explores the use of target funding as a financial planning tool used by deposit insurers in order to establish and maintain an adequate DIS funding. It explains the main methodologies used for setting the target fund size and provides example of arbitrary setting of a target and risk analysis models that could be applied by the deposit insurance

D. Ognjenovic, *Deposit Insurance Schemes*,
DOI 10.1007/978-3-319-51143-6_4

authorities. It discusses the impact the growth of deposits has on the real value of the DIF over an established time frame.

4.2 What Is Target Funding

Core Principles (IADI 2014, 29) advocate establishing the target fund size level after the establishment of an ex ante DIF. It may be argued whether the target fund size level should be determined prior to the establishment of an ex ante fund or at the same time, when the authorities have to decide on the level of the annual regular premium.

The sequence of events is important in order to utilize the target fund size as a methodology for the determination of a desirable and optimal DIF. Once the ex ante DIF is established, the target fund size should be closely managed and updated and adjusted over time, on a regular basis.

IADI provides a somewhat confusing definition of the term 'target fund size'. Core Principles define it as ex ante collected funds as a proportion of the 'assessment base' (which may be total or insured deposits) (IADI 2014, 10). Theoretically, this is correct, but total deposits are not a liability for the DIS. The DIS is liable only for the repayment of the covered (insured) deposits, not the total deposits. The difference between total and covered deposits may be significant in individual banks. Therefore, if ex ante collected funds are compared to the total deposits of banks, the result would not be precise.

In the IADI Guidance Paper on ex ante funding it is stated that 'the target fund should reflect the capability of the deposit insurer to meet its mandate, taking into account its overall sources of funding, as well as the financial exposure of the banks which the deposit insurance scheme is mandated to protect' (IADI 2015, 10). By carefully reading the above sentence, the target fund size definition (which refers to 'overall sources of funding', that is, ex ante, ex post and emergency funding), compared to its 'financial exposure' (i.e. the amount of covered deposits due to be paid to depositors in case of an insurance event occurrence), does not reflect the definition of the target fund size from the Core Principles (which refers to 'ex ante fund' to the 'assessment base', that may be the total or covered deposits).

Regardless of the somewhat confusing definition, target funding became relevant in the ex ante funded DIS for understanding the adequacy and sufficiency of a DIF. That was never the key question for ex post DISs because they collected funds only after the failure of a bank and in the amount of the failed bank's covered deposits.

Therefore, for the purpose of this book, we will use the term *target fund size ratio* to denote the *total DIF (ex ante funds) in relation to the total covered (insured) deposits of banks.*

In other words, the target fund size is the desired (targeted) level of the coverage ratio, expressed as a percentage of the total ex ante desired funds (to be collected over an envisaged number of years) over the total exposure of the DIS toward individual member banks expressed as covered deposits in each individual bank. In simple words, the target fund size is the desired payout capacity of the DIS.

However, additional funds (emergency funding) may be at the DIS' disposal resulting in a larger amount of available funds than those collected on a regular basis and consequently resulting in a larger 'overall payout capacity' of the DIS than those built through ex ante funding exclusively, though these funds are not taken into account when setting and adjusting the desired target fund.

International guidelines (IADI 2014, 29) suggest that the target fund size should be determined on the basis of clear, consistent and transparent criteria, which are subject to periodic review. In addition, a reasonable time frame should be set to achieve the target fund size.

Many DISs use the target fund size in order to achieve the desired level of the DIF.

IADI periodically conducts different surveys and it conducted a survey on the target fund size (Villegas 2015, 1–42) based on the date from the end of year 2014. Out of 64 respondents, 42 jurisdictions set the target fund size. Only 21 out of 42 jurisdictions used covered deposits when determining the target fund size level, and 28 set the target fund size in the legislation. There is no unique and recognized methodology implemented for determining the target fund size level.

The key question related to setting the target fund size is: *What is the desirable level of ex ante funds for a DIS, that is, how to determine a single figure which represents the desirable level of funds sufficient for a DIS to fulfill its mandate?*

The answer to this question is not simple and despite the fact that more and more jurisdictions use the concept of target fund size, very few of them reflect its true potential and use it to the fullest extent.

DIS methodology for determining the target fund size ranges from the discretionary approach to statistical modeling based on risk analysis.

The discretionary approach refers to the situation when the target fund size is not determined according to specific methodology. Instead, arbitrary decisions and judgments are made when establishing the target fund size. Judgments are based on ideas of analysts and experts and their 'feeling' where the 'margin of safety' for the DIF is. In other words, experts judge the sufficiency of the DIF or target fund size. The method is only an approximation of the needed funds without taking into consideration the potential liability for the DIS.

As evidenced by deposit insurers' implemented practices, although the concept of target fund size has been known for some years already, many DISs still determine it without a specific methodology or by using a simple rule of thumb in the form of an arbitrary approximation of the desired coverage ratio, without taking into account any kind of risk analysis.

Deposit insurers apply both covered (insured) deposits and eligible (insurable) deposits when setting the target fund size level. However, only the covered deposits represent DIS' a potential liability exposure.

Although there is no comprehensive accurate database on target fund size levels in all DISs, it is clear that the deposit insurance authorities have not yet accepted the target fund size as a standard measure for their payout capacities.

4.3 Setting the Target Fund Size Arbitrarily

As evidenced by many DISs, it is a common practice to set the target fund size arbitrarily, that is, to use expert opinions. Experts (policy makers, financial authorities, advisers) propose the most appropriate desirable size of the DIF expressed as a single number in relation to the DIS's exposure (total liabilities) at a certain point of time.

For example, if the target fund size is set at 2 per cent over five years, it reads that the DIS aims to collect funds in the amount of 2 per cent of the total covered deposits over five years.

Expert judgments are used to judge why the target fund size should be set at 2 per cent and not at some other figure and what the expected payout capacity of the DIS would be once it reached the target, that is, collected the targeted amount of funds. The expected payout capacity of the DIS is assessed using the bottom-up cumulative approach.

4.3.1 Example: Setting the Target Fund Size Using an Expert Opinion

In order to understand how to set the target fund size by an expert opinion, an example is given on a banking sector with ten banks where the DIS coverage level is €10,000.

When deciding on setting the target fund size level, there are two questions to be answered:

- How big is the DIF we want to build?
- In what time frame do we want to build the targeted DIF?

Authorities are focused on finding answers to these two questions

As the first step, the closer look will be given to distribution of covered deposits among individual banks, in order to be able to understand the payout capacity of the possible target fund size level. Therefore, a simple analysis of the ratio (market share) of each bank in the total covered deposits may provide an initial idea on the possible desirable size of the DIF.

Table 4.1 lists banks from the smallest to the largest one, where the smallest bank represents only 0.01 per cent and the largest bank represents 35.18 per cent in the total covered deposits. There are four banks with a larger market share and three banks with the market share under 1 per cent.

Authorities need to make the first policy decision in this stage; that is, they need to answer the question how big the DIF should be. There could be more than one answer, all of which are correct and based on an arbitrary policy decision.

Table 4.1 Comparison of payout capacity for two target fund size options

Banks	Covered deposits at coverage level of €10,000, in €	Ratio of each bank in total covered deposits, in percentage	Covered deposits bottom-up cumulative approach, in €
10	2,536,500	0.01	2,536,500
9	65,800,000	0.27	68,336,500
8	70,000,000	0.29	138,336,500
6	273,000,000	1.11	411,336,500
7	535,500,000	2.18	946,836,500
5	955,500,000	3.89	1,902,336,500
4	2,195,000,000	8.95	4,097,336,500
3	4,255,000,000	17.34	8,352,336,500
2	7,550,000,000	30.78	15,902,336,500
1	8,630,000,000	35.18	24,532,336,500
Total	**24,532,336,500**	**100.00**	
Target fund size 1.5 per cent	**367,985,048**		
Target fund size 4 per cent	**981,293,460**		

One answer to the first question could be: *We want to build a DIF so big to be able to repay eligible depositors in bank number 6 (which is the fourth-smallest bank in the banking system) with a market share of 1.11 per cent that is a minimum of €273 mil.*

Or the answer could be somewhat more ambiguous: *We want to build a DIF so big to be able to repay eligible depositors in bank number 5 (which is the sixth-smallest bank in the banking system) with a market share of 3.89 per cent.*

Authorities want to analyze the two possible ideas further and establish two possible options for the desired target fund size level: (i) 1.5 per cent and (ii) 4 per cent.

Clearly, four largest banks are large enough to be called 'systemic' for the purpose of the DIS and their resolution should be addressed by all safety net players. That is the reason why authorities usually exclude systemic banks from approximation on DIFs and from setting the target fund size.

After answering the first question, the decision should be made about the number of years necessary for achieving the set goal.

In order to understand the desired payout capacity of each target fund size level option, banks are sorted in accordance with the bottom-up cumulative approach, starting from the smallest to the largest, in the last column of Table 4.1.

If the target fund size is determined at 1.5 per cent of covered deposits, that is, at €367 mil, the DIS would be able to repay depositors in any of the four smallest banks in the system respectively or even in the three smallest banks simultaneously.

If a higher target ratio is chosen, as the proposed 4 per cent, such decision would accumulate almost one €1 billion and the payout capacity of the DIS would increase to the payout of depositors in any of the six smallest banks respectively or even in the five smallest banks at the same time.

Which of the two options is better? Is it better to be able to repay four or six of the smallest banks and over which time frame?

Obviously, the higher target fund size (4 per cent) is more reassuring for the public and ensures a certain comfort for the authorities in case of bank failure. Though the question is whether it is really necessary to target the DIF at 4 per cent. The target fund size level is usually set arbitrarily, with a time frame of three to five years. Furthermore, can authorities make a decision already at this point?

The answer is: *Yes and no*. Many DISs make a decision at this point. Consequently, authorities decided to establish the target fund size level over a five-year time frame.

If the decision was made now, it would ignore the impact of the target fund size level on individual banks and the impact of time (i.e. the growth of covered deposits over the established time frame).

In the next step, authorities should analyze what the minimum annual premium should be in order to achieve the proposed target fund size level for the two options over the suggested time frame of five years and how it would affect the banks' liquidity and profitability (i.e. how much the banks would need to pay for the DIS to collect the desired targeted amount).

Simple calculation results are as follows:

- target fund size at 1.5 per cent of covered deposits over five years would result in a minimum annual regular premium at 0.3 per cent (as 0.3

per cent × 5 = 1.5 per cent) where banks would pay €73.6 million with the largest banks paying €25.9 million annually;
- target fund size at 4 per cent of covered deposits over five years would result in a minimum annual regular premium at 0.8 per cent (0.8 per cent × 5 = 4 per cent) where banks would pay €196.2 million with the largest banks paying €69 million annually.

The decision to have a higher payout capacity and a larger target fund size over five years would consequently result in higher annual banks' contribution to the DIF and thus their higher direct expenses, resulting in a lower profitability over that period.

Additional analysis should be made for different time frames before making the final decision. Authorities may consider prolonging the time frame for gaining a higher target fund size in order to soften the impact of a higher annual regular premium. In other words, authorities may, for example, explore options to set the target fund size at 4 per cent over eight years instead of five. If the target fund size of 4 per cent should be achieved over eight years, the annual regular premium for banks would drop to 0.2 per cent.

Whichever option is chosen, it would always be arbitrary as long as the risk analysis is ignored.

4.4 Setting the Target Fund Size Using Risk Analysis

In addition to an expert opinion on the desirable size of the DIF, many DISs have taken one step further and applied risk analysis methods in order to capture the risks that may cause the insurance event and the consumption of DIFs.

This approach is based on the assumption that the DIF should be sufficient to ensure an efficient payout of the covered deposits in a failed bank, not just any bank. Accordingly, the DIF should grow as much as it is necessary to fulfill that task.

The common approach of risk analysis methods used for setting the target fund size is that systemic banks are not a primary focus and the value of their covered deposits is not relevant for the evaluation of DIF's sufficiency. This approach is based on the assumption that systemic banks should be dealt with on the level of the national safety net using other resolution tools (such as, for example, bridge bank, transfer of assets and liabilities, bail-in or a combination of several resolution tools). However, if the DIS has a mandate for bank resolution, a realistic assumption on the potential liquidity requirements and losses (non-recoverable funds from the DIF) should be assessed and taken into account when assessing the potential outflow from the DIF.

Therefore, the aim is to determine the target value of the DIF which is necessary for the DIS to fulfill its function, either by excluding systemically important banks whose failure will be dealt with by all safety net participants and through other resolution tools (if the DIS does not have a broadened mandate) or by including all banks with a realistic assumption of resolution methods and funding needs (if the DIS has a broadened mandate).

Another important assumption relates to the difference between the liquidity and solvency gaps where insolvency of an established DIS is not a trigger for the DIS's termination.

The sufficiency of the DIF must be reviewed and revised on an ongoing basis. Once the target size level is established, as either an optimal or a sufficient value of the DIF, it must be monitored or adjusted to the circumstances and requirements. Due to the fact that the banking risks are not static, neither should the target fund size be that way as well. In other words, the target fund size is constantly changing in line with the DIS's risk exposures.

In order to determine the target fund size, having in mind the risks of bank failure, one must assess the potential losses for the DIF, which are classified as expected and unexpected losses.

The sufficiency of the DIF in relation to the target fund size can be evaluated in the short term and in the long term. The short-term evaluation of the DIF is based on cash flow projections over a one-year time frame, taking into account all known inflows and outflows from the DIF. The long-term evaluation of the DIF stretches over the set target time frame.

In both cases, the forecast of a bank's failure is the most delicate part. Some jurisdictions use data from historical experience with bank failures. They determine the losses they experienced in historical bank failures and adjust the level of the target fund size accordingly. Such approach is a look backward rather than a look forward and does not take into account the current and future risk profiles of member banks.

Some DISs use early warning systems and other forward-looking methods for assessing risk profiles of member banks.

Based on Value at Risk principle, the DIF must be sufficient to cover both expected and unexpected losses.

In addition, the DIF should be sufficient to correspond to a certain level of the financial reliability of the deposit insurance authority. The financial reliability of banks is determined by credit rating. As deposit insurance authorities don't have credit ratings, their implied credit rating (the level of the DIF's deficit probability) may be assigned by a mapping procedure.

By doing so, the mapping procedure of credit rating agencies can be used in order to determine the implied credit rating of the deposit insurance authority. It should be in the range between the credit rating of the safest and soundest member bank and the sovereign credit rating.

Therefore, a simple formula for the DIS's expected losses may be used. Expected losses (EL) for the DIS are the sum of products of all Exposures at Default (EAD), Probabilities of Default (PD) and Losses Given Default (LGD):

$$EL = \sum EAD \times PDi \times LGDi$$

EAD is the amount of covered deposits in a member bank which has a certain probability of failure (PD), and LGD is the share of losses the DIF will suffer in case a particular bank fails and the DIS is obliged to payout its covered deposits. The probability of default (PD) can be determined based on:

(i) the standard approach and credit ratings of banks, if such ratings exist,
(ii) the improved approach on the basis of econometric models and
(iii) the advanced approach on the basis of market data models.

EAD is actually the DIS's potential liquidity outflow (the amount that the DIS pays to eligible depositors). LGDi is a real loss for the DIS (the amount that is not recovered). The DIS must worry about both that is its potential liquidity needs and its ultimate level of the DIF.

The standard approach is often limited by non-existing external credit ratings of banks, especially in less developed markets where many small national banks exist. However, the deposit insurance authority may develop its own internal credit rating model or use the same model used for the differential premium system.

The improved approach uses econometric models to estimate the financial condition of banks as a function of its financial parameters which then modify the PD of each bank on the basis of available statistics of the historical data on defaults.

The advanced approach is based on market data models, that is, the current financial condition of member banks, banking sector and economy as a whole.

The DISs don't assess the probability of the default of banks easily because in most cases there are no reliable historical data on losses in bank failures. However, the empirical evidence from many DISs show that even with the analysis of publicly available data any DIS can obtain a decent assessment of the risk profile of its member banks. Banks usually don't fail overnight and without warning signs which cannot be noticed. The delay is always made when deciding when and how to resolve a bank, but the financial condition of a bank hardly deteriorates overnight. If this is the case, risks were not captured on time.

There are several models developed for forecasting the failure of a company which can also be used for the prediction of the failure of a bank. These models are Moody's, Standard & Poor's, Z-score model and Vaziri's model (Vaziri et al. 2012, 122–123).

Moody's failure forecasting model is based on financial ratios such as:

(i) coverage ratios that show whether a bank is able to repay its debts (interest coverage ratio, asset coverage ratio),
(ii) leverage ratios that show the level of debt,

(iii) liquidity ratios that show whether a bank has sufficient liquidity to pay its current debt liabilities and
(iv) profitability ratios that show the level of earnings.

Standard & Poor's forecasting model is similar to the Moody's model and uses:

(i) coverage ratios,
(ii) leverage ratios and
(iii) profitability ratios.

Vaziri's model incorporates Moody's and Standards & Poor's financial ratios and expands them with efficiency ratios.

Altman's original Z-score model (Altman 1968, 589–609) was developed and improved over time by the author, where the model used for non-manufacturing industries can be adjusted for banks.

Z-score model uses the following formula:

$Z = 6.56\ X_1 + 3.26\ X_2 + 6.72\ X_3 + 1.05\ X_4$

Where:

X_1 represents working capital/total assets.
X_2 represents retained earnings/total assets.
X_3 represents EBIT (earnings before interest and taxes)/total assets and.
X_4 represents book value equity/total liabilities.

These models can be adjusted for the prediction of bank failure within a one-year horizon, with a certain level of precision.

LGD is 1 – recovery rate in case of failure. If the DIS recovers 20 per cent of its funds in bank failures, then LGD is 80 per cent.

4.4.1 Example: Calculating the DIS's Expected Losses

Let us assume that Bank number 6 from our example has an 80 per cent probability of default (failure), and that the DIS could recover 20 per cent of its funds. The total covered deposits deposited at Bank number 6 are €273 million. The DIS's expected losses are:

$$EL = \sum EAD \times PDi \times \text{LGDi}$$
$$EL = 273{,}000{,}000 \times 0.8 \times 0.8$$
$$= 174{,}720{,}000\,€$$

By using this method, under the given assumption, the DIF can expect losses in the amount of €174 mil.

It is not problematic to assess the EAD, but it may be challenging to assess the probability of default of member banks and the losses given default. The DISs can apply the credit portfolio approach method for assessing the probability of default (failure) of its member banks. The credit portfolio approach is an analytical method derived from Basel II principles for assessing bank risks, using, for example, Value at Risk indicators. Recalling that there are some similarities between the DIF and the CAR, the DIS may determine the 'risk of its portfolio of covered deposits' in a way similar to the banks' calculation of their CAR using the Basel risk assessment methodology.

If the banking sector is developed and if member banks have assigned credit ratings, the DIS may use credit rating models to determine the probability of default. In many jurisdictions, banks are not global credit institutions with assigned credit ratings; therefore, the DISs are developing internal ratings and early warning models of predictions of the probability of default of their member banks or combine different methods or simply use CAMELS rating or even ranking of banks that are used for the differential premium system.

If the deposit insurance authority is already applying the risk-based methodology for premium collection, it may use information on assessed risk-profiles of individual banks as a foundation for further analysis. For example, the deposit insurance authority may decide to target its funds in order to have sufficient funds if all banks categorized as a 'risky' fail.

By using the risk models, the DIS is much more aware of the risks of failures and a potential payout and it is able to manage its own funds in an optimal way. In order to do so, the DIS should establish and develop an analytical function responsible for the collection and analysis of data and information and for the development of a reliable methodology for assessing risks.

Unexpected losses may be determined using a statistical simulation method like Monte Carlo. DISs use statistical models, internal ratings, expert judgments and external ratings when conducting the risk analysis for the purpose of the DIF's sufficiency evaluation (IADI 2011, 45).

4.4.2 Example: Setting the Target Fund Size Using Risk Analysis

Exposure at Default (EAD) is the amount of covered deposits in each member bank.

Probability of Default (PD) for each bank is based on an early warning system developed in cooperation with the bank supervisor.

Results show that the probabilities of default of individual banks range from 10 per cent, for less risky banks, to 97 per cent for the riskiest banks.

Loss Given Default (LGD) is determined based on the historical experience of banks' failure and the recovery rate or using a more advanced approach, by analyzing the balance sheet structure of each individual bank, legal system and assessment of the recovery rate. In our example, based on the historical experience with failed banks, authorities estimated that the LGD is 70 per cent. In other words, it may be expected, on average, that the deposit insurance authority would be able to recover 30 per cent of the covered deposits in case of the deposit payout.

Summary of the used methodology with results is presented in Table 4.2. By multiplying the amount of the covered deposits of each bank with the probability of its failure and the losses of its failure, the DIS calculates its expected losses. The sum of all expected losses is the absolute value of its desired funds. In this case, the sum of all expected losses, based on the applied model, would be €3.9 billion, that is, 16.11 per cent of the total covered deposits.

However, some banks are systemically important and thus the DIS can exclude them from the final calculation. Based on the approximation, adjustment is made to expected losses with a result that the DIF should rise to at least 3.19 per cent of the total covered deposits.

In order to test our risk assessment based on the early warning system, we will conduct a similar assessment based on the applied risk-based premium methodology. Results of the applied risk-based premium methodology for calculating the desired fund size level that is the target fund size is given in Table 4.3.

Table 4.2 Use of risk analysis in setting target fund size, in €

Banks	EAD = covered deposits	Probability of default, in percentage	Loss given default, in percentage	Expected losses	Adjusted expected losses
10	2,536,500	90	70	1,597,995	1,597,995
9	65,800,000	95	70	43,757,000	43,757,000
8	70,000,000	97	70	47,530,000	47,530,000
6	273,000,000	88	70	168,168,000	168,168,000
7	535,500,000	50	70	187,425,000	187,425,000
5	955,500,000	50	70	334,425,000	334,425,000
4	2,195,000,000	40	70	614,600,000	0
3	4,255,000,000	30	70	893,550,000	0
2	7,550,000,000	20	70	1,057,000,000	0
1	8,630,000,000	10	70	604,100,000	0
Total	**24,532,336,500**			**3,952,152,995**	**782,902,995**
Target fund size, in percentage				**16.11**	**3.19**

Table 4.3 Use of risk-based premium methodology in setting target fund size, in €

Banks	EAD = covered deposits	Risk category	Expected losses
10	2,536,500	Risky	2,536,500
9	65,800,000	Risky	65,800,000
8	70,000,000	Risky	70,000,000
6	273,000,000	Risky	273,000,000
7	535,500,000	Risky	535,500,000
5	955,500,000	Watch	0
4	2,195,000,000	Watch	0
3	4,255,000,000	Watch	0
2	7,550,000,000	Watch	0
1	8,630,000,000	Watch	0
Total	**24,532,336,500**		**946,836,500**
Target fund size, in percentage			**3.86**

Based on the regularly applied risk-based premium methodology developed and implemented by the DIS, there are five banks identified as risky banks. The total covered deposits in those five risky banks are at €946 million, that is, 3.86 per cent of the total covered deposits.

There is a difference in results between the two approaches; hence the deposit insurance authority must decide which target fund size would be more appropriate: 3.19 per cent or 3.86 per cent. If the deposit insurance authority wants to be 'on the safe side', the higher target fund size is more desirable. Obviously, one bank is on the edge of being identified as risky and the deposit insurance authority should, over a short period of time, take a closer look at its financial statements and discuss with the bank's supervisor the financial condition of that particular bank in order to be sure it possesses sufficient financial resources in case of failure.

4.4.3 The FDIC Experience with the Target Fund Size

The FDIC desires to have a DIF that is sufficient at all times to ensure the payout of covered deposits (Ellis 2013, 3). As a consequence of a large number of bank failures during the 1980s when the FDIC spent 200 billion USD for resolving 2,900 banks, the US Congress instituted the target fund size in 1989, named the Designated Reserve Ratio (DRR), equal to at least 1.25 per cent of the covered deposits within 15 years (Congress 1989).

In 1996, the legislation changed, so the FDIC stopped charging a premium to the well-capitalized and well-managed banks once the DIF reached the target level of 1.25 per cent.

Another legislative change in 2006 prescribed the DRR within a range between 1.15 and 1.50 per cent.

In 2010, the Dodd-Frank law increased the DDR to 1.35 per cent (Congress 2010).

At a certain period of time, the FDIC used credit risk model and calculated the probability of failure, loss given default and exposure at default for each bank (Bennet 2001, 1–74). It used an economic model to determine the statistical relationship between the results and economic variables such as interest rates, stock prices and housing prices. The simulation model was used in order to assess the distribution of possible future failures and losses for the DIF.

At present the FDIC is mandated with the authority to determine the optimal fund size and to charge premiums to meet the fund's needs. In doing so, the FDIC uses historical experience to calculate (ex post based on historical data) how much funds would have been needed in the past in order to pay out the covered deposits in historical failures. Results show that if the DIF was able to grow to 2 per cent of the covered deposits prior to each of the two latest banking crises, the DIF would not have been depleted during these two banking crises. Therefore, a new level of DRR was set at 2 per cent.

4.5 Time Impact on Achieving the Target Fund Size

Target fund size is the desirable payout capacity of the DIF at a certain point of time in the future, determined at present. Although achieving the target fund size is envisaged over a predicted time frame, so far the effect of time and its impact on the value of the DIF have been ignored. However, the €1 collected in year 5 is worth less than the €1 collected today. In finance, this is a well-known fact.

If the DIS ignores the impact of time, its target fund will not be reached within the established time frame. Even if the DIS did not have to compensate depositors over the envisaged period, its funds at the end of the planned period could lag behind the targeted amount. The growth of deposits at rates higher than predicted may jeopardize reaching of the target fund.

Therefore, a DIS should proactively manage its funding over the established time frame.

4.5.1 Example: Target Fund Size and Impact of Growth of Deposits

An example is based on the following assumptions:

- Target fund size level is 4 per cent
- Annual premium is set at 0.8 per cent
- Target fund time frame is five years
- Annual growth of covered deposits is 10 per cent

The question is what happens with the target fund size at 4 per cent over five years.

The initial projections of the growth of deposits over a five-year time frame and the annual premium contribution to the DIF over the same period are given in Table 4.4.

When setting the target fund size at 4 per cent, authorities had in mind the desired size of the DIF to be collected in five years, in the amount which would be sufficient to compensate any of the six smallest banks in the system individually or 5 smallest banks simultaneously.

The difference between the planned target fund size and actual funds collected each year is presented in the line sufficiency/deficiency of funds over the target.

Due to the increase of covered deposits (because of the annual growth of covered deposits by 10 per cent), the annual premium is increasing in absolute terms up to €316 million.

At the end of year 5, instead of having 4 per cent of covered deposits, despite the collection of 0.8 per cent annual premium, the DIF would amount to only 3.34 per cent of covered deposits. The total DIF lacks more than €262 million compared to the desired targeted amount.

How was this possible if the annual premium was set at 0.8 per cent annually? The answer lies in the growth of the total covered deposits to €39 billion and consequently the depletion of the total DIF in relation to the total covered deposits. The impact of the high growth of deposits on the increase of the annual premium was smaller than the impact on the total DIS's liabilities (which increased more than the premium).

Therefore, in the banking sectors with historically high growth of deposits, the level of annual growth of deposits must be taken in calculation in order to understand the real implication of the growth of deposits on the DIFs.

Consequently, the payout capacity of the DIS decreased, resulting in the fact that, with €1,317 billion at end of Year 5, the DIS is able to repay any of the five smallest banks in the system (instead of six, as planned).

Figure 4.1 illustrates the desired and actual target fund size over five years.

Table 4.4 Targeted fund size and annual growth of deposits, in €

Banks	Year 0	Year 1	Year 2	Year 3	Year 4	Year 5
Coverage €10,000	Covered deposits, annual growth by 10 per cent					
10	2,536,500	2,790,150	3,069,165	3,376,082	3,713,690	4,085,059
9	65,800,000	72,380,000	79,618,000	87,579,800	96,337,780	105,971,558
8	70,000,000	77,000,000	84,700,000	93,170,000	102,487,000	112,735,700
6	273,000,000	300,300,000	330,330,000	363,363,000	399,699,300	439,669,230
7	535,500,000	589,050,000	647,955,000	712,750,500	784,025,550	862,428,105
5	955,500,000	1,051,050,000	1,156,155,000	1,271,770,500	1,398,947,550	1,538,842,305
4	2,195,000,000	2,414,500,000	2,655,950,000	2,921,545,000	3,213,699,500	3,535,069,450
3	4,255,000,000	4,680,500,000	5,148,550,000	5,663,405,000	6,229,745,500	6,852,720,050
2	7,550,000,000	8,305,000,000	9,135,500,000	10,049,050,000	11,053,955,000	12,159,350,500
1	8,630,000,000	9,493,000,000	10,442,300,000	11,486,530,000	12,635,183,000	13,898,701,300
Total	**24,532,336,500**	**26,985,570,150**	**29,684,127,165**	**32,652,539,882**	**35,917,793,870**	**39,509,573,257**
Annual premium 0.8 per cent		**215,884,561**	**237,473,017**	**261,220,319**	**287,342,351**	**316,076,586**
Total DIF		**215,884,561**	**453,357,579**	**714,577,898**	**1,001,920,249**	**1,317,996,835**
Planned target fund at the end of each year		**215,884,561**	**474,946,035**	**783,660,957**	**1,149,369,404**	**1,580,382,930**
Sufficiency/ deficiency over target		**0**	**–21,588,456**	**–69,083,060**	**–147,449,155**	**–262,386,096**
Actual target fund size level, in percentage		**0.80**	**1.53**	**2.19**	**2.79**	**3.34**

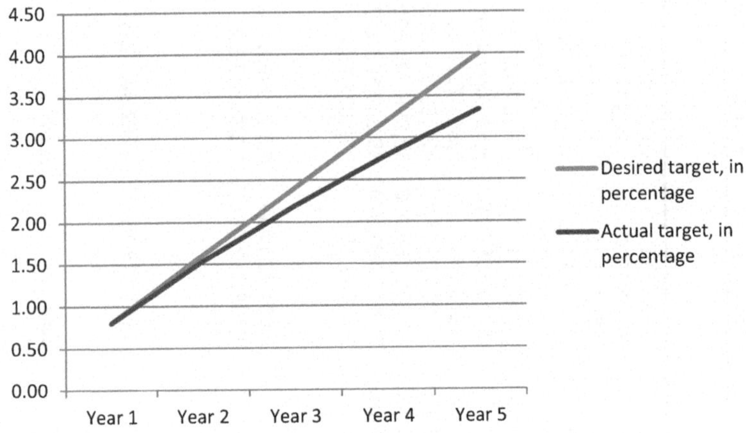

Fig. 4.1 Desired and actual target fund size

Having taken all into account, what could and should the deposit insurance authority do? There are two options:

- The first option is to ignore the annual growth of covered deposits and continue applying a steady annual premium of 0.8 per cent, although knowing that the targeted funds would not be achieved within the planned time frame and that most likely the time frame would have to be prolonged. This option is possible only if the banking sector is safe and sound and there is no immediate risk of bank failure. Actual practices of many DISs, where the annual regular premium is not adjusted on a regular basis, suggest that many authorities ignore the impact of time and deposit growth.
- The second option is to correct and adjust the annual premium every year for the correct amount in order to achieve the annual planned target fund level.

Table 4.5 presents adjustments in the annual premium level in order to achieve the planned target fund size of 4 per cent over five years if the covered deposits grow by 10 per cent annually.

The collected funds on an annual basis are lagging behind the targeted funds of Year 2. As a result, at the end of Year 2, the actual coverage ratio

Table 4.5 Correction of annual premium to target fund size

Banks	Covered deposits with coverage level of €10,000	Year 1	Year 2	Year 3	Year 4	Year 5
10	2,536,500	2,790,150	3,069,165	3,376,082	3,713,690	4,085,059
9	65,800,000	72,380,000	79,618,000	87,579,800	96,337,780	105,971,558
8	70,000,000	77,000,000	84,700,000	93,170,000	102,487,000	112,735,700
6	273,000,000	300,300,000	330,330,000	363,363,000	399,699,300	439,669,230
7	535,500,000	589,050,000	647,955,000	712,750,500	784,025,550	862,428,105
5	955,500,000	1,051,050,000	1,156,155,000	1,271,770,500	1,398,947,550	1,538,842,305
4	2,195,000,000	2,414,500,000	2,655,950,000	2,921,545,000	3,213,699,500	3,535,069,450
3	4,255,000,000	4,680,500,000	5,148,550,000	5,663,405,000	6,229,745,500	6,852,720,050
2	7,550,000,000	8,305,000,000	9,135,500,000	10,049,050,000	11,053,955,000	12,159,350,500
1	8,630,000,000	9,493,000,000	10,442,300,000	11,486,530,000	12,635,183,000	13,898,701,300
Total	**24,532,336,500**	**26,985,570,150**	**29,684,127,165**	**32,652,539,882**	**35,917,793,870**	**39,509,573,257**
Annual premium 0.8 per cent		**215,884,561**	**237,473,017**	**261,220,319**	**287,342,351**	**316,076,586**
Total DIF		**215,884,561**	**453,357,579**	**714,577,898**	**1,001,920,249**	**1,317,996,835**
Planned target fund at the end of each year		**215,884,561**	**474,946,035**	**783,660,957**	**1,149,369,404**	**1,580,382,930**
Sufficiency/deficiency over target		**0**	**−21,588,456**	**−69,083,060**	**−147,449,155**	**−262,386,096**

(continued)

Table 4.5 (continued)

Banks	Covered deposits with coverage level of €10,000	Year 1	Year 2	Year 3	Year 4	Year 5
Actual coverage ratio at 0.8 per cent premium		**0.80**	**1.53**	**2.19**	**2.79**	**3.34**
Corrected coefficient of premium, in percentage		**0**	**0.07**	**0.15**	**0.22**	**0.29**
Corrected annual premium level, in percentage		**0.80**	**0.87**	**0.95**	**1.02**	**1.09**
Correction (increase) of premium		0	21,588,456	47,494,603	78,366,096	114,936,940
Total collected corrected annual premium		0	259,061,473	308,714,923	365,708,447	431,013,526
Total DIF after adjustment		**215,884,561**	**474,946,035**	**783,660,957**	**1,149,369,404**	**1,580,382,930**
Corrected coverage ratio, in percentage		0.80	1.60	2.40	3.20	4.00

is 1.53 per cent, although it should have already been 1.6 per cent (i.e. 0.8 per cent × 2 years).

Authorities must determine how much banks must pay additionally, expressed as the corrected premium level coefficient.

The corrected coefficient is determined as a difference between the appropriate level of target fund size for a particular year and actually collected funds in that year.

The corrected coefficient for Year 2 is 0.7 per cent. The corrected coefficient is then applied to the total covered deposits in order to calculate the additional amount of premium in absolute figures to be collected if authorities want to 'keep the pace' with the targeted funds on an annual level.

As a result, in Year 2 banks should additionally pay €21.6 mil which results in a total premium of €259 mil instead of €237 mil. Therefore, the corrected annual premium applied in Year 2 is 0.87 per cent (instead of 0.8 per cent). By applying 0.87 per cent in Year 2, at the end of Year 2, the DIF would amount to 1.6 per cent of the targeted funds and to almost €475 million.

The same principle is used for the remaining years, resulting in the fact that in Year 3, Year 4 and Year 5 the corrected annual premium is 0.95 per cent, 1.02 per cent and 1.09 per cent, respectively.

The corrected annual premium is then applied to the amount of covered deposits for each bank if the flat premium is applied. If the differential premium system is applied, calculations are adjusted accordingly in order to reflect the risk profiles of each individual bank.

Over five years, banks must contribute 4.73 per cent of total covered deposits in order to ensure minimum 4 per cent of total covered deposits at the end of the planned horizon of five years, due to the annual growth of deposits by 10 per cent.

Hence, there is a trade-off between achieving the target fund size within the planned time frame and the adjusted (increased) level of annual premium each year.

The example showed how adjustments should be applied in each year in order to overcome the discrepancy between the targeted fund size and the actual coverage ratio at the end of each year and at the end of the planned time frame for the target fund size. Without annual adjustments of the premium level, the DIF would collect less than planned if the covered deposits grew. The higher the growth of the covered deposits, the bigger is the discrepancy between the target fund size and the actual coverage ratio over a longer planned period of time.

4.6 Conclusion

Target fund size is the desired level of the DIS's payout capacity ('future coverage ratio') over an established reasonable time frame. In order to use target funding for assessing the adequacy of the DIF, the DIS should choose among the risk analysis methods and focus on balancing its available financial resources with the potential financial needs. The DIS is going to be able to understand its potential financial needs only if it is aware of the risk assessment of banks. However, banks' risks are not static and banks' risk profiles change over time. Therefore, once the target fund size level is established, expressed as total ex ante available funds compared to the total covered deposits in banks, it must be regularly monitored, analyzed and adjusted to potential needs which are changing over time. If the targeted level of funding is not achieved, the deposit insurance authority should analyze overall financial conditions and probabilities of failures of each individual member bank in order to decide whether to prolong the previously established time frame or adjust the funding (increase or decrease the annual regular premium).

Bibliography

Altman, Edward I. 1968. Financial Ratios, Discriminant Analysis and the Prediction of Corporate Bankruptcy. *Journal of Finance* 23(4): 589–609.

Bennet, Rosalind L. 2001. *Evaluating the Adequacy of the Deposit Insurance Fund*. Washington, DC: FDIC.

Congress, USA. 1989. Financial Institutions Reform, Recovery, and Enforcement Act of 1989, Pub. L. No. 101-73, 103 Stat.

———. 2010. Dodd-Frank Wall Street Reform and Consumer Protection Act, Pub. L. No. 111-203, 124 Stat. 1376.

Ellis, Diane. 2013. Deposit Insurance Funding. Assuring Confidence. https://www.fdic.gov/deposit/insurance/assuringconfidence.pdf. Accessed 2016.
IADI. 2011. *Evaluation of Deposit Insurance Fund Sufficiency on the Basis of Risk Analysis*. Basel. IADI.
———. 2014. *The Revised Core Principles for Effective Deposit Insurance Systems*. Basel. IADI.
———. 2015. *Enhanced Guidance for Effective Deposit Insurance Systems: Ex-ante Funding*. Basel. IADI.
Vaziri, Mo, Rafiqul Bhuyan, and Ponkala Anand Vaseekhar Manuel. 2012. Comparative Predictability of Failure of Financial Institutions Using Multiple Models. *Investment Management and Financial Innovations* 9(2): 120–112.
Villegas, Anna Carmela L. 2015. IADI's Preliminary Results of Survey on DIF Target Ratio; PPTs Presented on a Workshop Organized by PDIC in June 2015. http://www.pdic.gov.ph/files/iadi/Session%201_Ma.%20Ana%20Carmela%20Villegas_presentation.pdf. Accessed 2016.

5

Optimized Funding

5.1 Introduction

Optimal or adequate DIF is the one which ensures sufficient financial resources in relation to the DIS's potential liability. Optimal DIF is neither overfunded nor underfunded. Is there a secret formula how to establish an optimal DIF? Is optimal funding a part of a long-term strategic financial planning process that each deposit insurer should conduct and adjust regularly? Many DISs use an established target fund size level, arbitrarily or by using the risk analysis methodology. Target funding, if used for strategic financial planning, enables adjustments of funding in accordance with the DIS's requirements on a regular basis. If the established target fund size level is a constant figure over a projected time frame, it does not capture the real needs of the DIS and there is a gap between the DIF and its potential liability. Target fund size level is the desired level of the DIF and as such it changes and moves in line with the DIS's potential exposure. Therefore, target fund size level is a dynamic (moving) rather than a static figure. Optimal funding enables the DIS to provide funding for a dynamic target fund.

D. Ognjenovic, *Deposit Insurance Schemes*,
DOI 10.1007/978-3-319-51143-6_5

This chapter explores the idea of the optimal size of the DIF and discusses how financial management techniques in interaction with the established target funding, based on risk analysis, enable deposit insurers to adjust the funding in accordance with their exposures on an ongoing basis. It provides examples how to adjust the time frame to the initially established target fund size level and how to adjust the annual regular premium to the initially established time frame. In addition, it discusses whether and how to revise and adjust the initially established target fund size level if the actual DIF is lagging behind the desired target. It discusses funding liquidity gaps and restoring the solvency of the DIF.

5.2 Implementing Optimized Funding in the DIS

Although some papers (Ellis 2013, 3) refer to an optimal reserve fund, they elaborate target funding without a deeper analysis on how target funding could be used further to facilitate optimal funding (IADI 2009, 17).

Optimal DIS should be the one with a sufficient level of the DIF which balances the benefits with the costs of funding. Establishing and implementing target funding is one step toward optimal funding. An optimally funded DIS is able to fulfill its main task and enable fast and efficient access to deposits when they become unavailable, based on the DIS's risk awareness, a proactive financial management policy and adjustments of established benchmarks and funding in accordance with the DIS's needs. Optimized (adjusted) funding leads to an optimal DIF size.

As evidence from many jurisdictions shows, regardless of the established target funding and implemented financial planning, the DISs often face liquidity and solvency challenges. *How does that happen? Could more advanced financial planning techniques prevent such situations? Is it possible to create and maintain an optimal level of the DIF?*

Optimal funding would enable the DIS to fulfill its mandate in a credible and efficient manner. It is based on active financial management and a regular adjustment of funding in accordance with the DIS's liabilities.

The target fund size that is established arbitrarily cannot prevent the insufficiency of funds even if the target has been accomplished. Clearly, if the target fund size is determined arbitrarily, without an applied methodology and by ignoring the risk exposure of individual banks, it is irrelevant whether the banks' paid premiums contribute to the total DIS's funds adequately and whether the total funds correspond to the needs of the DIS. The result is that there are either more than necessary or insufficient amounts of funds compared to the actual requirements; that is, the DIF is either underfunded or overfunded. The link between the size of the DIF and the actual requirements of a credible DIS is missing.

Ideally, the target fund size should be established based on the risk assessment of bank failures and used for the optimization of the DIS funding.

The DIS should use information gained from cash flow projections for further fine-tuning of its funding by adjusting the annual premium to the target fund size and by adjusting the target fund size level to the risks of bank failures.

5.2.1 Example: Financial Planning for the Purpose of Optimized Funding

The DIS conducts regular financial planning and has an established target fund size. Over the course of its operation, it faces challenges and consequences of the deposit payout due to the failures of smaller banks.

Assumptions used in this example are as follows:

- Covered deposit level is €10,000 per depositor per bank
- Annual regular premium is 0.2 per cent calculated on covered deposits
- Covered deposits grow by 3 per cent annually
- Target fund size is set at 0.8 per cent over a five-year time frame
- Liquidity reserve is €2 mil minimum
- Remaining funds above the liquidity reserve are invested in short-term government securities with the projected yield of 8 per cent annually
- Bank number 8 fails in Year 3.

The question remains how bank failure will affect funding of the DIS and its target fund size and what the DIS authority should do if the actual DIF diverged from the targeted one.

Table 5.1 Comparison of targeted and actual DIF, in €

Banks	Year 1	Year 2	Year 3	Year 4	Year 5
Coverage €10,000			Covered deposits		
10	2,536,500	2,612,595	2,690,973	2,771,702	2,854,853
9	65,800,000	67,774,000	69,807,220	71,901,437	74,058,480
8	70,000,000	72,100,000	**74,263,000**		0
6	273,000,000	281,190,000	289,625,700	298,314,471	307,263,905
7	535,500,000	551,565,000	568,111,950	585,155,309	602,709,968
5	955,500,000	984,165,000	1,013,689,950	1,044,100,649	1,075,423,668
4	2,195,000,000	2,260,850,000	2,328,675,500	2,398,535,765	2,470,491,838
3	4,255,000,000	4,382,650,000	4,514,129,500	4,649,553,385	4,789,039,987
2	7,550,000,000	7,776,500,000	8,009,795,000	8,250,088,850	8,497,591,516
1	8,630,000,000	8,888,900,000	9,155,567,000	9,430,234,010	9,713,141,030
Total	**24,532,336,500**	**25,268,306,595**	**26,026,355,793**	**26,807,146,467**	**27,611,360,861**
Annual premium 0.2 per cent	49,064,673	50,536,613	52,052,712	53,614,293	55,222,722
Projected DIF	**49,064,673**	**99,601,286**	**151,653,998**	**205,268,291**	**260,491,012**
Target level of DIF 0.8 per cent in Year 5					**220,890,887**
Actual DIF	**50,529,283**	**107,128,185**	**88,744,571**		
Difference between actual and projected	**1,464,610**	**7,526,899**	**−62,909,427**		

Table 5.1 presents the DIS's five-year projection of covered deposits, targeted DIF, annual premium, total projected DIF and actual DIF. At the time of the establishment of the target fund size at 0.8 per cent the projection value of the target fund size amounted to €220 million. The DIS judged that its desired level of the DIF over five years should be €220 million.

The projected cash flows indicated that the DIF would amount to €260 million, due to the growth of deposits over five years.

At the time of Bank number 8's failure, in Year 3, the DIS had €99 million, but faced a liquidity challenge and cashed a portion of invested securities. At the end of Year 3, as a result of a payout, the total DIF decreased to €88 mil.

Initial projections estimated that the DIF should be in the amount of €151 mil at the end of Year 3. Due to the risk analysis and awareness of the probability of bank failure, the deposit insurance authority ensured sufficient liquidity on time and prevented insufficiency of available financial resources. Nevertheless, the DIF is smaller than projected and targeted.

At the end of Year 3, the deposit insurance authority is facing a new challenge related to the future funding and authorities must ask themselves some important questions, such as: *Is there a need to modify the funding policy and how?! Is there a need to adjust the target fund size and how?*

Obviously, the target fund size will not be accomplished over a five-year time frame anymore.

First of all, the deposit insurance authority must examine the financial effect of the failure of Bank number 8 on its total funds and the overall funding policy.

There are two consequences of this event:

- the first consequence was the immediate liquidity impact in the amount of €75 mil for the covered deposits payout which decreases the total DIF for the same amount.
- the second consequence is the impact on the lower regular premium in the future due to a lower covered deposits base as Bank number 8 is no

longer on the market and will no longer pay the premium and contribute to the DIF.

However, the deposit insurance authority must assess whether and how much it may recover in the insolvency proceedings from its claim on the paid covered deposits. Will there be any recovery on €75 mil, when and in which year will this money be collected? In addition, due to the lower amount of the total funds, a smaller portion of funds will be available for investments, resulting in a lower yield on investments than initially planned. All this information should be taken into account in the following financial planning iteration.

We assume that the deposit insurance authority will not recover any money from the insolvency proceedings in the next three years due to long and cumbersome bankruptcy procedures. Most likely, not more than 10 per cent can be collected within five years.

Authorities have several options at hand at the end of Year 3 in order to optimize the overall funding with:

- adjustment (moving) of the time frame to comply with the target fund size
- adjustment (changing) of the annual regular premium to comply with the set target fund size
- adjustment (changing) of the target fund size to comply with the DIS exposure.

5.3 Adjustment of the Time Frame to the Target Fund Size Level

One way how to respond to the fact of a lower than planned DIF over a projected time frame is to retain an identical initial target fund size, but to adjust the time frame and extend (prolong) the planned targeted cycle as much as necessary.

Table 5.2 Adjusting target fund size by prolonging its time frame, in €

Banks	Year 1	Year 2	Year 3	Year 4	Year 5	Year 6
Coverage €10,000			Covered deposits			
10	2,536,500	2,612,595	2,690,973	2,771,702	2,854,853	2,940,499
9	65,800,000	67,774,000	69,807,220	71,901,437	74,058,480	76,280,234
8	70,000,000	72,100,000	74,263,000	0	0	0
6	273,000,000	281,190,000	289,625,700	298,314,471	307,263,905	316,481,822
7	535,500,000	551,565,000	568,111,950	585,155,309	602,709,968	620,791,267
5	955,500,000	984,165,000	1,013,689,950	1,044,100,649	1,075,423,668	1,107,686,378
4	2,195,000,000	2,260,850,000	2,328,675,500	2,398,535,765	2,470,491,838	2,544,606,593
3	4,255,000,000	4,382,650,000	4,514,129,500	4,649,553,385	4,789,039,987	4,932,711,186
2	7,550,000,000	7,776,500,000	8,009,795,000	8,250,088,850	8,497,591,516	8,752,519,261
1	8,630,000,000	8,888,900,000	9,155,567,000	9,430,234,010	9,713,141,030	10,004,535,261
Total	**24,532,336,500**	**25,268,306,595**	**26,026,355,793**	**26,730,655,577**	**27,532,575,244**	**28,358,552,501**
Annual premium 0.2 per cent	49,064,673	50,536,613	52,052,712	53,461,311	55,065,150	56,717,105
Projected DIF	**49,064,673**	**99,601,286**	**151,653,998**			
Target level of DIF 0.8 per cent (net of investment)				**213,845,245**	**220,260,602**	**226,868,420**
Actual DIF	**50,529,283**	**107,128,185**	**88,744,571**	**142,205,882**	**197,271,032**	**253,988,137**
Difference between actual and projected	**1,464,610**	**7,526,899**	**−62,909,427**			
Difference between actual and target				−71,639,363	−22,989,569	**27,119,717**

5.3.1 Example: Adjustment of the Time Frame to the Target Fund Size Level

Using the same assumptions, at the end of Year 3, the deposit insurance authority projected cash flow again, as presented in Table 5.2, taking into account the developments during Year 3 and consequences of bank failure on inputs that are used in the new projection of cash flow.

New calculations show that the target fund size, if it remained unchanged at 0.8 per cent of the covered deposits, may be reached within six years, that is, within the remaining three years, instead of 2 as it was initially projected.

The annual premium in Years 4, 5 and 6 are contributions from the remaining 9 banks, at an unchanged premium level of 0.2 per cent annually.

Assuming there would be no other bank failures in the following three years, the DIF would amount to €254 mil by the end of Year 6 which is above the target fund size at 0.8 per cent.

As a result of the adjustment of the targeted time frame, the DIF reaches the target in Year 6.

5.4 Adjustment of Annual Funding to the Target Fund Size Level

However, when it is clear that the initial targeted fund size cannot be reached within the initially established time frame, authorities may consider an option to retain the target fund size within the initial time frame and to adjust the level of the annual premium in order to collect the targeted funds as initially envisaged.

5.4.1 Example: Adjustment of Annual Funding to the Target Fund Size Level

An example uses the same initial assumptions.

After the failure of one bank, there are nine banks remaining on the market. *What is their financial condition? Was the failure of bank number 8 an isolated incident? What caused the failure of the bank? How does bank failure reflect on other banks? Does the DIS need a more robust DIF or is the banking sector stronger than ever?* These questions should be raised in order to assess whether the target fund size needs to be adjusted.

Even if the deposit insurance authority decides that the target fund size remains at 0.8 per cent as it was projected three years ago, the depletion of the total DIF, due to the compensation of eligible depositors of the failed bank, should be reflected on the future premium policy and funding decisions.

In this step, authorities analyze the options if they wish to retain the target of 0.8 per cent over the initial five years, regardless of the bank failure in the middle of that time frame, which depleted the financial resources of the DIF.

In order to do so, additional calculations are necessary to compare the targeted funds at the end of each year, under the same circumstances as earlier. A comprehensive calculation of the projected covered deposits, targeted and actual funds and premium adjustments necessary in order to achieve the established targets within the established time frame is provided in Table 5.3.

If the deposit insurance authority does not modify the annual premium level (but continues applying 0.2 per cent in Years 4 and 5), the DIF would amount to €130 mil and €185 mil at the end of Year 4 and Year 5 respectively. Clearly, in order to achieve the target fund size of 0.8 per cent within the initially set time frame of five years, the DIS must increase the annual regular premium.

In order to assess how much the annual regular premium should increase, we will calculate the gap between the actual DIF size and the targeted DIF size in Years 4 and 5.

At the end of Year 4 the DIF still lacks €29 mil, while at the end of Year 5 the gap is €23 mil.

In order to calculate the increased level of the annual regular premium, the amount that represents the gap between an actual and targeted DIF is divided by covered deposits at the end of each year.

Table 5.3 Adjusting annual regular premium within the initial target size fund time frame, in €

Banks	Year 1	Year 2	Year 3	Year 4	Year 5
Coverage €10,000			Covered deposits		
10	2,536,500	2,612,595	2,690,973	2,771,702	2,854,853
9	65,800,000	67,774,000	69,807,220	71,901,437	74,058,480
8	70,000,000	72,100,000	74,263,000	0	0
6	273,000,000	281,190,000	289,625,700	298,314,471	307,263,905
7	535,500,000	551,565,000	568,111,950	585,155,309	602,709,968
5	955,500,000	984,165,000	1,013,689,950	1,044,100,649	1,075,423,668
4	2,195,000,000	2,260,850,000	2,328,675,500	2,398,535,765	2,470,491,838
3	4,255,000,000	4,382,650,000	4,514,129,500	4,649,553,385	4,789,039,987
2	7,550,000,000	7,776,500,000	8,009,795,000	8,250,088,850	8,497,591,516
1	8,630,000,000	8,888,900,000	9,155,567,000	9,430,234,010	9,713,141,030
Total	**24,532,336,500**	**25,268,306,595**	**26,026,355,793**	**26,730,655,577**	**27,532,575,244**
Annual premium 0.2 per cent	49,064,673	50,536,613	52,052,712	53,461,311	55,065,150
Projected DIF	**49,064,673**	**99,601,286**	**151,653,998**		
Target level of DIF 0.8 per cent in Year 5	**39,251,738**	**80,858,581**	**124,926,508**	**171,076,196**	**220,260,602**
Actual DIF, if 0.2 per cent applied	**50,529,283**	**107,128,185**	**88,744,571**	142,205,882	197,271,032

Banks	Year 1	Year 2	Year 3	Year 4	Year 5
Coverage €10,000			Covered deposits		
Difference between actual and projected DIF in Years 1–3	**1,464,610**	**7,526,899**	**−62,909,427**		
Difference between actual and target in Years 3–5	11,277,545	26,269,604	−28,870,314	−28,870,314	−22,989,569
Necessary increase in annual premium in either Year 4 or 5, in percentage				**0.11**	**0.08**
New adjusted premium, in percentage				**0.31**	**0.28**

Based on the given calculations, the DIS has three options to accomplish the initially set target fund size level of 0.8 per cent within the initially set time frame of five years, as follows:

- to adjust (increase) the annual premium in Year 4 by 0.11 per cent and apply 0.31 per cent annual premium in Year 4, while keeping 0.2 per cent in Year 5;
- to adjust (increase) the annual premium in Year 5 by 0.08 per cent to 0.28 per cent while continuing to apply 0.20 per cent premium level on covered deposits in Year 4;
- to even out and spread the adjusted premium over the remaining two years in equal amounts and to apply 0.24 per cent premium in Years 4 and 5.

If deciding on the third option, the DIS must calculate the absolute amount of the financial gap. The deposit insurance authority has available €88.7 million at the end of Year 3 and it targeted €220 mil at the end of Year 5. Therefore, the financial gap is €131 mil (€220 mil – €88 mil = €131 mil). Dividing €131 mil by the average amount of the projected covered deposits in Years 4 and 5, the result is that the if the premium level is set at 0.24 per cent in the remaining two targeted years, the DIS would collect €220 mil at the end of Year 5.

Thus the deposit insurance authority must decide and choose one out of three possible options.

Table 5.4 Comparison of three options on adjusting annual premium level

Options	Year 4	Year 5
(i) Adjusted premium in Year 4, in percentage	0.31	0.20
New adjusted premium collected, in €	**82,865,032**	**55,065,150**
Adjusted DIF, in €	**171.819.293**	**226.884.444**
(ii) Adjusted premium in Year 5, in percentage	0.20	**0.28**
New adjusted premium collected, in €	**53.461.311**	**77.091.211**
Adjusted DIF, in €	**142.415.572**	**219.506.783**
(iii) Equally adjusted premium in Years 4 and 5, in percentage	**0.24**	**0.24**
New adjusted premium collected, in €	64.153.573	66.078.181
Adjusted DIF, in €	**153.107.834**	**219.186.015**

In order to make a decision, the financial effects of each option should be analyzed. Table 5.4 presents the financial effects for each option.

The first option increases the annual regular premium immediately in the year following the year in which the deposit payout occurred. If the deposit insurance authority decides to apply a 0.31 per cent premium in Year 4, the DIS would collect €83 million in Year 4 and €55 million in Year 5. The total DIF would amount to €226 million at the end of Year 5, which is slightly above the targeted fund size at the end of Year 5. However, the premium increase immediately after the bank failure may be a liquidity burden for the remaining banks.

The second option collects 0.2 per cent in Year 4 in the amount of €53 million, and 0.28 per cent in Year 5 that is €77 million. The total DIF would amount to €220 million which is the amount of the targeted fund.

Clearly, for the DIS, the first option is better as more funds are collected earlier. For banks, the second option is preferable since they pay the increased premium later and in a slightly lower amount compared to the first option.

The third option aims to 'even out' the effect of the increase of the annual premium and to spread it over Years 4 and 5 equally, by 0.04 per cent in both years, which would result in the total DIF in the amount of €220 million at the end of Year 5. This option is favorable both for the DIS and for the banks as it removes the cyclicality effect and smooths the impact on banks' liquidity.

The deposit insurance authority may simultaneously decide to combine the prolongation of the initial target time frame with adjustments on the premium level. That decision makes sense in the case when the financial gap between the actual fund size and the target fund size is large and it can't be adjusted in a short term and with a minimum increase of the premium level.

The deposit insurance authority should monitor and manage its target fund size on an annual basis and choose the most appropriate option. In order to be able to introduce such adjustments, legislation should be flexible enough and allow the board to make such decisions. If the legislation is strict and prescribes a fixed percentage of the annual premium level, the deposit insurance authority will not be allowed to make annual adjustments based on the real circumstances and requirements.

The deposit insurance authority chooses among the available options, taking into account the results of the analysis of the banking sector, particularly its liquidity, solvency, and profitability. The impact of the decision to increase the premium level will be analyzed from an individual bank's point of view and communicated with the banks so that they understand why the decision has been made and what the arguments in favor of the chosen option are.

5.5 Revision of the Initially Established Target Fund Size Level

In cases when the deposit insurance authority experiences a deposit payout and reconsiders options related to the accomplishment of its desired target fund size level, either by adjusting its funding (annual premium level) or by adjusting (prolonging) the initial time frame, there is one important question to be answered. Should the established target fund size level be revised (changed) prior to the expiration of its envisaged time frame?!

Referring to our example in this chapter, it is the question for the deposit insurance authority at the end of Year 3 *whether the initially set target fund size level of 0.8 per cent of covered deposits is still relevant or it should be adjusted to the fact that one out of ten banks failed. Is the target fund size in the amount of 0.8 per cent of covered deposits still sufficient to provide deposit insurance to the depositors of nine banks and what is the financial condition of these banks?!*

Bank failure and deposit payout are significant events in any banking sector. Authorities should analyze the consequences of each and every bank failure as well as the financial condition of the remaining banks. *Is there any other bank in the system vulnerable enough that it might fail in the near future?!* Authorities should ask these questions openly and analyze the possible answers.

Ideally, the deposit insurance authority should update its risk analysis of member banks and adjust the target fund size level to the results. After setting a new target fund size, the time frame for its achievement should be determined and an appropriate level of a new adjusted premium level should be set.

In general, although the target fund size is set for an envisaged time frame, it is changeable and variable as bank risk profiles change over time and consequently the DIS's potential exposure to the payout changes as well.

5.5.1 Example: Revision of the Initially Established Target Fund Size Level

Initial assumptions are the same as in the previous example.

There are only nine banks operating at the end of Year 3 since Bank number 8 failed in the first half of the year. Consequently, the DIS's funds were depleted by €75 million and are only at €89 million, resulting in the actual target fund size at 0.34 per cent of total covered deposits at the end of Year 3.

Table 5.5 Revised target fund size level

Banks	Covered deposits at the end of Year 3, in €	Risk category at the end of Year 3	Exposure at default, in €
10	2,700,000	Risky	2,700,000
9	68,000,000	Risky	68,000,000
8	0	–	–
6	290,000,000	Risky	290,000,000
7	550,000,000	Watch	0
5	1,000,000,000	Watch	0
4	2,330,000,000	Watch	0
3	4,520,000,000	Watch	0
2	8,001,000,000	Watch	0
1	9,200,000,000	Watch	0
Total	**25,961,700,000**		**360,700,000**
Adjusted target fund size level, in percentage			**1.39**
Proposed new premium level, in percentage			**0.46**

The remaining nine banks are not equally risky; some are more safe and sound and some are problem banks. The deposit insurance authority should understand the soundness of the banking sector on a regular basis, and especially at the moment when the appropriate level of the target fund size has to be re-assessed.

Therefore, the deposit insurance authority conducts a new risk assessment and learns that there are three risky banks operating at that time. Bank number 7, who had a risky profile three years ago, improved its soundness and its profile is now described as 'watch'.

Table 5.5 provides details on risk categories and total covered deposits in risky banks for the purpose of revision of the target fund size and premium adjustments.

Total covered deposits in three risky banks amounted to €360 million, which is the amount toward which the DIS should aspire to in order to be financially prepared if any of these three banks fail in the near future.

As a result, a new adjusted target fund size level is established at 1.4 per cent. If the deposit insurance authority decides that it is reasonable to collect at least a minimum of €360 million, it must also decide over which time horizon it should collect these funds. In our example, the deposit insurance authority decided that it would be reasonable to reach a newly set target fund size over the next three years.

In order to achieve the newly set target, banks must pay a minimum of 0.46 per cent over the next three years. More likely, the premium level will again be adjusted on an annual basis due to the growth of covered deposits.

Clearly, the target fund size level moves along the level of riskiness of member banks.

Risk profiles of banks change constantly; therefore, it is important not only to adjust the annual regular premium to the target fund size, but also to adjust the level of the target fund to foresee risks over time.

Banking risks are changing over time, for better or for worse, and the financial condition of each bank can improve or worsen. Consequently, the assessment of risks of member banks is not static. The DIS should develop a methodology for the constant monitoring of risks in its banking sector. As a result, the target ratio should adjust over time, due to the dynamics of the financial conditions of each bank and due to the economic conditions. The target fund size level should be updated and adjusted to reflect any significant increase of foreseen losses. It may be concluded that the target fund size is not a static figure; instead, it is a 'moving target'.

5.6 Assessing the DIF's Liquidity Gaps and Extraordinary Funding

As evidence from many DISs suggests, it is highly likely that the DIS will face a situation of a bank failure during its operation, where the available DIF is insufficient to promptly pay all covered deposits.

What options do the DISs have and what is the most feasible extraordinary funding source in case of a liquidity gap? Should the DIS borrow money and under what terms or should it focus on rebuilding its capital base (with non-refundable instruments)?

When the funds are insufficient, extraordinary funding becomes more relevant. Extraordinary funding often relies on budgetary transfers (either as a form of rebuilding the total funds or financing liquidity needs via borrowing or transfer of funds without a return) and on borrowing from the market. When applying risk assessment of member banks on an ongoing basis and for the purpose of planning of funding, the DIS is able to enhance its overall funding position and possibly avoid the use of extraordinary funding, unless it becomes extremely necessary. Contrary to that, poor financial management can lead to the use of borrowed funds even in cases when it could be avoided if proper financial planning was implemented, if the exchange of information with a supervisor was functional and if the DIS was properly prepared for the mandate.

5.6.1 Example: Assessing the DIF's Liquidity Gaps

In order to understand how to assess the situation and make a decision, we will modify and expand our initial example and assume that Bank number 6 failed in May of Year 3 (instead of Bank number 8). The total covered deposits of eligible depositors of Bank number 6 were over €289 million at the time of its failure.

Table 5.6 DIF size at end of April, Year 3, in €000

DIF at the beginning of Year 3	107,128
Increase (expected premium collection) January–May	26,500
Decrease (expected operating expenses) January–May	70
DIF at the end of April, Year 3	**133,558**
Out of which:	
Invested in government securities	118,360
Cash reserves	15,198
Total covered deposits in Bank number 6, end of March	**289,625**
Total liquidity gap for deposit payout	**–156,067**

Having learned of the possibility of bank failure, the deposit insurance authority should assess its financial situation as soon as possible and explore its funding options. The first step in assessing the financial options is to calculate the exact amount of the available DIF. The data on the DIF's size are available from the accounting department. Table 5.6 presents a summary of the cash flow for the first four months and the amount of the DIF at the end of April in Year 3.

As it is evident from Table 5.6, the deposit insurance authority collected financial resources in the amount of €133 mil by the end of April, Year 3. At the same time, €15 mil is readily available as cash at hand and €118 mil is invested in short-term government securities.

If the DIS uses all of its available funds, assuming that it can liquidate the government securities fast and without significant losses, there would still be a financial gap in the amount of €156 mil in order to compensate the depositors of the failed Bank number 6.

At first, the deposit insurance authority should explore the consequences of its decision to liquidate all its investments at minimum losses. Hopefully, the secondary market is liquid and the DIS would not have additional problems in selling securities.

If securities are sold prior to their maturity, the deposit insurance authority would not be able to achieve the full price and would have to sell them at a discounted price, based on the market price at the time of selling and based on the buyers' demand. Some DISs experienced situations where the secondary market did not exist, the market was not liquid enough or the state Treasury had liquidity problems as well, so it was not possible to liquidate the government securities in a short term and without losses. Therefore, when drafting legislation, laws and subordinate laws, national authorities should thoroughly analyze its financial market situation and the DIS should rely on realistic extraordinary funding options.

The deposit insurance authority should explore all options for extraordinary funding prescribed by the law and procedures for each of those options in order to determine the best option to fund the financial gap in the amount of €157 mil?

Should the deposit insurance authority collect the extraordinary premium? An extraordinary premium is a good option if the amount of the liquidity gap is sufficient to ensure a complete payout. This is the case if the financial gap is in the amount up to the level of the annual regular premium. If the collection of the extraordinary premium would not be sufficient to bridge the financial gap, it is better not to use this option as it may have negative effects on banks (drain their liquidity even further) and it would not resolve the problem at all.

In our example, the necessary amount is three times higher than the amount of the annual regular premium and can't be collected from the banks as the additional premium at once. By collecting the only portion of the total amount, the deposit insurance authority would not resolve the main problem. Therefore, the deposit insurance authority should focus on other funding options.

Can it borrow and where from? If the DIS takes a loan, what would be the price and what would be pledged? What would be the time frame of the loan? Is there sufficient time to obtain the loan in time for the deposit payout? All these questions should be analyzed before making the final decision.

It is very important that the DIS develop and adopt subordinate laws with prescribed details on procedures related to extraordinary funding in order to save time on exploring the procedural questions when time is precious. The experience of some DISs shows that when the DISs were not prepared sufficiently in advance in terms of the borrowing procedures, this option was not available at the time of financial need either because it was not possible at all or it needed much more time than envisaged or the lender requested a collateral which was not available.

The DIS may look for borrowing on the market or from the state budget if the legislation provides for such borrowing options. In our example, the financial gap is larger than three annual regular premium contributions. Actually, the liquidity gap in this case may be treated as a solvency gap.

Even if the deposit insurance authority ensured borrowing in the amount of €157 mil, it would not be able to repay the borrowed amount in less than three years (financing the repayment solely from the future annual premium's contributions). The deposit insurance authority should take into account its operating expenses and the need for building the DIF from scratch again. Therefore, the deposit insurance authority must conduct a comprehensive analysis of all its funding options:

(a) Funding of immediate liquidity/solvency gap in the amount of the necessary €157 mil
(b) Ensuring future funding by setting a new target fund size, appropriate annual regular premium in order to be able to:

   a. Repay the borrowed funds
   b. Build a desirable DIF within a desirable time frame.

If the deposit insurance authority overestimates or underestimates its funding position, it will be in a position to seek extraordinary funding in the near future again or it will not be able to repay its borrowing as agreed. There is more than one way how to structure its overall funding at this moment.

Assuming that it is not an issue that the deposit insurance authority would be able to collect the necessary €157 million, we can explore the consequences of the funding options.

Ideally and theoretically, the best option for the DIS would be to collect €157 million in the form of new capital, that is, funds that are legally non-refundable. Simply put, the best option is to recapitalize the DIS. Another important question is whether this is a realistic option and who could provide additional capital to the DIS?

The DIS is not a private entity where existing shareholders can ensure additional capital nor can the DIS look for new shareholders on the capital market. Historical evidence suggests that governments of some countries provided recapitalization of the DIS when necessary or funds were collected jointly from the remaining banks and the government. Each jurisdiction has to explore if there is such an option available.

On the other hand, the DIS should be financed by banks, not by the governments, unless there is a threat to the stability of the financial system. Governmental interventions should be present in extraordinary circumstances, not on a regular basis.

Therefore, the borrowing of €157 million on the market, under the market conditions, is a more realistic option.

The DIS must analyze its cash flow at the time of bank failure and conduct further analysis prior to finalizing a loan contract to ensure that it can meet the proposed loan conditions (repayment of the loan within the predicted period, repayment of the interest rate) and to ensure the normal functioning of the DIS.

Consequently, the deposit insurance authority decided to cash all its available securities and borrow additional funds in order to commence the payout of covered deposits in the total amount of €289 million in May and decided to borrow €157 million.

The borrowed funds must be repaid by the deposit insurance authority and therefore these funds only improve its liquidity and ensure the payout of covered depositors of a failing bank without disruption. Borrowed funds are not a part of the DIF's own funds, and therefore, the DIF has a negative value throughout Year 3.

If the financial gap in the amount of €157 million was financed by non-refundable funds, the total DIF would increase by the same amount.

Assuming that the DIS borrowed €157 million at a 5 per cent annual interest rate, on five years, its annual payment would be €36 million (the exact amount would vary depending on the repayment period—annual, semiannual, quarterly, monthly). Over a five-year period, the DIS would repay more than €24 million in interest.

As evident from Table 5.7, the DIS has a positive net cash at the end of Year 3, but a negative DIF in the amount of €127 million. Only a newly collected premium paid by banks would decrease the negative value of the DIF over time and slowly recapitalize the DIS. Therefore, the DIF has a positive value in Year 6. Interest repayment is a financial expense which decreases the DIF. However, principal repayment is not an expense and it influences only liquidity that is cash flow.

At the end of Year 8 when the DIS had fully repaid its €157 million loan increased by €24 million interest, the DIF already amounted to €145 million.

When analyzing the position of the DIF in relation to financing the liquidity gap and repayment of the borrowed amount, the DIS authority makes several assumptions, such as retaining the initial level of annual regular premium unchanged.

At the end of Year 8, with the DIF in the amount of €145 million, the coverage ratio is 0.48 per cent, therefore sufficient to repay the covered deposits in any of the three smallest banks.

At this point, the deposit insurance authority should consider whether to adjust (revise) its target fund size and the time frame, and accordingly the annual regular premium.

Hypothetically, the DIS has many options; however, decisions should be based on the analysis of the data and information and in compliance with the overall role and the DIS's mandate within the safety net regime.

5.7 Restoring the DIF' Solvency

A major event of a failure of a larger bank where the deposit insurance authority faces not only liquidity issues, but also solvency issues, is a good opportunity for the re-assessment of the target fund level which had been set earlier.

If the deposit insurance authority has to borrow money to finance insufficient financial resources, then it needs to restore the shaken credibility of the DIS. The only way of doing it is to recapitalize its DIF. In cases when the government does not want or cannot provide new capital to the DIS, and in order not to subsidize the banks, it may be justified to increase the annual level of the regular premium.

The deposit insurance authority should conduct a detailed analysis of deposits, in order to be able to project its growth over the following period of three to five years. In cooperation with the bank supervisor,

Table 5.7 Projection of the DIF after borrowing

Deposit Insurance Fund, in €000	Year 3	Year 4	Year 5	Year 6	Year 7	Year 8
DIF at the end of previous year	107,128	−126,908	−80,568	−30,858	23,322	82,172
Initial premium	0	0	0	0	0	0
Regular premium	52,400	53,000	54,000	56,000	58,000	60,000
Yield on investments	3,400	1,400	2,200	3,100	4,200	5,600
Borrowed funds	157,000					
Operating expenses	210	210	210	210	210	210
Non-current assets	0					
Deposit payout	289,626					
Principal repayment		31,400	31,400	31,400	31,400	31,400
Interest repayment		7,850	6,280	4,710	3,140	1,570
DIF at the end of the year	**−126,908**	**−80,568**	**−30,858**	**23,322**	**82,172**	**145,992**
Net cash flow, at the end of the year	30,092	14,940	18,310	22,780	27,450	32,420

each remaining bank's risk profile should be analyzed in order to understand the DIS's risk exposure toward any other bank's failure.

5.7.1 Example: Restoring the DIF's Solvency

As a result of a failure of Bank number 6 during Year 3, all DIS's funds were depleted and in, addition, the deposit insurance authority borrowed

Table 5.8 Restoring a DIS' solvency

Deposit Insurance Fund, in €000	Year 3	Year 4	Year 5	Year 6	Year 7	Year 8
DIF at end of previous year	107,128	−126,908	31,332	202,542	386,922	584,872
Initial premium	0	0	0	0	0	0
Regular premium, adjusted, 0.6 per cent	52,400	159,000	164,000	169,000	174,000	179,000
Yield on investments, 5 per cent	3,400	7,300	13,700	20,300	27,300	34,500
Borrowed funds	157,000					
Operating expenses	210	210	210	210	210	210
Non-current assets	0					
Deposit payout	289,626					
Principal repayment		31,400	31,400	31,400	31,400	31,400
Interest repayment, 5 per cent		7,850	6,280	4,710	3,140	1,570
DIF at end of the year	**−126,908**	**31,332**	**202,542**	**386,922**	**584,872**	**796,592**
Net cash flow, at the end of the year	**30,092**	**126,840**	**139,810**	**152,980**	**166,550**	**180,320**
Actual coverage ratio, in percentage	**−0.49**					
Adjusted target fund size over 5 years, in percentage	**2.80**					
Projected adjusted coverage ratio, in percentage		**0.12**	**0.74**	**1.38**	**2.02**	**2.67**

€157 million on the market, at a 5 per cent interest rate, for a five-year loan.

At the end of Year 3, the DIS had a negative coverage ratio at −0.49 per cent (−€127 million). The positive cash flow at the end of the year was the result of the borrowing and collection of the regular premium.

Detailed risk analysis showed that the remaining smaller banks are the risky banks with their ratio toward total covered deposits at 2.8 per cent. Therefore, the deposit insurance authority could consider adjusting the target fund size level to a minimum 2.8 per cent over the next five years, as presented in Table 5.8. In order to reach the revised target, the annual premium level should be set at 0.6 per cent.

Before deciding, the deposit insurance authority should explore the effects of the increase of the level of the annual regular premium up to 0.6 per cent onto banks' liquidity and solvency, in order to:

(i) repay the borrowed funds, as envisaged, within a five-year time frame, at a 5 per cent annual interest rate and to
(ii) restore the DIF within the following five-year time frame at a minimum of 2.8 per cent.

A triple increase of the annual regular premium would also increase the yield on investment over the years, as it is evident from Table 5.8. However, a higher annual premium would increase banks' expenses and decrease banks' profits. In addition, a higher annual premium could be a liquidity challenge for the remaining banks.

If the analysis shows that neither banks' liquidity nor solvency would be jeopardized, authorities should adjust its target fund size, impose a higher annual premium, repay the borrowed funds, and restore the solvency of the DIF.

Indeed, the deposit insurance authority could, through collecting an increased annual regular premium, repay the loan earlier. The decision is strategic and it depends on the fact whether the authorities want to restore the total DIF earlier or to repay the borrowed funds earlier. The amount of borrowing is not very high and the interest expense can be offset with the yield on investments. There is no right or wrong answer, as both options would have pros and cons. If borrowing is not very costly, the deposit insurance authority may decide to continue its repayment as originally envisaged, regardless of the higher collection of the annual regular premium, rather than benefit from the restored DIF which can be a reassuring element of the much-needed public confidence.

5.8 Conclusion

Optimal DIF is one which is adequately funded and adjusted to the DIS' needs over a medium- and long-term period of time. In order to ensure an optimal DIF, deposit insurers should apply optimized funding which is based on adjustments to the established target fund size level and time frame on a regular basis, using comprehensive financial planning, assessment of banks' risks and adjustments of funding to DIS's needs. If the DIS does not adjust its desired DIF's size to its potential liability, there is a chance of facing liquidity or solvency issues in case of bank failure over the established target time frame. Extraordinary funding ensures funding options in case when additional resources are necessary. The DISs should establish a comprehensive financial planning function to be able to determine feasible and adequate funding options for restoring liquidity and the DIS's solvency without jeopardizing its credibility.

Bibliography

Ellis, Diane. 2013. *Deposit Insurance Funding: Assuring Confidence*. https://www.fdic.gov/deposit/insurance/assuringconfidence.pdf. Accessed 2016.

IADI. 2009. *Guidance Paper: Funding of Deposit Insurance Systems*. Basel. IADI.

6

Deposit Insurance in the European Union

6.1 Introduction

To minimize the negative effects of bank failures and to harmonize the standards of practice, the EU has redesigned its legislative framework modifying and introducing Directives on deposit insurance and bank recovery and resolution, respectively. The DIS plays an even more important role in the bank resolution process, although being primarily mandated with a payout function, financing bank resolution under certain conditions.

Member countries of the EU must comply with the EU laws (Directives) on national levels which is challenging. The process of the development of a new financial architecture within the EU has not been finalized although the skeleton of the future banking union is visible. Therefore, the impact of the implementation of a new regulatory framework can only be partially assessed at this point.

This chapter provides an overview on development of EU legislative framework on deposit insurance and investigates new deposit insurance and bank resolution rules for the EU member countries.

D. Ognjenovic, *Deposit Insurance Schemes*,
DOI 10.1007/978-3-319-51143-6_6

The EU rules on imposing a risk-based premium are discussed with the examples of calculation. A newly proposed regulation on the establishment of the European DIS (EDIS) is presented.

6.2 Deposit Insurance in the EU During 1980s

In the 1980s, deposit insurance, although the term 'deposit guarantee' is primarily used in the EU legislation and documents, was already a known concept in Europe and several European Union member countries that had introduced formal DISs.

By end of 1986, Belgium, the Federal Republic of Germany, Spain, France, the Netherlands and the UK had established their DISs. At the same time, Italy, Ireland and Portugal had drafted their first laws on deposit insurance awaiting their formal adoption and implementation.

The established DISs differed in many features among the member countries, and the European depositors of the same banking group, operating in different countries within the EU, enjoyed a very different level and scope of protection.

The European Commission (EC) instinctively felt that at least some features of the established schemes should be harmonized. Therefore, it published Recommendations concerning the introduction of the deposit guarantee schemes within the Community (EC 1986, 16–17). At the time of their issuance and adoption, Recommendations were not obligatory for member countries and were written in a simplified and general tone (the whole document is written on one page only).

The EC set out four recommendations, as follows:

(i) to guarantee compensation to be granted to less financially sophisticated depositors,
(ii) to cover depositors of all authorized credit institutions including depositors in branches established in other member countries,
(iii) to distinguish clearly the intervention prior to the winding-up process and compensation of depositors at winding-up credit institutions and
(iv) to clearly set up the criteria for compensation.

It is clear that the EC wanted to harmonize the minimum features of deposit insurance and the recommendations reflected the most important features at the time. Individuals have always been considered as less financially sophisticated depositors than legal entities and institutional investors. Therefore, the EC wanted to ensure that the less sophisticated depositors are covered and protected by the deposit insurance.

Another important common feature was a compulsory membership in the DIS. Whenever a credit institution is authorized for deposit collection it should participate in an established DIS. The EC recognized the need for the geographical harmonization of rules. Therefore, the 'home-host' rule was recommended and introduced. The 'home-host' rule indicates that depositors of a branch operating in another country are covered by the DIS established in the home country of a bank, not in a host country where the branch operates. This rule was followed by the EU member countries for many years after.

Furthermore, the EC emphasized that deposit insurance would differ from the financial interventions into problem banks. Although not stated explicitly, it is clear that the simple paybox deposit guarantee was promoted within the EU.

Historically, the EU countries have different legal systems and bankruptcy practices from the United States. Therefore, it was logical to structure a simple DIS with a simple mandate when banks legally fail. By that time, the FDIC had already had a lot of experience with bank resolution and had established itself as a DIS with the bank resolution mandate.

At that time, the European countries, with a few exceptions, did not have experience with failures of large problem banks. When large banks had liquidity and solvency issues, individual member countries dealt with them within their complex legal framework through national bank rehabilitation and restructuring processes, that is, through a form of the state bailout programs.

Clearly, the EC wanted to create a uniform and simple protection of unsophisticated depositors in case when banks were unable to repay their deposits. Therefore, it also recommended setting up clear rules for the compensation of depositors.

Although the EC published its Recommendations in the *Official Journal*, recommendations were too general and not compulsory, resulting in many different variations of the established deposit guarantee systems in the EU member states in the following years.

6.3 Directive on Deposit Guarantee Schemes 94/19/EC

In 1994, the EU adopted the first Directive on Deposit Guarantee Schemes. It was Directive 94/19/EC of the European Parliament and of the Council of 30 May 1994, on deposit guarantee schemes (Directive 94/19) which obliged the EU member countries to establish DISs within a prescribed timeline for compliance and national legislation adoption (Directive 1994, L 135/5–14).

Directive 94/19 set forth some specific features of the uniformed European deposit guarantee schemes, although at the same time national jurisdictions had many options related to the institutional setup and the DIS's arrangements. The EU used the minimum harmonization approach.

Directive 94/19 was structured with a Preamble, 16 Articles and 3 Annexes. The Preamble sets out the main principles of harmonization established in the main text. The language of Directive 94/19 was peculiar, and some member countries had problems in translating the document and understanding the terminology.

Although the EU member countries must follow the European legislation, at home, the national legislation seemed to be more important and the full transposition of the text of Directive 94/19 was questionable. The deposit insurance authorities were in compliance with the national legislation rather than with the European legislation, although, formally and in theory, they copy-pasted the exact wording from Directive 94/19.

Looking back at Directive 94/19, it may be described as 'simple and liberal' though a legally binding regulation which prescribed minimum specific rules to be complied with, almost like the principles within boundaries where each member country could create its own rules.

The document was based on a number of general statements allowing member countries full freedom in the design and implementation of the legislation. It resulted in numerous variations of DISs across the EU.

Directive 94/19 had never explicitly expressed that it was written for the DIS with the paybox mandate, but it had also never referred to any broadened mandate of the DIS. It may be implicitly concluded that it was written for the paybox DIS.

The Preamble sets forth the main general principles emphasizing, for example, the 'home-host' principle where the branches of banks licensed in one country belonged to the DIS of that home country, whereas, if offered and if the deposit coverage amount in the home country was lower, branches could become members of the DIS in the host country if the host country offered membership. In addition, if a branch of a non-EU country operated within an EU country, the host country could opt to offer to the branch of the bank licensed in the non-EU country to join the DIS of the host country, according to its prescribed rules in the national legislation.

The 'home-host' rule was well written and envisaged to improve harmonization within the EU territory but that was easier said than done. The case of the failure of an Icelandic bank and the ensuing diplomatic disputes showed all obstacles of implementation of the 'home-host' principle and the deficiency of Directive 94/19 in practice.

The Directive also stated that in principle, member banks must bear the cost of deposit insurance. It was clear that the DIS funding is based on regular funding ensured by member banks. However, Directive 94/19 did not prescribe other rules related to funding. As a result, some member countries established ex ante funds while others introduced ex post funded DIS. There were many differences among the countries in relation to the initial and extraordinary funding.

Directive 94/19 also promoted the set-off principle where the compensation amount would be decreased for any (due or total) liabilities of the depositor toward the bank. This rule created a number of practical problems. Bankruptcy laws in some countries did not permit the set-off or the set-off would be possible only if the depositor (debtor) explicitly accepted it (in a written form). Problems arose with long-term liabilities if they became due in the total amount at once, resulting in a negative compensation; that is, depositors had to repay the net amount to the bank instead of receiving a deposit payout, after the set-off calculation. In cases when only due liabilities were taken into calculation, the net deposit payout balance was only slightly decreased (the financial effect of the whole set-off exercise was minimum) but the deposit insurance authorities had a lot of work which delayed the payout time.

Directive 94/19 also promoted exclusion of certain categories of depositors or deposits and listed all recommended excluded deposits in Annex 1 of the Directive itself. Many countries prescribed in their national legislation those recommended exclusions of deposits as obligatory exclusions.

In addition, many countries covered only retail depositors. Directive 94/19 did not prescribe details on funding at all, nor did it promote ex ante or ex post funding, but it emphasized that the DIS should have sufficient funds in relation to its liabilities.

Directive 94/19 did not prescribe the governance of the DIS, nor whether the deposit insurance entity should be a separate legal entity or integrated within another legal entity. Every country should establish at minimum one DIS, allowing existence of more than one DIS if member countries wanted such an institutional solution.

The minimum coverage amount was set at €20,000 regardless of the number of deposits the depositor kept in the bank.

In its main text, Directive 94/19 provided a definition of the occurrence of the insurance event which was the trigger for the DIS's legal liability to commence a deposit payout. The idea was to ensure fast access to deposits. Therefore, the term 'unavailability of deposits' was introduced to define due and payable deposits which had not been paid to depositors. In other words, if depositors wanted to withdraw the money from their accounts and were not able to do it, for them these deposits were unavailable which would trigger the obligation of the deposit insurance entity to compensate for the deposits.

Therefore, Directive 94/19 established a maximum time frame of 21 days, starting from the deposits' unavailability during which either a judicial authority had to make a ruling (initiate bankruptcy or liquidation procedure) or relevant authorities had to declare officially unavailability of deposits.

Clearly, the EU wanted to foster the compensation of insured deposits. And, evidently, in order to activate the paybox deposit insurance, it was not necessary for the bank to officially fail; it was rather sufficient that the bank was illiquid for a period of three weeks. It was a simple assumption but it created problems in implementation and the EU member countries reluctantly followed this rule. A strict legislation on national insolvency proceedings prevented the payout of deposits by the deposit insurance authorities if the bank was still operational.

In simple words, if a bank had its license, regardless of its financial position and health (insolvency or illiquidity), its business was governed by the banking law and supervisory prudential measures as long as the banking license had not been withdrawn. Bankruptcy law and deposit insurance law are laws that are not applicable during the time when the bank is still operational, even if the bank stops paying out deposits to depositors.

Therefore, in compliance with their national legislations, member countries prescribed the deposit insurance event only in case when the banking license had been withdrawn, which triggered either liquidation or a bankruptcy (some form of winding up) procedure, formal appointment of a bankruptcy trustee and official closure of the bank.

In addition, in many European countries bankruptcy is under the jurisdiction of the Commercial court. Judicial systems are independent and have their own procedures (including petition time frames) and rules.

In reality, it was rarely possible to declare bankruptcy or liquidation procedure within 21 days. This status quo position of the Directive which could not be transposed into national jurisdictions or at least could not be easily transposed into national jurisdictions resulted in that very few deposit insurance entities were able to initiate compensation within 21 days, which prolonged the time for depositors to access their deposits.

While Directive 94/19 was applicable, only a few countries, if any, were able to fully comply with the 'unavailable deposits' time frame rule. However, not so many banks failed in the EU member countries in the 1990s and 2000s, and the deposit insurance authorities mostly compensated deposits of individual failures of smaller- and mid-sized banks. Deposit insurers were aware of non-compliance with 'unavailable deposits' rule but never raised this issue as a big problem.

However, circumstances changed over time and by the end of 2008 it was not only small individual banks that had failed. Nowadays, depositors are more financially educated and less patient.

Based on the definition of the unavailability of deposits, the deposit insurance authority should have paid duly verified claims of eligible depositors within three months from the deposits' unavailability. Exceptionally, the time frame could be prolonged for additional three months and no more than two more such prolongations were possible. At the end, it was possible to compensate depositors within 12 months, based on a discretionary judgment made by the national financial authorities, according to Directive 94/19.

The word 'within' raised many discussions and interpretations as many argued whether the deposit insurance authority must initiate the compensation process or compensate all depositors within the prescribed time frame of three months.

6.3.1 Failure of 'Home-Host' Principle in Case of the Icelandic Landsbanki Failure

Landsbanki was one of the 3 largest Icelandic banks whose online branch, Icesave, operated on the UK and the Netherlands' territory offering savings accounts to British and Dutch citizens. Iceland is not an EU member country but its membership in the European Economic Area (EEA) came into force in 1994.

Iceland's DIS was established as a private foundation in 1999 when Depositors' and Investors' Guarantee Fund (Guarantee Fund) was established by a separate law which, at that time, 'transposed Directive 94/19 into the Icelandic national legislation'. In accordance with the EEA Agreement, Iceland was bound to implement into the Icelandic law EC directives on deposit guarantee schemes and investor protection, equally as any other EU member with full membership.

The Guarantee Fund began its operation in January 2000. However, Iceland had enjoyed deposit insurance since 1941 in different forms for state-owned banks and commercial savings banks, where state-owned banks within the deposit guarantee scheme enjoyed the backup guarantee from the Ministry of Finance and commercial savings banks deposit guarantee scheme was backed up by private savings banks. So, historically, Iceland had known what deposit insurance was prior to the mandatory scheme due to the EU regulations.

By merger of the two existing funds and incorporation of an investor protection fund under the same protection 'umbrella' of the Guarantee Fund, it was assumed that there was no need for an explicit state guarantee, although the Guarantee Fund was a private one. In the case of insufficient funds, the Guarantee Fund was able to obtain a loan (theoretically) and its board members believed that such a stipulation in the law provided sufficient financial protection to depositors.

According to the legal act, by which the Guarantee Fund had been established, its board consisted of six members, out of which four members were representatives from the banking and investment industry and two were representatives of the Ministry of Business Affairs that also appointed the chairman of the board. Board members were appointed for a term of two years only (SIC 2010, 10). The board could employ a managing director or contract a legal entity for management. Since its establishment in 2000, the Central Bank of Iceland had been contracted for the management of the Guarantee Fund. In short, the Guarantee Fund is a private fund under the public management. Namely, the entity was established as a private one, where the majority of its board members (4 out of 6) were representatives of banks and investment companies, but the chairman was a government official working for the Ministry of Business Affairs. In accordance with the contract with the Central Bank of Iceland, its officer of the Financial Stability Department was employed as the manager of the Guarantee Fund, from 2005 until October 2008.

The coverage amount was established at approximately €20,000 (expressed in the local currency). The law prescribed the minimum target fund size in the amount of 1 per cent of the total guaranteed deposits which banks had to contribute.

The law was silent about the deposits of Icelandic banks' branches abroad as they were, by default, considered to be a part of the Icelandic deposit guarantee scheme (banks' branches are not separate legal entities). In other words, deposits collected by the branches of Icelandic banks abroad were guaranteed in the same manner as the deposits collected within the territory of Iceland.

By September 2008, the Guarantee Fund had signed 'topping-up' agreements with Norway, Finland, Denmark, the UK and the Netherlands. At the same time, Italian, French and Swedish DISs either delayed or refused to sign such an agreement with Iceland. The minimum target size of 1 per cent of total guaranteed deposits was satisfied at all times and banks were supplementing it once per year, by March of the current year for the liabilities of the previous year, but not more than 0.15 per cent (SIC 2010, 10–11). In addition, except contributions in cash, banks were able to provide contributions in the form of letters of guarantee.

Since 2006, Icelandic banks had been aggressively collecting deposits abroad, via the established subsidiaries (separate legal entities established in host countries and belonging to the DISs of host countries). However, soon Icelandic banks started the collection of deposits through its branches abroad (not subsidiaries).

Landsbanki bank established Icesave accounts for retail depositors, usually at high interest rates. Deposits were highly popular among host depositors (UK and Dutch) and rose rapidly in a short period of time. Such steep rise in the deposits of Icelandic banks due to a rise in foreign retail deposits in branches operating abroad had not been reflected in the appropriate rise of funds of the Guarantee Fund. By autumn 2008, Landsbanki bank had more than 300,000 depositors in the UK and more than 125,000 depositors in the Netherlands who deposited more than €5 billion and €1.7 billion in Icesave savings products online, respectively (SIC 2010, 36–54).

Throughout 2008, there were rumors and concerns about the stability of the Icelandic financial system at home and abroad. Icelandic financial authorities, consisting of representatives from the Government, the Financial Supervisory Authority and the Central Bank of Iceland, held regular meetings where the situation in the banking sector, and especially in large banks like Landsbanki, was discussed, however without a clear conclusion or imposed measures. In August 2008, questions were raised from abroad, namely, from the UK, Sweden and the Netherlands on whether and how the state would support the Guarantee Fund if needed.

On 6 October 2008, the Icelandic Parliament adopted an Emergency Law to combat the consequences of the financial crisis (Act 2008, 1–6). The Financial Supervisory Authority, in accordance with the Emergency

Law, put Landsbanki into receivership the very next day with a statement that deposits placed in the bank's branches in Iceland would be fully guaranteed (SIC 2010, 22). Landsbanki was split into the Icelandic business operations and business operations in other countries (such as the UK and the Netherlands). Icelandic assets and liabilities were then transferred into a new state-owned bank, while all foreign liabilities and other borrowings remained in the 'old Landsbanki' in receivership (€12.1 billion of assets and €22.2 billion of liabilities).

Both diplomatic meetings and meetings with the financial authority colleagues from the UK and the Netherlands were held in the next few days. The UK representatives proposed to transfer all deposits from the UK branch into the UK subsidiary of Landsbanki (which would then automatically be a part of the UK deposit guarantee), but this idea did not materialize. As a counter measure, the UK government imposed financial sanctions on Iceland (by freezing the assets of Landsbanki and the Central Bank of Iceland and the Iceland's government) which turned into a diplomatic scandal and instigated patriotic reactions among the Icelanders in support of the measures of their government.

There were several attempts of solutions, but all of them failed. In November 2008, the International Monetary Fund approved a loan to Iceland and the UK, and the Netherlands offered loans for deposit compensation up to the minimum coverage amount of €20,000, as a part of the solution.

The UK and the Netherlands required from the Icelandic state to guarantee repayment of the Icelandic minimum deposit guarantees (€4.0 billion) to retail depositors, and did not require any repayment guarantee for the other €18.2 billion creditors' claims in the bankrupt Landsbanki (Bergmann 2016, 19). The Icelandic state was offered a €2.7 billion repayment loan by the UK and a €1.3 billion repayment loan by the Netherlands, where the Landsbanki receivership should repay it with all the funds they could collect from the liquidation of assets in 2009–2015, and where the Icelandic state, starting from 2016, should subsequently assume the liability for the remaining repayments (including accrued interest) to the UK and the Netherlands.

Those offers were rejected and instead a solution was seen at the European Free Trade Association (EFTA) court in Luxembourg. It took several years to decide, but the EFTA court in 2013 freed the Icelandic state from accusations and ruled that Iceland did not break European free trade laws (EFTA 2013, 1–36).

To prevent the run on other banks, the British and Dutch authorities decided to repay in full amount their depositors in the branches of the Landsbanki bank. However, later they demanded from Iceland remuneration at a minimum of €20,000 per depositor, which was the minimum coverage amount in Iceland at the time of Landsbanki's collapse.

The case of the Landsbanki bank is an excellent example of how things do not work in practice and how fragile the 'compliance' with the EU regulation is and, in fact, how harmonization did not exist in practice. Obviously, in theory, Iceland's legal framework on the deposit guarantee was in compliance with Directive 94/19, but when problems were detected each side interpreted them in their own way. Iceland used as many as possible legal tools to justify its decision of the refusal of compensation to foreign depositors. Legal battles challenged every aspect of Directive 94/19 on the 'home-host' principle, systemic bank failure, compensation of depositors, equal treatment of depositors, funding, extraordinary funding and so on.

Through a careful study of the chronology of events and how Icelandic authorities handled the case, it is obvious that the Icelandic deposit guarantee scheme had many deficiencies (SIC 2010, 1–138). The Guarantee Fund had not developed in line with the circumstances and the development of its financial sector. Subordinate laws and internal acts had not been amended for years. It was the failure of Landsbanki that revealed that up until that point there had existed no systematic supervision or an overall understanding of the amount of insured deposits held in foreign branches. The data on deposits were discussed from time to time but without a thorough analysis and without understanding the real scope of the problem. During 2008, authorities discussed many times the situation in the financial sector, particularly in the banks, although these discussions were 'passive', without specific conclusions or imposed measures. The concept of state support to the Guarantee Fund had not been discussed until foreign authorities posed questions.

Although Iceland is a small country and it was cost effective not to establish a separate legal entity with full-time employees fully responsible for daily operation of the DIS, eventually the overall costs of negligence and ruined international image were much higher, despite the positive ruling of the EFTA court.

6.4 Directive 2009/14/EC Responding to the 2008 Crisis

The financial crisis in 2008 that spread all over the world, in addition to the EU's own weaknesses, urged the need for improvements of the regulation related to deposit insurance. Individual measures adopted by the national authorities prevented a further spread of the domino effect and panic among the depositors of European banks.

The EU authorities realized the importance of stronger common mechanisms and amended Directive 94/19 in March 2009 with the aim to restore the confidence of depositors.

New Amendments to the Directive (Directive 1999, L 68/3–7) introduced a gradual increase of the coverage amount from €20,000 first to €50,000, after which to €100,000 as of January 2011.

Another important novelty was the length of the compensation period that was shortened from 3 months to 20 working days.

And, finally, an even more important change was shortening of the period of unavailability of deposits (which was initially 21 days) to 5 working days in order to shorten the payout period.

All three key improvements such as the increase of the coverage amount, shortening of the period during which authorities must make a decision on the failing bank's destiny (in order to avoid a delay in decision making) and shortening of the period in which the deposit insurance authority should compensate the depositors were significant changes and a challenge for the member countries. The most challenging task was to comply with an increased coverage level which automatically increased the total potential liabilities of the DIS and urged for a better DIS funding.

6.5 Directive 2014/49/EU

6.5.1 New DIS Rules for EU Members

In spring 2014, after several years of consultations and numerous discussions among the EU member countries, a new recast Directive on the DIS (DGSD) was adopted by the European Parliament, marking a new era and setting new rules on harmonization within Europe (Directive 2014/49/EU 2014, L 173/149–178).

EU member countries had to comply with DGSD by 3 July 2015. However, by the end of 2015, ten member countries had failed to implement these rules into their national laws. Consequently, the EC issued a request for compliance where member countries were given two more months to comply. Otherwise, the EC might have decided to refer them to the European Court of Justice. These countries were Belgium, Cyprus, Estonia, Greece, Italy, Luxembourg, Poland, Romania, Slovenia and Sweden (EC 2015a, 1).

The 'new' Directive is, compared to the preceding one, very detailed, in its attempt of uniformity. If the 'old' Directive was based on minimum harmonization, the 'new' Directive is based on maximum harmonization.

Lessons learned from the 2008 financial crisis, fragile financial stability in many member countries at that time (Iceland, Cyprus, Spain, Ireland, Greece), fear for the future of the EU and of the European Monetary Union, instability and fragility of European banking and economic system all influenced and inspired European legislative authorities to undertake a slightly different approach with a detailed regulation on deposit insurance.

Simultaneously with DGSD was adopted the Directive on Bank Recovery and Resolution (BRRD), which set rules for restructuring, rehabilitation and resolution of banks in the European Union. Two directives are interrelated and national authorities have the freedom in the institutional setup and division of responsibilities.

The Preamble of DGSD is comprehensive where 56 items present many important principles used in the new deposit insurance legislative framework. In order to fully understand what is new and how to implement this comprehensive legal act, one must carefully read the Preamble and the main document comparing them.

One of the new ideas regulated by DGSD is the possibility of mergers of two national DISs or creation of a cross-border DIS. The idea is good in theory, but it would be interesting to learn whether and how the member countries would implement it due to numerous open issues on financing and governance of such scheme.

From the case of Icelandic bank failure it was clear that the 'cooperation' among member countries is based on very fragile foundations. When the times are 'good', for depositors it is irrelevant whether the deposit insurers cooperate or not, whether they exchange information and the know-how. For depositors, it is only important whether they have equal treatment on the whole EU territory and what would happen if a bank that was licensed for business in one country, operating in another country, failed. The questions remain on how depositors would be compensated and whether their national and geographical position in the EU would make a difference in the case of a merged DIS.

Therefore, at present, it is optimistic or unrealistic to expect any kind of operational merger of the two DISs from different countries, at least not in the short term. However, the DGSD laid down a foundation for such mergers.

The DGSD emphasizes that deposit insurers should have a functionally sound governance and publish annual reports on their activities. Even nowadays, there are deposit insurance authorities that don't publish annual reports and share very little, if any, information to the public. Often the information offered to the public was scarce and general, websites were not always updated, so the public could not obtain information easily and the overall level of transparency was not satisfactory.

The new DGSD sets more uniformity in deposit protection, broadens and clarifies the scope of coverage, encourages faster payout, improves funding and prescribes obligatory providing of information to depositors.

The general observation is that the text of the DGSD is very detailed, articles are long and the language is more complex and challenging for the general public. It is clear that the European authorities wanted to harmonize and uniform features of deposit insurance as much as possible, but it is also understandable that the final text is a result and reflection of long discussions and many compromises, as there are many exemptions and allowed procedures which have been retained due to the existing practice of some member countries.

In addition, the prescribed transitional periods of over ten years for the full compliance with the shortened payout time frame of seven working days may be criticized as too long since the hurdles that prevent operational efficiency should be removed in a year or two at most.

Before the new text of the DGSD was proposed, the EC had conducted research and analysis of the then established regulatory framework on the DIS. As a result, the analysis identified nine key areas with weaknesses, such as:

- differences and appropriateness of the level and scope of coverage
- inadequate payout procedures
- insufficient depositor information
- differences in DISs funding mechanisms
- insufficient and different level of funding
- banks' contributions not based on risks
- limited mandate of the DISs only onto paybox
- lack of cross-border cooperation among the DISs
- mutual and voluntary schemes exempted from the DIS,

that needed to be improved (EC 2010, 29).

Each of the identified problem drivers was addressed in the new DGSD.

6.5.2 Uniform Level and Scope of Coverage

Prior to the crisis, the European Union set the minimum harmonized level of insured deposit coverage to €20,000 allowing members to provide higher coverage. Some of its member countries established a higher coverage (e.g. Italy) and some provided a higher coverage for certain categories of depositors (e.g. pensioners). It was revealed that the average household deposit size in at least five member banks was above €50,000 (JRC 2010, 68).

In addition, the 'old' Directive suggested a number of exclusions which the countries could follow based on discretionary rights. The new DGSD does not support different coverage levels among the member countries. It is allowed, though on a temporary basis, to introduce coverage over €100,000 only for specific purposes arising from the personal situation of depositors and taking into account their social aspect. More explicitly, the DGSD advocates the same coverage level regardless of the member country's economic strength and regardless of the national currency.

The DGSD keeps the deposit insurance per depositor principle but provides clearer rules on the calculations of the coverage amount in the case of joint deposits and beneficiary rules. The set-off rule is permitted only if liabilities are due and the member countries are not encouraged to implement it any more.

The DGSD prescribes in detail which deposits should be excluded from the coverage. Deposit insurance is provided to retail and legal entities depositors. There is no different treatment or discrimination of depositors based on their nationalities. Deposit insurance excludes deposits of other credit institutions, own deposits of failed credit institutions, deposits arising from money laundry, deposits of financial institutions, deposits of investment firms, unidentified deposits, deposits of insurance undertakings, deposits of collective investment undertakings, deposits of pension funds, deposits of public authorities and debt securities issued by credit institutions. The DGSD allows that certain categories of deposits may be the subject of a payout such as deposits held by personal pension schemes of small- or medium-sized companies and deposits held by local authorities with a low annual budget of less than €500,000.

In order to identify eligible deposits (those deposits that are not excluded thus are included in deposit insurance), member states will ensure that credit institutions are able to identify and mark the eligible deposits. National deposit insurance authorities may prescribe in detail in subordinate laws or in written instructions how to mark the eligible deposits and ensure their immediate identification.

Although the coverage level is harmonized in the amount of €100,000, national legislations are allowed to prescribe coverage in a higher amount for special cases and on a temporary basis (from 3 to 12 months, but no longer), for deposits arising from real estate transactions on private residential properties, deposits that serve for social purposes such as marriage, divorce, retirement, dismissal, redundancy, invalidity and death, and deposits arising from insurance benefits or compensations.

6.5.3 Shortened Payout Time Frame

In order to build greater depositors' confidence, deposit insurers must compensate depositors in seven working days. As many EU members do not have appropriate management information systems (MIS), they have been allowed to comply with this rule gradually and implement it as follows:

(i) in 20 working days until the end of 2018,
(ii) in 15 working days until the end of 2020,
(iii) in 10 working days until the end of 2023 and
(iv) in 7 working days, as of 2024.

During the transitional periods, the deposit insurance authorities must ensure advanced payouts to depositors in order to cover their costs of living. If the deposits were inactive for at least 24 months and the balance of the deposit is lower than the administrative payout cost, such deposits are not a subject of payout.

The DGSD clarifies the details how the payout amount will be determined if several depositors are entitled to one account or when the depositor may not be identifiable. Depositors are also entitled to interest on their deposits until the date of the insurance event occurrence.

After the payout, the deposit insurance authority is entitled to the subrogation to the rights of depositors for the amount equal to their payments to depositors.

In order to compensate for a longer payout period, the DGSD advocates advance payouts to depositors in prescribed circumstances such as when depositors need money for payments of bills and covering of their cost of living. Such exemptions may create additional work and technical problems which must be resolved with software solutions. The payout of covered deposits should be efficient and simple. It is easier to ensure fast access to eligible sums of money rather than payments of small sums of money in advance and payments of remaining amounts later. It is likely that national jurisdictions will recognize the issue and enable a faster payout of entire amounts.

As the time frame for the deposit payout is becoming very short, it is important that the DISs are fully prepared at all times. Therefore, the EU regulators highlight the right of the DIS to access the required data at all times. Commonly, the DISs prescribe regular reporting obligations for member banks, but most of these data are on an aggregate basis. Member banks must supply at any time and upon request all information necessary for the preparation of a payout. This implies that at any time during the year, the DIS may request detailed data on depositors and deposits prepared and delivered in the same manner as for the deposit payout preparation. If the competent authority detects problems in the bank, which may potentially cause intervention of the DIS, the deposit insurance authority must be informed about the case and the problems. Such information is necessary much more in advance regardless of the DIS being only paybox or having a much larger role in the resolution process.

The deposit insurance authorities must perform stress tests on their systems, on a regular basis, at least every three years or more often if it is necessary. Based on the results of the performed stress tests, the European Banking Authority (EBA) will conduct peer reviews of the DISs, at least every five years, in order to examine their resilience. Bank failures are rare events and some European DISs have never experienced the payout process. Although the DISs could prepare for the payout, adopting payout procedures and developing MIS, such preparation is 'theoretical' as long as it does not simulate a real-case scenario and test all activities of the involved parties. The DISs would benefit from the annual testing of the system. Such test should be based on a developed scenario involving some or all member banks. The DIS should conduct the exercise with all activities that are usually performed when a bank fails and analyze the test results and prepare a report with recommendations for improvements.

If the DIS is mandated with paybox tasks, in such case, MIS and tested procedures for payout are the first things to be established in the DIS. A MIS should be designed in accordance with the DIS features. Even when the banking sector is safe and sound and no banks are failing for a longer period of time, the deposit insurance authority should regularly check its readiness and level of preparation for bank failure.

In 2014, the Bulgarian Corporate Commercial Bank's (KTB) failure showed failure in the implementation of the prescribed time frame for payout by the Deposit Guarantee Fund of Bulgaria.

6.5.3.1 Bulgarian KTB Collapse

A good example of collision between the national legislation and the EU Directives relates to the 'unavailability of deposits' rule and the compensation of insured deposits, as is the case of the Bulgarian KTB in 2014.

Bulgaria is a member of the EU and therefore liable to comply with all European Union Directives.

The KTB bank was the fourth-largest bank in Bulgaria with total assets of €3.7 billion (as of end of March 2014 data) that held more than 8 per cent of the market share and had more than 220,000 depositors. The Bulgarian banking legislation at the time did not allow for a fast and efficient bank resolution and a full audit of assets and liabilities was required prior to the Bulgarian National Bank making a decision on the bank's solvency and taking any measures toward revoking the banking license.

In addition, the existing law on Bulgarian Deposit Guarantee Fund triggered the compensation of depositors only after the revocation of the bank's license. Obviously, although during its accession period Bulgaria had to comply with Directive 94/19, neither the Bulgarian financial authorities nor the EC noticed non-compliance of the national legislation with the EU Directive 94/19.

In June 2014, after a publicly distributed email statement on the bank's financial situation, depositors ran on the bank and during a frantic week withdrew one-fifth of total deposits. Consequently, KTB became illiquid and requested financial assistance from the Bulgarian National Bank. Soon the Bulgarian National Bank issued prudential measures and placed KTB into a special supervisory regime of provisional administration for a period of three months, in accordance with its banking legislation, with an embargo on paying out deposits (deposit freeze).

During the period of provisional administration (conservatorship), the Bulgarian National Bank was trying to grasp the seriousness of the bank's financial condition and 'buy the time' in finding the solutions. Depositors were protesting on the streets because of the unavailability of deposits. Clearly, according to the European Union rules, 21 days of unavailability of deposits soon passed but the bank's doors remained closed. In September and October 2014, the EC reacted (EU 2014), as well as the European Banking Authority (EBA 2014, 1–8) by issuing recommendations and ordering the Bulgarian authorities to compensate depositors, in line with Directive 94/19 by 21 October 2014.

The Bulgarian authorities claimed that the Bulgarian law superseded the EU Law and that Bulgaria was under no obligation to comply with Directive 94/19. In September 2014, after the three-month period of provisional administration expired, the Bulgarian National Bank prolonged it for additional two months and further irritated the European Union's financial authorities.

In its published audit report on October 22nd, the Bulgarian National Bank (Novinite 2014, 1) disclosed to the public all the shortcomings in the bank's operation and desperate measures that were taken in order to preserve the 'illusion' of the bank's solvency. In other words, the bank self-funded its own Tier2 capital with circular lending transactions involving a number of inside and interrelated companies (by lending them loans which those companies later lent back to KTB in the form of subordinated loans recognized as a part of Tier2 capital).

Under the pressure from Europe, the Bulgarian authorities initiated a revision of its banking legislation and prepared a set of laws to be approved, in line with the European Directives. In the meantime, due to the political crisis, the Bulgarian Parliament was dismissed and the laws could not be enacted.

Similarly, like in many failing banks, it was revealed that KTB had inadequate internal controls and credit approval processes with wrong collateral valuation and missing or misleading documentation (for more than two-thirds of loans), as well as excessive insider lending. A group of investors connected to the bank's owner offered to put a rescue bid jointly with the Bulgarian government, but the idea failed and the bank's owner ran from the country. The Bulgarian National Bank filed a lawsuit against a major shareholder for the embezzlement of 140 million USD.

Finally, on November 6th, the Bulgarian National Bank (BNB 2014, 1) revoked the banking license which was the trigger date for the Bulgarian Deposit Insurance Fund to initiate compensation of insured deposits to KTB's depositors, in the amount of 1.9 billion Eur. The compensation of depositors commenced on December 4th, more than five months after the deposits initially became unavailable (DIF 2014, 1). However, the Bulgarian authorities claimed that all was in accordance with and in line with the Bulgarian legislation. Indeed, that is true, as well as the fact that the Bulgarian legislation was non-compliant with the European legislation which the EU authorities claimed superseded the national legislation.

Regardless of the legal uncertainties and significant legal obstacles, the fact is that in theory it is easy to comply with the most demanding rules, but sooner or later real-life situations will confirm whether the theory complies with the practice. The crucial lesson for Bulgaria learned from this case, but also for other countries that may face a similar issue sometime in the future, is that it is important to understand its own legislation, assume liability and be prepared for the enforcement of the legislation as copy-paste laws may be counterproductive.

6.5.4 Better Informed Depositors

In order to ensure sufficient information to depositors, standardized information sheet is prescribed with the standardized scope of information to be given to depositors where depositors must acknowledge the receipt of such information.

Member countries must ensure that banks provide depositors with all necessary information before entering into the deposit contract, in the manner prescribed by the law and in the language agreed at the time of the contract. The DISs must publish the information on their websites.

The deposit insurance authority is obliged to provide a full set of information to depositors, including the information on the payout currency. National jurisdictions may opt to choose the payout currency among the following options: €, local currency of the DIS, local currency of the depositor, currency of the deposit, local currency of the country where the deposit is made.

6.5.4.1 Example on Payout Currency Options Within the EU

This example is given for a better understanding of the currency options. Assumption is that a Croatian bank fails. It had a branch operating in Bosnia where an Italian depositor held a deposit in British pounds (GBP). Croatia is an EU member country, while Bosnia is not. The local currency of Croatia is Croatian Kuna (HRK). The Croatian deposit insurance authority has many options to choose for the payout currency. The chosen option should be prescribed in the national legislative. In this particular case, options provided by the DGSD are to conduct the payout in the following currencies:

(i) in € (local currency of the depositor, in which case, GBP must be converted in €, using the exchange rate at the date of the insurance event occurrence),
(ii) in HRK (local currency of the Croatian DIS),
(iii) in GBP (currency of the deposit) or
(iv) in Bosnian Mark (BAM) that is the local currency in Bosnia, where the deposit is deposited in a Croatian bank's branch.

6.5.5 Uniformed Ex Ante Financing

The EC characterized its member countries DISs' financing as insufficient and inadequate to cope with the financial crisis challenges. Out of 27 member countries at that time, 21 had established an ex ante DIF while 6 had ex post DIFs.

The actual coverage ratios (available funds over total covered deposits) in member countries DISs with established ex ante DIFs ranged between 0.01 per cent in France and 2.3 per cent in Lithuania, in 2007. The EC launched a research on the payout capacity of its member countries' DIS'. The research then showed that the DISs in 6 member states (Belgium, Cyprus, Ireland, Italy, Latvia and Malta) would not be capable of paying out depositors of a midsize bank with approximately 0.81 per cent of covered deposits (EC 2010, 21).

Therefore, one of the key features of the DGSD is the prescription of harmonization of ex ante funding. Member banks must bear the costs of funding DIS and the financing capacity of the DIS must be in proportion with its liabilities. In order to achieve this supreme goal, the EU has decided to introduce a uniform ex ante financial target for all DISs operating in its territory. It is set at the level of 0.8 per cent of insured (covered) deposits. Member countries must comply with the set target level of ex ante funds by 2024. In addition, it is prescribed that investments must be made only in low-risk assets.

In order to improve alternative funding options, the EU authorities encourage mutual DISs borrowing (from other national DISs). Although the idea is good, in principle, it raises many questions in its implementation within the prescribed borrowing limits. Therefore, it is unrealistic to expect its fast implementation and a practical value of such loans. It is highly optimistic to believe that in times of need and due to solidarity, countries are ready to assist each other for the DIS' purposes.

Another new principle introduced with the new DGSD was the obligatory risk-based premium calculated on the level of insured deposits. The EBA issued guidelines for the risk-based premium methodology but member countries may develop their own methodology with a prior consent of the EBA and the EU authorities (EBA 2015a, 1–86).

6.5.6 EU's DISs Are Given a Broader Mandate

The very explicitly DGSD states that the main task of the DIS is to protect depositors from the consequences of bank insolvency where such protection can be ensured in different ways, but the DIS should primarily be used to repay depositors, that is, for the paybox function. It is clear that the Directive was written for the paybox DIS, which has the narrowest mandate to compensate the depositors when the supervisory authorities make a decision on insolvency and consequently on the revocation of the license. Traditionally, the DISs in Europe were rarely involved in financing a P&A and many of national DISs across Europe were established as paybox systems in the past.

The Directive allows for the paybox DIS to assist in financing of the resolution of credit institutions where resolution mainly means 'rehabilitation of a bank', not the final closure of a failed bank.

However, as the EU in principle advocates the paybox DIS, the use of deposit insurance funds for open-bank assistance to a problem bank is not advocated by default. The DGSD states that it is possible to use deposit insurance funds for the prevention of bank failure, but only if the national legislation allows it (it is up to the national authorities whether they want the deposit insurance entity to be involved in it through national legislation). If it is so, in such case there must be clear rules and procedures in place, and any financial assistance must comply with the EU State Aid rules (EC 2008, 1).

At the same time, the deposit insurance authority must have set appropriate systems and procedures in order to select and monitor measures imposed on banks and manage risks affiliated with such measures. In other words, the deposit insurance authority should not provide financial assistance to the problem bank just because the problem bank has a low capital adequacy ratio or in order to improve its prudential ratios. The deposit insurance authority should not provide financial assistance without clear rules and procedures which could result in an unjustified financing of the problem bank or selective financing of individual banks. Request for financial assistance should be accompanied with a restructuring plan, list of imposed measures and a time frame in which assisted credit institutions must provide evidence on improved financial conditions. The deposit insurance authority must be able to monitor and manage its risks and improvements of the credit institution to which it provided financial assistance.

6.5.7 Improved Cross-Border Cooperation

The DGSD retained the 'home-host' rule where depositors of any branch of a bank in any member country authorized for operation in one member country should be protected by the home DIS equally as home depositors. In other words, if any Icelandic bank fails again in the future, the depositors in Iceland and the depositors in the bank's branch in the UK should be equally protected by the Icelandic deposit guarantee scheme. Although this equal treatment had not been so explicitly stated in Directive 94/19/EC, the principles are the same and there is not much difference in the new EU Directive, except for a more explicit wording. However, the Icelandic authorities decided that a special situation caused by the failure of systemic banks required a special solution in an emergency law and state intervention which excluded depositors in foreign branches outside Iceland from protection. Although the text of the DGSD does not prevent similar cases in the future, if such cases do occur, it will be much harder to justify actions of unequal treatment of depositors according to their nationality or geographical position.

The DGSD puts in focus the compulsory membership of authorized credit institutions in the DIS in the country where authorization was issued. Member countries have freedom to decide how to treat branches of credit institutions authorized in third countries (outside the EU).

The DGSD prescribes that the payout is executed by the DIS in which the branch of the bank operates, that is, a host DIS. The home DIS (established in the member country where the bank was authorized) is obliged to compensate the host DIS and provide information and payout instructions in a timely manner. In order to implement this rule, member countries are encouraged to sign contracts on mutual cooperation and on the specific task of the payout of depositors.

6.5.8 Role of Other National Authorities in the DIS

The DGSD uses the same term, the 'Deposit Guarantee Scheme' (DGS), for the DIS and for the deposit insurance authority and avoids even prescribing anything in regard to the DGS's legal status. It gives absolute freedom to national jurisdictions to opt for the most appropriate institutional setup and legal form. The only reference made is in regard to sound and transparent governance practices where the DGSs should produce annual reports on their activities.

The Directive introduced new terminology and acknowledged different authorities within national jurisdictions, each of which has its own role in respect to the DIS, such as competent authorities, designated authorities, resolution authorities and relevant administrative authorities.

Competent authority is a national competent authority responsible for the supervision of credit institutions and which has the power to revoke the license of credit institutions. In many cases, as prescribed by the DGSD, the DIS must consult its national competent authority, for example, on the risk-based methodology, on imposing the extraordinary premium, on investments in financial assets other than low-risk assets and so on.

Designated authority is an entity, a national body which is selected to administer and supervise the DIS in relation to the DGSD. In other words, the designated authority is responsible that the DGSD is transposed properly into the national law and implemented by the national DIS. Designated authority is either a central bank or the Ministry of Finance, but it may be any other entity designated with this task.

Resolution authority is an entity designated with the task of credit institutions' resolution. In some countries, this is a specialized resolution agency or even a supervisory entity, if it has been entrusted with the resolution mandate. However, if the deposit insurance authority is also given the resolution mandate, in such case the resolution authority and the deposit insurance authority are placed within one single legal entity.

Relevant administrative authority is a body identified by member countries for the purpose of determination of unavailable deposits, as prescribed by the DGSD. It is logical that the competent authority (the supervising entity of credit institutions) is given the role to act as the relevant administrative authority that will be responsible for the determination of unavailability of deposits within five working days. However, the national authorities may give such role to another entity as well.

6.6 EBA's Methodology on Differential Premium System

In its attempt to harmonize funding among the EU member countries, the DGSD prescribes that the contributions paid by banks will be based on the amount of covered deposits and the degree of risk incurred by each bank.

The DISs were obliged to comply with it starting from July 2015, exceptionally a year later, but no later than July 2016.

The EBA was obliged to issue Guidelines (EBA 2015a, 1–86) to specify methods for calculating the banks' contributions in accordance with the risk. The EBA intends to review individual members' risk-based methodologies by July 2017 and regularly at least every five years.

During the process of development of the Guidelines, the EBA tested three different methodologies with the selected EU member countries and finally decided on the one which was considered to be the best option.

The EBA provided a formula for the calculation of annual contributions to the DIS by individual member banks (EBA 2015a, 8) as follows:

$$C_i = CR \times ARW_i \times CD_i \times \mu$$

Where:

C_i	=	Annual contribution to the DIF from the member bank '*i*'
CR	=	Annual contribution (premium) rate, linear for all banks
ARW_i	=	Aggregate risk weight for the member bank '*i*'
CD_i	=	Covered deposits for the member bank '*i*'
μ	=	Adjustment coefficient, identical for all banks in a given year.

The EBA suggests starting with the calculation of the annual target amount each year, based on the set target fund size level and in accordance with the risk of each individual bank. For example, if the DIS sets a minimum target fund size level at 0.8 per cent over a ten-year time frame, the DIS would calculate an appropriate portion of the total target fund size level in Years 1/10, 1/9, 1/8 and so on until the final 1/1. Upon the result of the calculated target fund amount in each year, the DIS would calculate the necessary annual premium rate by dividing the required target amount by total covered deposits.

The DIS should calculate the Aggregate Risk Weight (ARW) for every member bank, by using the Aggregate Risk Score (ARS) for that bank. The EBA suggests ranging the ARW between 50 per cent and 200 per cent in order to avoid that all banks, despite their different risk profiles, fall into one risk category.

The purpose of the adjustment coefficient is to ensure that the sum of individually charged annual premium amounts equals the calculated annual premium amount.

An individual bank's annual premium contribution is then calculated by applying the annual regular premium (linear), adjusted by its ARW and the adjustment coefficient to the total covered deposits of that bank.

The EBA in its Annex 1 (EBA 2015a, 26–32) presents details on the bucket and the sliding scale methods for the calculation of ARW allowing countries to choose the one that suits them better.

6.6.1 Example: The EBA's Proposed Method for the Calculation of the Annual Premium Level

The following example illustrates how the EU's DIS may implement the EBA's proposed methodology for the calculation of the risk-based premium and reaching the desired target fund size, based on the following assumptions:

- The target fund size level is set at 0.8 per cent over seven years, starting from Year 1.The DIS conducts the initial calculation of the target fund size in comparison to its total covered deposits using the EBA's proposal.

As presented in Table 6.1 at the end of Year 1, the total target level of 0.8 per cent of covered deposits would amount to €355,139 million. The corresponding 1/7 of that amount is €50,734 million which the DIS should collect in 2018. When transforming the desirable annual premium amount into an annual premium level, it is 0.114285714 per cent of the covered deposits where 0.114285714 represents the annual premium level for Year 1.

Table 6.1 EBA's method for setting annual premium level, in €000

	Year 1	Year 2	Year 3	Year 4	Year 5	Year 6	Year 7
Total covered deposits	**44,392,364**	**45,724,134**	**47,095,858**	**48,508,734**	**49,963,996**	**51,462,916**	**53,006,804**
EBA's methodology							
Min. target 0.8 per cent	355,139	365,793	376,767	388,070	399,712	411,703	424,054
Appropriate annual premium amount	50,734	52,510	54,705	57,530	61,411	67,407	79,758
Annual premium level, in percentage	0.114285714	0.114840499	0.116155825	0.118597888	0.122910	0.130981	0.150467
Total DIF	**50,734**	**103,244**	**157,949**	**215,479**	**276,890**	**344,297**	**424,054**
Alternative methodology							
Annual premium level 0.1246651 per cent	55,342	57,002	58,712	60,473	62,288	64,156	66,081
Total DIF	**55,342**	**112,344**	**171,056**	**231,529**	**293,817**	**357,973**	**424,054**

Using the same analogy, the DIS calculates 0.8 per cent on covered deposits at the end of Year 2, which is €365,793 million. However, the DIS has already collected the first annual premium in the amount of €50,734 million, resulting in the amount of €315,059 million that should have been collected over the remaining six years. When calculating the annual regular premium for Year 2, the DIS uses the formula 315,059/6 = €52,510 million, that is, 0.114840499 of annual premium level.

By applying the same method, by the end of Year 7, the DIS would collect €424,054 million, which is the exact amount of the target fund size (0.8 per cent of the covered deposits).

The formula could be criticized because it is focused on the exact calculation of the relevant portion of 0.8 per cent at any year during the target fund size time frame, regardless of the risk exposure of the DIS and its need to build a credible DIF. By reading the EBA's Guidelines, it could be concluded that the minimum target fund size level of 0.8 per cent is optimal for any DIS. At that moment, it was rather a political decision among the EU member countries that 0.8 per cent of the covered deposits is sufficiently optimal for the EU as a whole. Therefore, it is irrelevant to calculate the exact amount of the target fund size each year with mathematical precision, because the target fund size is prescribed as a 'minimum'. The EU member countries should be encouraged to determine their own target fund size, preferably in accordance with the risk exposure.

Clearly, the EBA's proposed method results in constant adjustments of the annual premium amount and the annual premium level toward 0.8 per cent.

Table 6.1 provides a comparison of the EBA's proposed method for calculating the annual target level using an alternative approach. The same amount of funds may be collected applying calculations already used in this book. The projected target of the DIF by the end of Year 7 is €424,054 million which should be collected over a period of seven years and result in a minimally required annual premium amount of €60,579 million, during that period. When applying the required premium amount to average covered deposits during that period, the calculated minimum annual premium level is 0.12466513 per cent over the next seven years. Using the alternative approach, the annual premium level has evened out and additional adjustments would be necessary if the projection assumptions change significantly, such as the annual growth of deposits, in case of significant deviation of projected figures.

As presented in Table 6.1, if the EBA methodology is used, the annual premium level ranges from 0.11 per cent in Year 1 to 0.15 per cent in Year 7, whereas the alternative method uses a constant level of the annual premium level at 0.12 per cent.

In addition to complying with the DGSD target fund size requirement, the member countries should adjust their target fund size levels according to their risk exposures and probabilities of failures of member banks, which would result in the collection of funds in the necessary amount regardless of the EU minimum. The main purpose of a robust DIS's funding is to be financially prepared when necessary while compliance with the DGSD rules is only to assist with the minimum EU standards. Pure compliance with the DGSD rules doesn't guarantee credibility and robustness of the DIS.

6.6.2 Example: Calculation of Individual Bank's Annual Premium

This example illustrates how the EU's DIS, based on the proposed EBA's methodology, should recalculate the annual premium amount into individual banks' premiums, based on their assessed risks.

After the calculation of the desired annual premium amount for Year 1 in the amount of €50,734 million, that is, at 0.114285714 per cent of covered deposits, as presented in Table 6.1, the DIS must apply it to individual banks, in respect to their risk profiles.

If the DIS applies the linear annual premium, the annual premium level as calculated, at 0.114285714 per cent would be applied to each individual bank's covered deposits amount. However, banks don't represent the same risk exposure to the DIS. In our particular case, banks are categorized as high, medium and low risky banks with aggregate risk weights of 150 per cent, 120 per cent and 75 per cent respectively. Therefore, each bank's annual linear premium amount is adjusted for each bank's risk category (ranging from 75 per cent to 150 per cent), as presented in Table 6.2. By applying individual risk categories, the DIS would collect €40,880 million, which is lower than required at the end

Table 6.2 FRA's risk based premium in line with target fund amount, in €000

Banks	Covered deposits	Annual premium (linear) 0.114285714	Risk category	ARW	Annual risk-adjusted premium	Final risk-based premium adjusted by 1.24105 coefficient
10	3,422	4	High	1.50	6	7
9	101,296	116	High	1.50	174	216
6	1,238,060	1,415	High	1.50	2,122	2,634
7	1,463,161	1,672	Medium	1.20	2,007	2,490
5	1,800,814	2,058	Medium	1.20	2,470	3,065
4	4,502,035	5,145	Low	0.75	3,859	4,789
3	7,203,256	8,232	Low	0.75	6,174	7,662
2	11,480,190	13,120	Low	0.75	9,840	12,212
1	16,600,129	18,972	Low	0.75	14,229	17,658
Total	**44,392,364**	**50,734**			**40,880**	**50,734**

of the first out of seven years during which the DIS aims to collect at least 0.8 per cent of its covered deposits.

Therefore, the annual risk-adjusted premium amounts must be further adjusted to the adjustment coefficient μ, which in our case is 1.24105 (50,734/40,880). Adjustment coefficient should be applied to each individual bank's annual risk-adjusted premium amount in order to collect the aimed 50,734 million μ in Year 1 and to apply the risk based premium.

6.6.3 Risk Categories and Core Risk Indicators

The EBA Guidelines (EBA 2015a, 15) list five risk categories and a set of specific risk indicators for individual member banks:

(i) capital
(ii) liquidity and funding
(iii) asset quality
(iv) business model and management
(v) potential losses for the DIS.

Banks fail when they don't have sufficient capital to absorb losses. Higher amounts of capital decrease the likelihood of a failure. Liquidity enables a bank to pay its due debt. If the asset quality of a bank is poor, the bank will experience high levels of provisioning which might increase losses and, consequently, decrease the capital cushion. Business model and management indicators reflect profitability, balance sheet development and concentration levels. Finally, the DIS faces potential losses if a bank fails and its recovery rate is low due to the high encumbered assets.

Capital and liquidity and funding have the highest minimum weights, 18 per cent each. The remaining three risk categories have a minimum weight of 13 per cent. The DIS may increase minimum weights, that is, adjust some risk categories or specific risk indicators, in order to determine the risk profiles of member banks. The EBA set a sum of minimum weights to 75 per cent, in the following way:

- 18 per cent minimum weight for capital
- 18 per cent minimum weight for liquidity and funding
- 13 per cent minimum weight for asset quality
- 13 per cent minimum weight for business model and management and
- 13 per cent minimum weight for potential losses for the DIS (EBA 2015a, b, c, 23).

In addition, the DISs are allowed to use additional risk indicators if they consider them relevant, such as, for example, large exposure, growth of the balance sheet, return on equity, cost to income ratio and others.

The DISs are flexible on using the remaining 25 per cent of weights as they feel, under the following conditions:

- the minimum weights of risk categories and core risk indicators are preserved;
- where only core risk indicators are used, the flexible 25 per cent weight should be allocated in the following way:

    - Capital – 24 per cent;
    - Liquidity and funding – 24 per cent;
    - Asset quality – 18 per cent;
    - Business model and management – 17 per cent and

    - Potential use of the DIS' funds – 17 per cent;

- the weight of any additional indicator, or the increase in the weight of a core risk indicator, should not be higher than 15 per cent, except for additional qualitative indicators (EBA 2015a, 23–24).

Aggregate risk weights may be calculated using the 'bucket' or 'sliding scale' method (EBA 2015a, 31–37).

6.7 European Deposit Insurance Scheme

In November 2015, the European Union authorities presented the proposal for the regulation on establishment of the EDIS which evolved into a draft regulation proposal (EC 2015b, 1–69), although some EU member countries (especially Germany) are strongly opposing the idea. National jurisdictions are afraid of losing the power and financial resources. Many of the EDISs have sufficient experience and confidence in the fulfillment of their mandates. Naturally, they fear that all what had been created over years would disappear in an attempt to transfer the powers onto EDIS. There are still so many unknown details on its design, governance, processes, appropriate funding and similar.

The main idea is to develop the EDIS gradually, starting from 2017 and finalizing the process by 2024. The EDIS is the final of the three building blocks missing for the creation of the envisaged concept of the banking union, while the Single Supervisory Mechanism (SSM) and the Single Resolution Mechanism (SRM) had already been established.

The role of the Single Resolution Board would be expanded into the Single Resolution and Deposit Insurance Board in order to administer the EDIS. The EDIS would apply to the DISs established in the participating member states as defined by Regulation (EU) 806/2014 and Regulation (EU) 1024/2013, that is, to the ones in the Euro area and the ones in the non-Euro area who chose to participate in the SSM. Banks which are established in the member countries not participating in the SRM are not subject to the SRM, and thus not subject to the EDIS.

The first stage is the so-called re-insurance phase and would last until 2020. During that period, the national DISs would be re-insured by the EDIS and would be entitled to access the EDIS's funds for the purpose of:

(i) funding liquidity shortfalls up to 20 per cent and
(ii) covering 20 per cent of excess loss.

In both cases, the maximum funding provided by the EDIS should not exceed 20 per cent of the initial target level for the EDIS and ten times the target level for the national DIS, that is, 8 per cent of covered deposits.

The second stage is the so-called co-insurance phase and would last until 2024. During that period, the EDIS would participate in the deposit payout starting from a low level of the contribution share ranging from 20 per cent to 80 per cent over a four-year period.

The final stage is the so-called full insurance phase where the EDIS would fully insure national DISs as of 2024.

The intention of the EU authorities is to create and build a European DIF with the EDIS, where banks, members of national DISs, would make contributions, based on their risk assessment. Banks would pay their contributions directly to the Single Resolution Board, although the national DIS would calculate and invoice the contribution for the EDIS.

As proposed, in all three stages—reinsurance, co-insurance and full insurance—the EDIS would both provide funding and cover losses of the national DISs. The funding provided by the EDIS would address the initial liquidity need of a national DIS to compensate depositors within the payout deadline (seven working days) and to satisfy the request for contribution to the resolution procedure in time. The EDIS's funding must be reimbursed by the participating DIS and the due amount could be decreased by the amount of the DIS's losses, in particular the bank's payout.

During the re-insurance stage, EDIS would provide liquidity funding to the national DIS, in case of deposit payout when the national DIS' total financial resources, increased by ex post extraordinary contributions are lower than the total covered deposits in the failing bank, in the amount of a maximum of 20 per cent of the liquidity shortfall.

Funding would be provided only when they had first exhausted their own resources. The purpose of enabling liquidity to national DISs is that the national DISs become less dependent on alternative (extraordinary) funding on national levels (e.g. national budgets).

During the co-insurance stage, the EDIS would provide liquidity funding and loss coverage when national DISs experience payout, from the 'first euro'. For example, at the beginning, the share of the EDIS's contribution would only be 20 per cent of covered deposits.

The EDIS would rigorously monitor national DISs payout procedures and the use of funding in order to confirm justification of the funding and to determine the final loss amount for a national DIS.

The EDIS's financial means must meet two target levels:

(i) initial target level of 20 per cent of four-ninth of the sum of all national minimum target levels by the end of the three-year reinsurance phase and
(ii) a final target level equal to the sum of the minimum target levels that participating

DISs must reach by mid-2024.

As the EDIS will be financed by banks, paid contributions will count toward the target level at their national DIS and thus are cost neutral.

If the EDIS's DIF would be insufficient, the EDIS would be able to raise ex post extraordinary contributions and borrow funds from the non-participating EU member countries, as being allowed by the DGSD.

At present, it is difficult to assess how the EDIS would contribute to the financial stability, especially in its third phase of full insurance. It is either a brilliant idea or a great fiasco. Clearly, in case of financial crisis and contagious effects, without fiscal financial assistance on national levels it is difficult to believe that the EDIS would be enough to ensure sufficient financial resources for the deposit payout. In case of repetitive weaknesses in the same countries, the EDIS would be in the danger of soon becoming insufficient and ineffective and could easily create discomfort because 'the good would pay for the bad'.

Differences in the level of development of the banking sectors, business discipline, tradition and many other differences arising from national peculiarities could become important obstacles. Time will show eventually whether the EDIS is the last brick in the strong and safe banking union wall, as the EU authorities claim.

6.8 EU Bank Resolution Model

Before 2008, European countries dealt with banking resolution issues within their national legal frameworks using a limited set of resolution tools. More developed EU countries relied on private solutions, whereas the developing countries relied on state support when resolving bank failures. In addition, just a few years ago banking was less cross-bordered and there were fewer international banks.

Nowadays, banking does not have limits related to national borders. Banks that are established under the EU legal framework are allowed to operate freely on the territory of any other EU member country. These banks don't need a banking license from their host supervisor and moreover, they are supervised by their home supervisors. In order to understand the condition and soundness of banks that offer their services to their citizens, bank supervisors must establish formal ways of close cooperation.

The turmoil on the European financial markets in the last decade and especially the deposit run on Cyprian and Greek banks, where national authorities failed to support the banks without financial assistance from Europe, were the trigger for the development of modern supranational legal framework for dealing with failing banks. Not only that the EU provided €141.8 billion to Greece from its European Financial Stability Facility from 2012 to 2014, but the whole EU feared the spread of the contagious deposit run on other countries (EFSF 2012, 1).

Therefore, the EU decided that new, modern, uniform standards for bank resolution and deposit insurance must be implemented within the EU. And as deposit insurance was already obligatory for EU member countries, it was decided to expand its role in support of the resolution tools.

The EU, with its views on the bank resolution process, somewhat diverges from the traditional understanding of bank resolution that was implemented internationally, especially in the United States. Although it was implicitly designed for dealing with failing of systemically important banks (too big to fail banks), any bank, even the smallest one, may be resolved in accordance with the new EU bank resolution rules if authorities assess that it is in the public interest and that the financial stability is endangered.

EU members did not have much practical experience on a larger scale with bank resolution tools such as P&A or bridge bank prior to the financial crisis compared to the United States. In the past, bank failures were rather incidental and did not happen often.

If a big bank was insolvent, 'too big to fail' rule was applied, relying rather on public, not on private solutions. Other (smaller by size and importance) banks were allowed to fail and in such cases, insolvency proceedings with deposit payout were initiated.

However, the 2008 financial crisis changed the entire philosophy on bank resolution within the EU's turmoil because it was clear that the existing solutions were limited and expensive not only for the individual member states but for the EU as a whole.

The idea is to provide authorities with a credible set of tools to intervene in the bank sufficiently early and quickly in order to ensure the continuity of the bank's critical financial and economic functions while minimizing the impact of its failure on the economy and the financial system in general. In other words, bank resolution, prescribed by the BRRD, is a bank restructuring process, when there is public interest.

In the Euro area countries, the BRRD is implemented through the SRM and a complex design of cooperation between the national authorities and the Single Resolution Board, as a supreme decision-making body for banks participating in the SSMs. The Single Resolution Fund is created to finance the resolution process of banks within the Euro area, starting from January 2016. Its target fund size is 1 per cent (approximately €55 billion) of covered deposits that is going to be collected over eight annual contribution cycles, by 2024.

For all other EU member countries, the bank resolution process is executed on national levels. Policy makers have choices on administrative and operational responsibilities for bank resolution and one of the first choices was related to a decision on the bank resolution authority. Authorities may decide to establish a new legal entity responsible for bank resolution or to give this mandate to a bank supervisor or a deposit insurance authority, or to divide the responsibility between the bank supervisor and the deposit insurance authority.

For EU, the concept of financial stability comes first. The main principle governing the idea of recovery and resolution of banks within the EU is that any failing bank should be able to exit the market, irrespective of its size and interconnectedness, without causing systemic disruption and as such should, in principle, be liquidated under normal insolvency proceedings, as prescribed by the BRRD.

The winding up of a failing bank through normal insolvency proceedings should always be considered before resolution tools are applied. In reality, normal insolvency proceedings may jeopardize financial stability, interrupt the critical functions of a bank and affect the protection of depositors. If that happens, it is likely that there would be a public interest in placing the institution under resolution and applying resolution tools rather than conducting normal insolvency proceedings. By providing such a strong statement, it is clear that public interests are those that authorities should consider when deciding whether to liquidate a bank in normal insolvency proceedings or enter the resolution process. It is hard to measure the justification for the 'public interest' before the failure, especially when smaller banks fail. Therefore, resolution authorities have serious responsibilities when deciding to apply resolution tools instead of normal insolvency proceedings.

Although, traditionally, normal insolvency proceedings are also considered as a resolution tool, the EU approach is slightly different and bank resolution should not be confused with normal insolvency proceedings. Bank resolution is an addition to normal insolvency proceedings. However, resolution tools may be implemented in combination with insolvency proceedings (such as bank liquidation or bank bankruptcy). In such case, the resolution process results in the bank's partial liquidation. In other cases, resolution process will result in the bank's recovery and rehabilitation.

Namely, if the bank is sold as a whole and recapitalized by its new owner or if the bail-in resolution tool is used, the resolved bank may continue its operation on an ongoing concern basis. This is one of the key differences in bank resolution between the EU and traditional bank resolution, where resolution actually means disposition ('death') of a bank.

In the EU, resolution can ensure either 'life' or 'death' of a bank, depending on the selected resolution tool. Bank resolution can actually also be understood as a form of rehabilitation (remediation) of a bank if it ensures that the bank continues its operation on an ongoing concern basis.

Government financial stabilization tool such as public equity support or temporary public ownership, in accordance with the state aid rules, may also be implemented, under the specific conditions and as a last resort when other resolution tools have been exhausted, for the purpose of maintaining financial stability (Directive 2014/59/EU 2014, L 173/287). In other words, it is still possible to use public funds to recapitalize the failing banks, but only in exceptional cases and after shareholders and creditors bear losses up to 8 per cent of bank's liabilities, under the conditions set out in the state aid rules. However, there is room for exception in case of severe liquidity shortages and use of liquidity loans by the central bank, guaranteed by the government, provided under the state aid rules, in order to preserve financial stability or in case when a bank needs recapitalization due to the results of the stress tests. In such exceptional cases, a bank that facilitates liquidity support should not be resolved, nor should the bail-in rule be applied (Directive 2014/59/EU 2014, L 173/196–197)

The whole idea of recovery and resolution is based on the principle of timely interventions and obligation for banks to prepare in advance their recovery plans. Recovery plans should set out measures to be taken by banks themselves in order to restore their financial position, if necessary. In other words, the recovery plan of a particular bank is a document which describes how that particular bank plans to self-rehabilitate itself (recover) and improve its financial condition. If we simplify it further, recovery plans will help problem banks to restore their financial health. Recovery plans should not assume any usage of extraordinary public financial support. They should be sufficiently detailed and based on realistic assumptions. Each bank is obliged to develop its recovery plan and submit it to the resolution authority for evaluation. Recovery plans should be regularly updated.

One of the key principles in dealing with problem or failing banks is to seek private solutions prior to any resolution and intervention in the public funds.

Based on the BRRD, supervisors should have the right to appoint a temporary administrator as part of their early intervention powers. Early intervention powers may include requirements to the management of the bank to implement one or all measures listed in the recovery plan, to examine the situation and develop a program to overcome problems within a specific time frame, to convene a shareholders' meeting and require decisions to be made, require one member of the management or the entire management to remove themselves from the position, to develop a plan for restructuring debt with creditors, require changes in the business strategy, require changes of the legal or operational structure of the bank, acquire all the information and prepare for the possible bank resolution. Given the above listed, supervisors have many powers at their disposal prior to the decision on resolution.

Under the BRRD guiding principles, resolution actions can be taken by the resolution authorities only when an institution is considered as failing or likely to fail, where private sector solutions and supervisory actions are not likely to prevent the failure of an institution within a reasonable time frame, and where normal insolvency proceedings would not meet the public interest test.

The BRRD defines resolution as an application of a resolution tool or a tool in order to achieve one or more of the resolution objectives. And resolution objectives are listed as:

(i) ensuring the continuity of critical functions of the institution,
(ii) avoidance of a significant adverse effect on the financial system and maintaining market discipline,
(iii) protection of public funds by minimizing reliance on extraordinary public financial support,
(iv) protection of deposits and
(v) protection of client's funds and client's assets.

However, one of the conditions for resolution is determination that the institution is failing or about to fail, which is made by the competent authority in consultation with the resolution authority. The idea is to enter into resolution before the bank is 'balance sheet insolvent and before all equity has been fully wiped out' (Directive 2014/59/EU 2014, L 173/196). Historically, bank failures showed that, in many cases, failed banks were deeply insolvent and the value of their asset deterioration resulted in a small recovery in the resolution process (and/or insolvency proceedings). However, entering into bank resolution which is 'likely to fail' is like 'skating on a thin ice'. The rationale is good and valid, but the implementation may lead to misuse of powers whenever discretionary decisions are made.

A bank should be considered failing or likely to fail (EBA 2015b, 6) when it 'infringes or is likely in the near future to infringe the requirements for continuing authorization, when assets are or are likely in the near future to be less than its liabilities, when the bank is or is likely in the near future to be unable to pay its debts as they fall due or when the bank requires extraordinary public financial support'. The EBA states that the authorities will make a decision based on comprehensive quantitative and qualitative objective elements, primarily based on the outcomes of the supervisory review and evaluation process (so-called SREP) such as capital position, liquidity position and other requirements for bank's authorization.

There are three conditions that must be simultaneously met before resolution actions are taken:

(i) competent authority makes a decision that the bank is failing or about to fail,
(ii) there is no reasonable prospect that any alternative private sector actions or supervisory measures would prevent bank failure within a reasonable time frame and
(iii) the resolution is necessary and in the public interest.

Figure 6.1 illustrates envisaged steps in bank recovery and resolution process within the EU. As long as the bank operates as usual, for the purpose of its risk management, it must develop its contingency liquidity and capital plan. For the purpose of its better overall preparation, the bank must develop its recovery plan. In addition, the competent author-

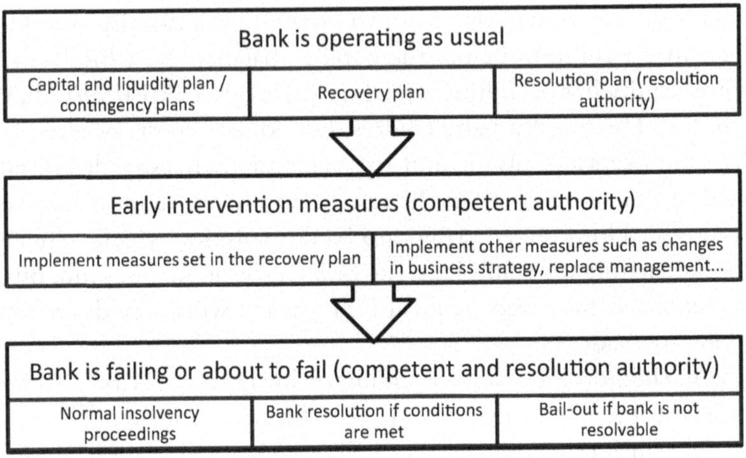

Fig. 6.1 Banking resolution within the EU

ity (usually banking supervisory authority) is responsible for the preparation of the bank's resolution plan, which should be updated regularly.

If the bank has problems, the competent authority should intervene sufficiently in advance with early intervention measures, assisting the bank to implement measures prescribed in its recovery plan or imposing other measures that it deems necessary, such as, for example, appointment of a temporary administrator.

If the bank is resolvable (in accordance with the BRRD), and that is if it may be liquidated under normal insolvency proceedings or resolved by applying one of the resolution tools and if it is failing or about to fail (prior balance sheet insolvency), the competent authority, having consulted the resolution authority, decides whether to initiate bank resolution if other conditions are met, or to put a bank under normal insolvency proceedings, if conditions for the resolution are not met. However, one or more several resolution tools may be combined with normal insolvency proceedings (bank liquidation).

The BRRD defines four main resolution tools as:

(i) sale of business,
(ii) bridge bank,

(iii) asset separation and
(iv) bail-in.

Sale of business means that the resolution authority is entitled to sell shares of a bank or all or some of its assets and liabilities to another purchaser.

The bridge bank tool is used for the transfer of shares or all or any assets and liabilities into bridge bank which is established for that particular purpose. In the second phase, the transfer of shares and/or all or any assets and liabilities may be returned to the previous shareholders, that is, bank in resolution or to a third party.

Asset separation tool is the transfer of assets, rights and liabilities of an institution under resolution or a bridge bank into an asset management vehicle which is established as a legal entity with a mandate to maximize their value through sale or potential wind-up.

The bail-in tool may be applied only if there is a reasonable prospect of restoring the institution to its financial soundness and long-term viability. The main goals of the bail-in tool are recapitalization of the institution under resolution or conversion to equity or reducing the principal amount of claims or debt instruments that are transferred to a bridge institution or under the sale of business or asset separation tool. The bail-in tool is the most controversial of all resolution tools and it has triggered many discussions within the EU as it gives the right to the resolution authority to easily convert the bail-in-able instruments (non-secured creditors, bondholders, depositors for portion of deposits above €100,000) to bank equity. The provision on bail-in entered into force in January 2016. There are many unanswered questions on the treatment of specific instruments such as derivatives and swaps, which are traditionally a significant part of the banks' liabilities. Banks are obliged to hold a minimum requirement of the eligible liabilities, that is, the minimum percentage of own funds or shares, contingent capital and unsecured liabilities in order to have sufficient bail-in-able instruments. In some countries (e.g. Italy) citizens are unsecured bondholders and if the bail-in tool is applied, as prescribed by the BRRD, their claims from banks would be converted into equity and, although indirectly, citizens would recapitalize a bank directly, for the sake of the public interest. Many technical details related to the conversion are still unknown.

Resolution of a bank within the EU is, in fact, an alternative to normal insolvency proceedings with no use of the public funds. Therefore, banks must contribute to national ex ante resolution funds, in accordance with their risk profiles. The BRRD set a minimum target level for the resolution fund at 1 per cent of covered deposits, by the end of 2024. Sources of funding bank resolution at national levels are ex ante and ex post contributions by banks and borrowing and other forms of support. The use of financial resources which is going to be collected into the resolution fund is strictly prescribed by Article 101 of the BRRD, where funds may be used for providing loans to a bank in the resolution process, bridge bank or asset management vehicle, to guarantee the assets or the liabilities of the bank, bridge bank or asset management vehicle, to purchase assets from a bank, to contribute to the bridge bank or asset management vehicle, to compensate shareholders and creditors in accordance with the BRRD, to provide loans to other national resolution funds (Directive 2014/59/EU 2014, L 173/325).

Up to 30 per cent of total bank's contribution to the bank resolution fund may be in the form of irrevocable payment commitments.

When funds are insufficient, authorities may impose ex post premiums and use alternative funding options (such as borrowing).

Deposit insurance funds and bank resolution funds, although they may be administrated and managed by the same authority, must be kept separate and should not be mixed. Nevertheless, the key question remains for both funds and that is how to ensure sufficient liquidity and solvency in case of a large bank failure especially since resolution funds have only recently been created (in 2015). In situations when the market is small and in development, with a relatively small number of banks that operate, bank resolution may be limited not only by financial resources but also because some resolution tools may not be feasible (sale of a bank) due to the imposed limitations (lack of interested buyers).

In addition, it is a challenge for the policy makers to transpose the EU harmonized rules into the national legislation. The BRRD is written with a high level of harmonization based on many guiding principles which yet have to be developed in regulation or guidelines. In order to be pragmatic and to comply with the basic rules, EU member countries adopted the same principles into their national legislation where details which are relevant for implementation are still in the process of development.

Standardization and harmonization of processes can create many problems for EU member countries that have already had experience with resolution or bank rehabilitation in the past. On the other hand, a large level of discretion when making important decisions and at the same time within the established complex rules on the EU level may create obstacles or prevent quick interventions and solutions.

The decision-making process on bank resolution for the global SIFIs established under the banking union is much more complex, and its success would depend on the close coordination between national and the EU authorities due to a short time frame.

Despite the initial confusion, complexity and many unanswered questions, the EU authorities indicated a strong will to complete the banking union project and develop an overall regulatory framework for banks, in order to minimize fiscal costs in case of bank failures.

However, despite the uniformity of rules and tools, implementation remains challenging, especially for smaller and less developed EU member countries.

First results of the reform will be visible only in case of a cross-border bank's failure which would be a serious test for the EU's deposit insurance and bank resolution framework.

6.9 Conclusion

In spring 2014, after several years of consultations and numerous discussions among the EU member countries, a new recast Directive on the DIS (DGSD) was adopted by the European Parliament, marking a new era and setting new rules on harmonization within Europe. The new DGSD sets more uniformity in deposit protection, broadens and clarifies the scope of coverage, encourages faster payout, improves funding and prescribes obligatory providing of information to depositors.

In parallel, in its attempt to standardize the bank resolution process, the EU introduced a complex set of rules through the BRRD setting new guiding principles and a new philosophy for policy makers when recovering and resolving banks. The BRRD, in principle, prescribes that banks must be better prepared developing their own recovery plans. Supervisors have more powers to intervene sufficiently early, prior to the deterioration of the financial condition of a bank, imposing early intervention measures. If, after all, the bank is failing or about to fail, although still not being insolvent, and if normal insolvency proceedings could jeopardize the financial stability and if the bank is resolvable, one or several standardized resolution tools are at disposal when making a decision on bank resolution. Although bank resolution is in the public interest, its main source of funding is private where costs of banking failure should be borne by bank's shareholders and creditors, not the taxpayers. Contrary to the traditional bank resolution, a failing bank may continue its operation on an ongoing basis, under given circumstances and selected resolution tool.

Two years after the adoption of the two Directives, many controversies remain, many questions still don't have answers and the success of the new regulatory framework is hard to assess. Future bank failure cases will show whether national policy makers are overly concerned about the BRRD implementation and what the critical areas for improvements are.

The relationship between deposit insurance and resolution authorities should be close and formalized and, although the two ex ante funds are separate, their use is strictly prescribed with the same purpose, to minimize the costs of bank failure and to ensure to depositors a faster access to money, in order to preserve financial stability.

Bibliography

Act. 2008. https://eng.forsaetisraduneyti.is/news-and-articles/nr/3037. *Act No. 125/2008*. pokušaj pristupa 2016.

Bergmann, Eirikur. 2016. *The IceSave Disput: Case Study into Crisis of Diplomacy During Credit Crunch*. Unpublished conference proceeding, Draft paper under review. Presented at the conference at University of Akureyri March 19, 2016.

BNB. 2014. http://www.bnb.bg/. http://www.bnb.bg/PressOffice/POPressReleases/POPRDate/PR_20141106_EN.

DIF. 2014. http://dif.bg. http://dif.bg/en/%d0%b8%d0%b7%d0%bf%d0%bb%d0%b0%d1%89%d0%b0%d0%bd%d0%b5-qa/. pokušaj pristupa 2016.

Directive. 1994. *Directive 94/19/EC on Deposit Guarantee Schemes*. Bruxelles. EU.

———. 1999. *DIRECTIVE 2009/14/EC OF THE EUROPEAN PARLIAMENT AND OF THE COUNCIL of 11 March 2009 amending Directive 94/19/EC on Deposit-Guarantee Schemes as Regards the Coverage Level and the Payout Delay.*

Directive 2014/49/EU. 2014. *Directive 2014/49/EU of the European Parliament and of the Council of 16 April 2014 on Deposit Guarantee Schemes*. http://eur-lex.europa.eu/legal-content/EN/TXT/?uri=CELEX:32014L0049. Accessed 2016.

Directive 2014/59/EU. 2014. *Directive 2014/59/EU of the European Parliament and of the Council of 15 May 2014 Establishing a Framework for the Recovery and Resolution of Credit Institutions and Investment Firms and Amending Council Directive 82/891/EEC, and Directives 2001/24/EC, 20*. http://data.europa.eu/eli/dir/2014/59/oj. Accessed 2016.

EBA. 2014. www.eba.europa.eu. https://www.eba.europa.eu/documents/10180/856039/EBA+REC+2014+02+*(Recommendation+to+the+BNB+and+BDIF).pdf*. Accessed 2016.

———. 2015a. Guidelines on Methods for Calculating Contributions to Deposit Guarantee Schemes. https://www.eba.europa.eu/documents/10180/1089322/EBA-GL-2015-10+GL+on+methods+for+calculating+contributions+to+DGS_EN. Accessed 2016.

———. 2015b. *Guidelines on the Interpretation of the Different Circumstances When an Institution Shall Be Considered as Failing or Likely to Fail Under Article 32(6) of Directive 2014/59/EU*. London. EBA.

EC. 1986. *87/63/EEC: Commission Recommendation of 22 December 1986 Concerning the Introduction of Deposit-Guarantee Schemes in the Community Official Journal L 033, 04/02/1987 P. 0016–0017*. Official journal NO. L 033, 04/02/1987 P. 0016–0017.

———. 2008. http://ec.europa.eu. http://ec.europa.eu/competition/state_aid/overview/index_en.html. Accessed 2016.

———. 2010. *Report from the Commission to the European Parliament and to the Council, Review of Directive 94/19/EC on Deposit Guarantee Schemes*. Bruxelles. EU.

———. 2015a. http://europa.eu/rapid/press-release_IP-15-6253_en.htm. Accessed 2016.

———. 2015b. *Proposal for a REGULATION OF THE EUROPEAN PARLIAMENT AND OF THE COUNCIL Amending Regulation (EU)*

806/2014 in Order to Establish a European Deposit Insurance Scheme. http://eur-lex.europa.eu/legal-content/EN/TXT/PDF/?uri=CELEX:52015PC0586&from=EN. Accessed 2016.

EFSF. 2012. http://www.efsf.europa.eu/about/operations/Greece/index.htm. pokušaj pristupa 2016.

EFTA. 2013. www.eftacourt.int. http://www.eftacourt.int/uploads/tx_nvcases/16_11_Judgment_EN.pdf.

EU. 2014. http://europa.eu. September 2014.

JRC. 2010. *JRC Report Under Article 12 of Directive 94/19/EC as Amended by Directive 2009/14/EC; Annex 1*. Bruxelles. European Commission.

Novinite. 2014. http://www.novinite.com. http://www.novinite.com/articles/164266/Audit+Finds+BGN+4.2+B+Impairment+Costs+on+KTB+Balance+Sheet,+Bulgaria+C.+Bank+Says.

SIC. 2010. http://www.rna.is/media/skjol/RNAvefKafli17Enska.pdf. *Chapter 17*. Accessed 2016.

7

Funding Deposit Insurance Schemes in the European Union

7.1 Introduction

Since the DGSD approval, funding the DIS of the EU member countries has become stricter than outside the EU, with a focus on a minimum target fund size at 0.8 per cent of covered deposits, obligatory ex ante regular premium based on banks' risk profiles and the prescribed use of the DIS' funds.

This chapter discusses specifics related to new financing rules in the EU and the use of DIFs for a deposit payout and bank resolution, within the established limitations on target funding, regular and extraordinary DIS funding and cases when the DIS finances the bank resolution process and faces liquidity insufficiency. Using the DIS' funds is enabled with the aim of financing alternative measures, as well.

Examples are given related to the compliance with the established minimum target fund size and the required adjustments of the annual regular premium, as well as to the mutual DIS borrowing options.

D. Ognjenovic, *Deposit Insurance Schemes*,
DOI 10.1007/978-3-319-51143-6_7

7.2 Implementing New Financing Rules in the EU Member DISs

The DGSD prescribed financing and uses of funds in a strict manner. When compared to the rest of the world, it is more rigid and specific. One of the policy's principles set out in the DGSD is that member countries shall ensure that their national DISs have adequate financial resources or relevant financial arrangements to meet their obligations.

The DIS funding, as prescribed by the DGSD, may be collected via:

(i) annual regular premium,
(ii) extraordinary premium up to 0.5 per cent of covered deposits and
(iii) alternative funding arrangements.

In addition, the DISs are, conditionally, allowed to use two other financing options:

(iv) soft-borrowing from the resolution fund and
(v) borrowing from other DISs on a voluntary basis.

The DGSD prescribes the target level of funds in the amount of 0.8 per cent of the insured deposits to be reached by July 2024.

The Directive prescribes that the banks pay a regular premium at least on an annual basis. It is more convenient to pay premiums on a quarterly basis in order to offset the cyclical effects of a onetime premium collection and for easier financial management of DIFs. Some member countries collect premium once per year, usually by the end of Quarter 1 of the current year for the previous year.

The DGSD does not prescribe other details regarding the premium except that the premium level should be applied to the amount of covered deposits and that it should be based on risk exposure toward individual banks. In addition, a maximum of 30 per cent of the annual premium contribution may be in the form of payment commitments.

Evidently, there was a need to make uniform the premium basis and the minimum target fund size, allowing individual member banks to apply the annual regular premium to the level which they consider appropriate to be proportional to their potential liabilities. In other words, individual member banks must understand their potential liabilities in order to be able to collect sufficient funding. The prescribed minimum target fund size is the minimum harmonized level and member countries are encouraged to establish the target fund size level which would be the most appropriate in their national circumstances.

As evidenced from Table 7.1, EU member countries applied different funding options prior to the harmonization of funding prescribed

Table 7.1 DIS' funding in EU member countries, 2010

	EU member countries	Annual premium, in percentage	Premium base	Extra-ordinary premium	Borrowing
1	Austria	ex post	Covered deposits	No	Possible
2	Belgium	0.0175	Eligible deposits	Possible	Not allowed
3	Bulgaria	0.5	Eligible deposits	No	Possible
4	Croatia	0.5	Covered deposits	Possible	Possible
5	Cyprus	0.3	Eligible deposits	Possible	Possible
6	The Czech Republic	0.1	Eligible deposits	Possible	Possible
7	Denmark	Only when the DIF is below minimum	Covered deposits	Possible	Possible
8	Estonia	0.36	Eligible deposits	Possible	Possible
9	Finland	0.175	Covered deposits	No	Possible
10	France	risk-based	Eligible deposits	Possible	Possible
11	Germany	0.016	Eligible deposits	Possible	Possible
12	Greece	up to 0.625	Eligible deposits	No	Possible
13	Hungary	up to 0.05	Eligible deposits	Possible	Possible
14	Ireland	0.2	Total	Possible	Not allowed

(*continued*)

Table 7.1 (continued)

	EU member countries	Annual premium, in percentage	Premium base	Extra-ordinary premium	Borrowing
15	Italy	ex post	Covered deposits	No	Not allowed
16	Latvia	0.2	Eligible deposits	No	Not allowed
17	Lithuania	0.45	Eligible deposits	No	Possible
18	Luxembourg	ex post	Eligible deposits	No	Possible
19	Malta	0.1	Eligible deposits	No	Possible
20	The Netherlands	ex post	Other	No	Not allowed
21	Poland	12.5 times the sum of total capital requirements	Other	No	Possible
22	Portugal	up to 0.27	Eligible deposits	No	Possible
23	Romania	0.1	Eligible deposits	Possible	Possible
24	Slovakia	up to 0.75	Eligible deposits	Possible	Possible
25	Slovenia	ex post	Covered deposits	No	Not allowed
26	Spain	up to 0.08	Eligible deposits	Possible	Possible
27	Sweden	0.1	Covered deposits	No	Possible
28	The United Kingdom	ex post	Other	No	Possible

by the DGSD. Six member countries used ex post funding. Member countries with an established ex ante DIF charged the annual premium level ranging from a fixed 0.01 per cent up to a maximum of 1.875 per cent. Some member countries had the possibility to adjust annual regular premium. Many member countries did not have the option to apply an extraordinary premium in case of liquidity gaps at all. Even the premium base differed, where only seven member countries used covered deposits as a premium base.

The differences among EU member countries related to the target fund level are even more obvious. As evidenced from Table 7.2, half of the member countries did not have the target fund size level in 2007. A few of those member countries which had established target levels projected the required funds in an absolute amount, not in relation to their potential liabilities. Only six member countries established the target fund size level in relation to the covered deposits, that is, to their potential liability. It may be concluded that target funding was not used as a tool for financial planning in EU member countries before the adoption of the DGSD.

However, the situation has changed in favor of target funding. Target funding is obligatory and, although the DGSD prescribed the minimum target fund size level at 0.8 per cent of covered deposits, some member countries decided to establish an even higher target fund size (Poland and Croatia lead with 2.6 per cent and 2.5 per cent of total covered deposits, respectively), which is evident in Table 7.2.

Table 7.2 Comparison of target fund size level in EU member countries in 2007 and in 2016

	EU member countries	Target fund level, 2007		Target fund level, May 2016	
		Per cent	Basis	Per cent	Basis
1	Austria	No	No	0.80	Covered deposits
2	Belgium	No	No	na	na
3	Bulgaria	5.00	Eligible deposits	1.00	Covered deposits
4	Croatia	2.50	Covered deposits	2.50	Covered deposits
5	Cyprus	No	No	0.80	Covered deposits
6	The Czech Republic	No	No	1.50	Covered deposits
7	Denmark	€429.5 million	No	0.80	Covered deposits
8	Estonia	2.00	Eligible deposits	0.80	Covered deposits

(*continued*)

Table 7.2 (continued)

	EU member countries	Target fund level, 2007		Target fund level, May 2016	
		Per cent	Basis	Per cent	Basis
9	Finland	2.00–10.00	Covered deposits	0.80	Covered deposits
10	France	€1.5 billion	No	na	na
11	Germany	No	No	0.80	Covered deposits
12	Greece	No	No	1.00	Covered deposits
13	Hungary	Confidential	Confidential	Confidential	na
14	Ireland	0.20	Covered deposits	0.80	Covered deposits
15	Italy	0.80	Covered deposits	0.80	Covered deposits
16	Latvia	No	No	0.80	Covered deposits
17	Lithuania	3.00–4.00	Eligible deposits	2.00	Covered deposits
18	Luxembourg	No	No	0.80	Covered deposits
19	Malta	€7 million	No	1.30	Covered deposits
20	The Netherlands	No	No	0.80	Covered deposits
21	Poland	No	No	0.8–2.60*	Covered deposits
22	Portugal	No	No	na	na
23	Romania	2.30	Covered deposits	0.80	Covered deposits
24	Slovakia	1.50	Covered deposits	0.80	Covered deposits
25	Slovenia	No	No	0.80	Covered deposits
26	Spain	1.00	Eligible deposits	1.00	Covered deposits
27	Sweden	No	No	0.80	Covered deposits
28	The United Kingdom	No	No	0.80	Covered deposits

"Poland established two target funds for member banks:

(a) minimum target fund level of 0.8 per cent of covered deposits (by the end of 2016) and
(b) target fund level of 2.6 per cent of covered deposits (by 3 July 2030).

Additionally, the Polish DIS established two identical target fund levels with the same time frame for credit unions.

Now, all member countries must set their target fund size in relation to covered deposits. As in the past some member countries applied an established target fund size level to eligible deposits (which is higher than covered deposits), a newly established lower target fund size which is applied to covered deposits would result in, de facto, a lower target funding. Member countries which applied ex post funding are now focusing on building the DIF almost from scratch.

Member countries must comply with the minimum target fund size within ten years, that is, by July 2024, with some possible exceptions.

The initial timeframe may be prolonged for four years, that is, until July 2028, if during the transition period the DIS experienced a cumulative deposit payout in excess of 0.8 per cent of the covered deposits.

However, if the DIS had already reached the minimum target fund size level, yet its funds are being decreased to less than two-thirds (0.666 per cent), the regular annual premium could be set to the level allowing reaching the target level again within six years.

The decision on the target level was a very important issue where the European Parliament and the EU Council could not reach the agreement which delayed the adoption of the DGSD. The European Parliament wanted the target level to be set at a minimum of 1.5 per cent, while the EU Council did not want it higher than 0.5 per cent. After several years of negotiations, it was finally agreed to set the minimum target level at 0.8 per cent of the covered deposits.

The EU authorities may be criticized for setting a uniform minimum target ratio at 0.8 per cent which is linear for all member countries ('one fit for all' approach). The EU's minimum target fund does not take into account specific characteristics of the national banking sectors; nor does it capture the risks they face.

The concentration of the banking sector and the ratio of SIFIs in total banks are important elements for the credibility of the target fund size.

The DGSD even allows that banking sectors which are highly concentrated may, as an exception, set the minimum target fund size at 0.5 per cent.

However, in countries with a small number of banks and with a highly concentrated banking sector, the target ratio of 0.8 per cent can be reached easily and fast, but the collected funds would not provide sufficient assurance to the public and the DIS would lack financial robustness.

By complying with the 0.8 per cent prescribed target fund size, the DIS does not ensure sufficient funding at all as long as the covered deposits of its risky banks represent more than 0.8 per cent of the total covered deposits. This is the strongest criticism on the target ratio for EU member countries.

Indeed, the EU's DISs are allowed to set the target fund size to levels higher than 0.8 per cent if they think it is appropriate and necessary. Therefore, the EU members should be encouraged to conduct an analysis of their banking sector regularly and adjust the rules as much as possible to their national circumstances, within the prescribed limits and benchmarks.

The DGSD implies that once the DIS reaches the target level and if there are no payouts which would exhaust the amount of available financial resources, the collection of premium might stop or decrease. This was not said explicitly, but it may lead to such a conclusion as the DGSD states in Article 10(2) the following: 'Where the financing capacity falls short of the target level, the payment of contributions **shall resume** at least **until the target level is reached again**'(2014/49/EU 2014, L 173/164).

More specifically, Article 10(2) of the DGSD further prescribes in detail how to proceed with financing if the target level is reached for the first time and if financial resources fall below two-thirds of the target funds, allowing a six-year timeframe in order to reach the target level again.

7.2.1 Example: Target Funding in the DIS' of EU Member Countries

The example below illustrates target funding for the DIS of EU member countries, using the basic assumptions:

- covered deposits at €100,000
- annual growth of covered deposits by 5 per cent,
- target fund size is 0.8 per cent by Year 10, that is, €518,000,000 by the end of Year 10
- annual regular premium is set at 0.2 per cent,
- when the DIS reaches the target fund size of 0.8 per cent (planned at the end of Year 6), the DIS plans to reduce the annual regular premium by 50 per cent for the remaining period,
- however, Bank number 8 fails at the beginning of Year 7
- in Year 7, the DIS must project how much the annual regular premium should apply in order to reach the target by the end of Year 10 and adjust the annual premium level accordingly.

The projected target funding of an EU member's DIS for a ten-year period is given in Table 7.3. The initial calculation (without any bank failures) projects the target fund size by the end of Year 10 in the amount of €518mil. With the applied 0.2 per cent annual premium, the target will be reached much more in advance by the end of Year 6. Although the DIS can set the annual regular premium lower than 0.1 per cent, it was decided to initially collect the annual premium at 0.2 per cent annually and, once the target fund is reached, to apply a lower annual regular premium level.

Due to the unexpected failure of Bank number 8 at the beginning of Year 7, where the DIS had to compensate more than €527 million of covered deposits (0.99 per cent of covered deposits at the end of Year 6), the total DIF was decreased to a 0.24 per cent of the covered deposits at the end of Year 7.

Table 7.3 Projection of target fund in EU DIS, in €000

Banks	Year 0	Year 1	Year 2	Year 3	Year 4	Year 5	Year 6	Year 7	Year 8	Year 9	Year 10
10	3,040	3,192	3,352	3,519	3,695	3,880	4,074	4,278	4,491	4,716	4,952
9	90,000	94,500	99,225	104,186	109,396	114,865	120,609	126,639	132,971	139,620	146,601
8	375,000	393,750	413,438	434,109	455,815	478,606	502,536	0	0	0	0
6	1,100,000	1,155,000	1,212,750	1,273,388	1,337,057	1,403,910	1,474,105	1,547,810	1,625,201	1,706,461	1,791,784
7	1,300,000	1,365,000	1,433,250	1,504,913	1,580,158	1,659,166	1,742,124	1,829,231	1,920,692	2,016,727	2,117,563
5	1,600,000	1,680,000	1,764,000	1,852,200	1,944,810	2,042,051	2,144,153	2,251,361	2,363,929	2,482,125	2,606,231
4	4,000,000	4,200,000	4,410,000	4,630,500	4,862,025	5,105,126	5,360,383	5,628,402	5,909,822	6,205,313	6,515,579
3	6,400,000	6,720,000	7,056,000	7,408,800	7,779,240	8,168,202	8,576,612	9,005,443	9,455,715	9,928,501	10,424,926
2	10,200,000	10,710,000	11,245,500	11,807,775	12,398,164	13,018,072	13,668,976	14,352,424	15,070,046	15,823,548	16,614,725
1	14,749,000	15,486,450	16,260,773	17,073,811	17,927,502	18,823,877	19,765,071	20,753,324	21,790,990	22,880,540	24,024,567
Total	**39,817,040**	**41,807,892**	**43,898,287**	**46,093,201**	**48,397,861**	**50,817,754**	**53,358,642**	**55,498,911**	**58,273,857**	**61,187,550**	**64,246,927**
Target 0.8 per cent											**513,975**
Premium 0.2 per cent; 0.21 per cent	79,634	83,616	87,797	92,186	96,796	50,818	53,359	116,548	122,375	128,494	134,919
Payout								527,000			
DIF	**79,634**	**163,250**	**251,046**	**343,233**	**440,029**	**490,846**	**544,205**	**133,753**	**256,128**	**384,622**	**519,540**
Actual coverage ratio, per cent	**0.20**	**0.39**	**0.57**	**0.74**	**0.91**	**0.97**	**1.02**	**0.24**	**0.44**	**0.63**	**0.81**

The DIS must reconsider its funding policy and re-calculate the annual regular premium level in order to reach the minimum target fund size level either:

(a) within the prescribed time frame or
(b) to use the legal possibility to prolong the initial time frame for a maximum of 4 years in accordance with Article 10(2) of the DGSD (2014/49/EU 2014, L 173/165).

A DIS has to conduct simple recalculation of target fund size by the end of Year 10 and determine its financial gap, in order to establish new annual regular premium.

As evidenced in Table 7.4, a DIS conducted two calculations for each possible option.

First, a DIS considers reaching the target within initial prescribed timeframe of ten years. Recalculated target fund size by the end of Year 10 is €514 million, whereas a DIS has a gap in amount of €496 million to be collected over four years (because a failure of a bank occurred at the beginning of Year 7 there are four years to reach the target by the end of Year 10).

Table 7.4 Recalculation of target and annual premium

Reaching the target fund size level by the end of Year 10	
Re-calculated target DIF by the end of Year 10, in €000	513,975
Actual DIF after payout in Year 7, in €000	17,205
Target DIF gap to be collected over 4 years, in €000	496,770
Minimum required annual premium over 4 years, in €000	124,193
Average covered deposits over 4 years, in €000	59,801,811
Minimum annual premium level, in percentage	0.207673668
New annual premium level, in percentage	0.21
Reaching the target fund size level by the end of Year 14	
Projected target DIF by the end of Year 14, in €000	624,740
Actual DIF after payout in Year 7, in €000	17,205
Target DIF gap to be collected over 8 years, in €000	607,535
Minimum required annual premium over 8 years, in €000	75,942
Average covered deposits over 4 years, in €000	66,245,643,14
Minimum annual premium level, in percentage	0.114636792
New annual premium level, in percentage	0.11

By dividing the amount of needed annual premium (€124 million) by remaining number of years (4), a minimum annual premium level is recalculated at 0.21 per cent. If a DIS applies 0.21 per cent of annual premium level over the next four years, it would be able to reach the target as prescribed by the DGSD by the end of Year 10.

Alternatively, the DIS could use the option to prolong the time frame for reaching the minimum target fund size level by the end of Year 14. Therefore, the DIS conducts another calculation in a similar manner and determines that in such case the annual premium level could be set at 0.11 per cent over eight years in order to be able to comply with the target fund size level by the end of Year 14.

Legally, both options are possible and in line with the DGSD. However, the DIS must decide whether it is better to be 'on the safe side' and collect 0.8 per cent of the total covered deposits rather earlier than later. The structure of its banking sector is such that 0.8 per cent does not provide sufficient assurance to the DIS and depositors. Therefore, unless the recalculated annual premium level at 0.21 per cent of the covered deposits jeopardizes liquidity and profitability of the member banks, for the system as a whole it is better to establish a more robust DIF earlier by the end of Year 10.

Obviously, the DIS must analyze its financing more seriously and in parallel with understanding the soundness of the banks, at all time. As a result of the learned facts, the deposit insurance authority should be able to conduct a proactive financial management and adjust its funding to real situations and funding needs in order to be able to establish and maintain its credibility over a longer period of time. Therefore, it should be able to adjust the annual regular premium to ensure not only compliance with the EU deposit insurance rules but also the financial robustness of the DIS. Pure compliance with the DGSD requests would not guarantee the sufficiency of funds. The DIS might fully comply with the DGSD but be financially weak and unable to repay the depositors on time.

In order to be a credible DIS, the national authorities should decide to set the target fund size which is higher than the prescribed minimum EU target fund size and apply an active risk assessment of banks, however, not breaking the established EU minimum thresholds.

The DIS might use a strategy, similar to our example, to set the target fund size at the minimum level as prescribed by the DGSD, but to shorten the time frame for reaching it. However, after the initial compliance with the minimum set target fund rules, national DISs should adjust the target fund size level and the annual premium level to their circumstances. When deciding to do so, the DIS is given more options on a proactive financial management compared with the DIS that set the minimum target level as prescribed by the DGSD over an allowed timeframe.

It is clear that the projections are not 100 per cent certain as they are based on various assumptions and uncertainties. It is also clear that the DIS can't ignore the need for a better understanding of the banks' risk profiles. Ignorance and passive financial management may result in the insufficiency of required funds. Regular monitoring of developments in the real economy and the banking sector as a whole, as well as in individual member banks, will facilitate the DIS to respond to the changing circumstances.

The DGSD envisages that the premium may be collected in cash, but member banks may also provide payment commitments, in the amount not higher than 30 per cent of the total DIFs. Those payment commitments must be fully collateralized providing that the collateral consists of low-risk assets and is unencumbered by any third-party rights and is at disposal to the DIS. A similar funding option existed in Iceland, prior to the financial crisis in 2008, and payment commitments (in the form of different 'I owe you' instruments) were of little use in the moment when the banks became insolvent.

Obviously, this form of funding is a legacy of different funding options that existed in the past in some EU member countries. Most likely, the member countries which used ex post funding would use a certain share of payment commitments in total funding. It is less likely that those DISs which had never used payment commitments or other form of ex post funding would start using them from now on. Payment commitments, as prescribed by the EU legislation, are a legacy from the past and a form of transition from ex post to ex ante funding of the deposit insurance schemes in the European Union.

The DGSD allows a member country to establish the minimum target level lower than 0.8 per cent, but not lower than 0.5 per cent of insured deposits, if it justifies its assumptions to the European Commission which has the authority to approve or disapprove them. The DIS must meet two conditions in such case. The first condition is based on the assumption that a significant amount of DIFs is unlikely to be used for alternative measures as prescribed by Article 11 of the Directive (instead for the deposit payout), for financing the transfer of deposits and assets into a sound bank and for financing the resolution, as prescribed in Article 109 of the BRRD (Directive 2014/59/EU 2014, L 173/331–332). The second condition is that the banking sector is highly concentrated with a small number of banks holding a large quantity of assets and their failure would be, according to their size, subject to resolution proceedings, not deposit payout.

The DGSD allows 'soft borrowing' from the resolution fund up to the amount of the target level, if own available funds are below it, in case the DIS is not able to raise funds through extraordinary contributions, based on an opinion provided by the competent authority, and for the purpose of the deposit payout and usage of funds as prescribed by the DGSD. The DIS must repay the borrowed money through the collected membership premium.

If the DIFs are not sufficient, the DIS is entitled to collect an extraordinary premium, not higher than 0.5 per cent of insured deposits in one calendar year. Exceptionally, the DIS may collect the extraordinary premium in the amount higher than 0.5 per cent of the insured deposits annually, with the prior consent of the national competent authority and under exceptional circumstances. Based on its findings and assumption on the possible jeopardized liquidity or solvency of the banks, the national competent authority may postpone, partially or entirely, the bank's payment of the extraordinary ex post premium to the DIS. Such delay should be granted only up to six months and may be prolonged upon the request of the bank.

In addition to the extraordinary premium, the DGSD prescribes that the DIS must ensure adequate alternative funding arrangements in order to obtain short-term funding for the deposit payout. The DGSD does not provide any details on possible alternative funding arrangements, leaving the options to national jurisdictions. Alternative funding arrangements are, in fact, borrowing facilities from the public and private sources which would enable the DIS to gain fast access to liquidity when necessary and to conclude pre-arranged agreements with the government which would provide additional assurance in case when the financial stability is in jeopardy. Pre-arranged standby facilities, although not free of charge, are efficient and credible financial instruments in case of liquidity gaps.

7.3 Rules on the Use of Funds in the EU's DISs

The DGSD triggered many discussions among its member countries on issues related to the use of the DIS funds. It prescribes the use of the DIS funds in Article 11 (2014/49/EU 2014, L 173/166–167), as follows:

- The DIS financial resources shall be used for:

  (i) payout of depositors, primarily and, in addition, for
  (ii) financing resolution of credit institutions, in accordance with Article 109 of the BRRD.

- Conditionally, the DIS financial resources may be used for:

  (iii) alternative measures in order to prevent bank failure.

- In addition, when the DIS financial resources are used in the context of insolvency proceedings, funds may be used to finance measures to preserve access of depositors to covered deposits including:

  (iv) transfer of assets and liabilities (and deposit transfer), provided that the costs do not exceed the net amount of the covered deposit.

In other words, there are: (i) mandatory and (ii) voluntary use of the DIS funds.

The mandatory use of the DIS funds refers to the payout of depositors in insolvency proceedings and in financing bank resolution.

The voluntary use of the DIS funds is for alternative measures, in the pre-resolution period and in the payout of deposits when the transfer of assets and liabilities occurs.

Clearly, the EU's DISs are, by default, becoming paybox plus DISs, although primarily they use financial resources for the deposit payout, within a prescribed timeframe. In addition, the use of DIFs in financing resolution procedures is mandatory.

Namely, Article 11(2) of the DGSD states that funds '**shall** be used in financing resolution procedures' (Directive 2014/59/EU 2014, L 173/166). Resolution authorities are entitled to determine the amount of the DIS's liability, after consultations with the DIS.

It means that the resolution authority, which in some cases differs from the deposit insurance legal entity, would calculate the amount of the DIS's obligation, share the information with the deposit insurance authority and then discuss it jointly.

Member countries may decide to expand the use of DIFs for alternative measures, in order to prevent bank failure only if certain prescribed conditions are met. In such cases, DISs would be given a broadened least cost mandate.

And, lastly, the use of DIFs in P&A transactions within insolvency proceedings is a possibility, although this is, obviously, a copy-paste situation from the international practice where the P&A is a resolution method per se.

It is noted that the DIS has a limitation for using funds in resolution but such limitation does not exist if funds are used for financing alternative measures in banks. That is unusual given the fact that the DIS use funds as mandatory tools in financing bank resolution.

Strong criticism relates to the fact that the use of DIFs is not fully prescribed within the DGSD. Namely, for a clear understanding of the use of the DIFs, one must carefully read the DGSD (Article 11) and the BRRD (Article 109) in parallel.

7.3.1 Use of the DIS' Funds for Payout

The DGSD does not provide any details on how the DIS should organize the payout of covered deposits. It is up to each country to determine its envisaged payout procedure. The payout process starts when a bank is in insolvency proceedings (liquidation or bankruptcy). Deposits may be paid in cash or transferred into accounts of another bank. Some countries send checks or use special cards for the withdrawal of insured amounts at ATMs. The chosen method of payout is based on usual transactions used by banks, the kind that the depositors are familiar with.

In addition, the DIS may use funds to finance the transfer of assets and liabilities in the context of insolvency proceedings where the financing amount must be lower than the covered deposits at that particular bank.

7.3.1.1 Example: The EU's DIS' Use of Funds for a Deposit Payout: Options for Funding Liquidity Gaps

The following example illustrates a challenging situation for a EU member DIS facing insufficient liquidity required for a deposit payout, using the following assumptions:

- Covered deposits growth of 3 per cent annually.
- Target fund size is at 0.8 per cent within the prescribed timeframe by the end of Year 10.
- The DIS set the annual regular premium at 0.0828 per cent.
- The bank number 8 fails at the beginning of year 3.

The DIS uses the projection of its funding over ten years, using the given assumptions, as illustrated in Table 7.5. At the end of Year 2, the DIS collected €102 million, which is insufficient to compensate the insured depositors of Bank number 8, where the total required funds are €410 million. At that particular moment, the deposit insurance authority must make certain decisions in order to finance its liquidity insufficiency, such as either:

(i) collecting the extraordinary premium up to 0.5 per cent of covered deposits unless the competent authority defers its payment and if the

Table 7.5 Financing the liquidity insufficiency with extraordinary premium and borrowing, in €000

Banks	Year 0	Year 1	Year 2	Year 3	Year 4	Year 5	Year 6	Year 7	Year 8	Year 9	Year 10
10	3,040	3,131	3,225	3,322	3,422	3,524	3,630	3,739	3,851	3,967	4,086
9	90,000	92,700	95,481	98,345	101,296	104,335	107,465	110,689	114,009	117,430	120,952
8	375,000	386,250	397,838	**409,773**	0	0	0	0	0	0	0
6	1,100,000	1,133,000	1,166,990	1,202,000	1,238,060	1,275,201	1,313,458	1,352,861	1,393,447	1,435,251	1,478,308
7	1,300,000	1,339,000	1,379,170	1,420,545	1,463,161	1,507,056	1,552,268	1,598,836	1,646,801	1,696,205	1,747,091
5	1,600,000	1,648,000	1,697,440	1,748,363	1,800,814	1,854,839	1,910,484	1,967,798	2,026,832	2,087,637	2,150,266
4	4,000,000	4,120,000	4,243,600	4,370,908	4,502,035	4,637,096	4,776,209	4,919,495	5,067,080	5,219,093	5,375,666
3	6,400,000	6,592,000	6,789,760	6,993,453	7,203,256	7,419,354	7,641,935	7,871,193	8,107,329	8,350,548	8,601,065
2	10,200,000	10,506,000	10,821,180	11,145,815	11,480,190	11,824,596	12,179,333	12,544,713	12,921,055	13,308,686	13,707,947
1	14,749,000	15,191,470	15,647,214	16,116,631	16,600,129	17,098,133	17,611,077	18,139,410	18,683,592	19,244,100	19,821,423
Total	**39,817,040**	**41,011,551**	**42,241,898**	**43,509,155**	**44,392,364**	**45,724,134**	**47,095,858**	**48,508,734**	**49,963,996**	**51,462,916**	**53,006,804**
Min target 0.8 per cent											**424,054**
Regular premium (0.0828 per cent; 0.15 per cent)	32,988	33,977	34,996	36,046	**66,589**	68,586	70,644	72,763	74,946	77,194	79,510
ex post premium 0.5 per cent – option				217,546							
DIF	**32,988**	**66,965**	**101,961**	**-54,219**	**9,619**	**76,328**	**146,010**	**218,773**	**293,719**	**370,913**	**450,423**
Borrowing				**55,000**							
DIS liquid funds				**781**	**67,369**	**115,759**	**166,206**	**218,773**	**293,719**	**370,913**	**450,423**
Loan repayment (3 yrs, 5 per cent)					**-20,196**	**-20,196**	**-20,196**				
DIS liquid funds after loan					**47,173**	**95,562**	**146,010**				
Actual coverage ratio, per cent	0.08	0.16	0.24	-0.12	0.02	0.17	0.31	0.45	0.59	0.72	0.85

total available funds are still insufficient to borrow money on the market; or

(ii) borrowing the funds from the resolution fund, if possible.

Before the DIS makes its final decision, it should conduct analysis of two possible options: collection of extraordinary premium and alternative funding or soft borrowing from the bank resolution fund.

(i) *Collection of extraordinary premium and alternative funding (borrowing on the market)*

When the DIS faces insufficient funds, the first option it should consider is to raise the extraordinary premium, as it is prescribed by the DGSD. The DIS is allowed to collect the extraordinary premium at the highest possible level of 0.5 per cent annually, or alternatively seek permission from its competent authority to impose an even higher extraordinary premium. The DIS lacks €272 million in total, whereas the extraordinary premium could provide only €217 million, leaving a liquidity gap in the amount of €55 million. However, the competent authority advised not to apply a higher extraordinary premium than 0.5 per cent, due to the liquidity burden on banks. Thus, the DIS must turn to alternative funding that is borrowing in the amount of €55 million.

Assuming that the DIS had pre-arranged alternative funding options and approved procedures, a loan in the amount of €55 million should be arranged in a fast manner.

The DIS successfully arranged a three-year loan at a 5 per cent interest rate. Payments would be made in equal annual installments over the next three years.

Table 7.5 illustrates the DIS' projection of the funding requirements, extraordinary and alternative funding options and loan repayments over the agreed timeframe. In addition, Table 7.5 presents the recalculated annual regular premium in the amount that is sufficient to repay the loan and comply with the recalculated target fund level by the end of Year 10.

The DIS financed its liquidity gap as follows: €217 million are provided by banks (non-refundable funds) in Year 3 and €55 million is a loan, at a 5 per cent interest rate over three years.

The obtained loan is not a part of the DIS's own funds and thus it does not increase the total DIF. The obtained loan is only an instrument for financing liquidity insufficiency. Therefore, at the end of Year 3, the DIS has €781,000 liquid funds, although its DIF is insolvent by €54 million. When the DIS obtains a loan it increases its liquidity. When the DIS repays the loan, the principal amount of repayment decreases the liquidity, but the interest rate payment finances the expense for the DIS, decreasing the total amount of the DIF.

As presented in Table 7.5, the DIS would repay its loan in the amount of €20,196,000 annually (€60,589,000 total) in Years 4 to 6, whereas the total interests are €5,589,000.

Based on the projections of the initial repayment of the loan, the DIS recalculates the annual regular premium level and projects the cash flow for the whole period of reaching the target fund size.

The DIS recalculated the target fund size in the amount of €424 million by the end of Year 10 and the total financial gap to the targeted amount in the amount of €478 million (target fund size increased by the negative DIF amount of €55 million).

Based on the initial recalculation of the annual regular premium, the DIS decides to apply 0.15 per cent of the annual regular premium starting from Year 4 to the end of Year 10. By applying the regular premium level at 0.15 per cent, the DIS would be able to repay the loan as envisaged by the loan agreement and reach the target fund size by the end of Year 10.

Additionally, the DIS again has the option to prolong the timeframe for the target fund size by four years. In such a case, the new recalculated annual premium should provide sufficient funds over the remaining 11 years. If a larger bank failed, this could be an option. However, in the case when the financial gap is not significant and it is feasible to reach the target fund size level over the initial established timeframe, the DIS decided not to prolong the timeframe for four years.

(ii) *Borrowing from the resolution fund up to the target fund size*

The DIS had another legal option, that is, to borrow from the resolution fund. If the DIS cannot obtain extraordinary premiums from member banks due to the negative opinion of its competent authority, it is entitled to raise funds from the resolution fund, up to the target fund size level, as prescribed by the DGSD Article 10(4) paragraph 2(2014/49/EU 2014, L 173/165).

The DIS may borrow from the resolution fund up to the 0.8 per cent of its covered deposits and the borrowed money must be used exclusively for the purposes prescribed by Article 11 of the DGSD. The DIS must return the borrowed funds from the collected regular premium by mid-2024.

The DIS continues analysis of its funding options, as presented in Table 7.6. It faces liquidity insufficiency in the amount of €272 million, so it qualifies for the liquidity borrowing from the resolution fund. By arranging the borrowing from the resolution fund without interest payment, under the assumption that the funds are repaid on time, the DIS must raise the regular premium to 0.24 per cent annually in order to collect sufficient funds over the remaining 7 years to: (i) repay the amount of €272 million and to (ii) reach the minimum target of 0.8 per cent by Year 10.

The DIS must repay almost €39 million annually to the resolution fund, over the remaining seven years.

The DIS has an overall financial gap in the amount of €696 million (424 million target increased by 272 million loan). The new recalculated annual regular premium at 0.24 per cent would ensure sufficient liquidity over the next seven years to restore the solvency of the DIF up to 0.8 per cent and repay the borrowed funds to the resolution fund.

The question is whether the resolution fund may provide sufficient liquidity and whether it can afford to provide the loan during the required timeframe (in this example seven years).

However, it is once again proven that the deposit insurance authority and the bank resolution authority must cooperate. The final decision on the financing options must be made in line with what is feasible and favorable for all parties involved.

When considering all possible funding options, the DIS must take into account many variables. In this particular case, it weights the costs and benefits for the DIS and for the banks. In case when the banks must supply 0.5 per cent annually in the form of an extraordinary premium payment, they may face a sudden liquidity pressure due to the fact that the funds must be obtained in a short period of time and at once. In

Table 7.6 Financing the liquidity insufficiency with the borrowing from the resolution fund, in €000

Banks	2014	2015	2016	2017	2018	2019	2020	2021	2022	2023	2024
10	3,040	3,131	3,225	3,322	3,422	3,524	3,630	3,739	3,851	3,967	4,086
9	90,000	92,700	95,481	98,345	101,296	104,335	107,465	110,689	114,009	117,430	120,952
8	375,000	386,250	397,838	**409,773**	0	0	0	0	0	0	0
6	1,100,000	1,133,000	1,166,990	1,202,000	1,238,060	1,275,201	1,313,458	1,352,861	1,393,447	1,435,251	1,478,308
7	1,300,000	1,339,000	1,379,170	1,420,545	1,463,161	1,507,056	1,552,268	1,598,836	1,646,801	1,696,205	1,747,091
5	1,600,000	1,648,000	1,697,440	1,748,363	1,800,814	1,854,839	1,910,484	1,967,798	2,026,832	2,087,637	2,150,266
4	4,000,000	4,120,000	4,243,600	4,370,908	4,502,035	4,637,096	4,776,209	4,919,495	5,067,080	5,219,093	5,375,666
3	6,400,000	6,592,000	6,789,760	6,993,453	7,203,256	7,419,354	7,641,935	7,871,193	8,107,329	8,350,548	8,601,065
2	10,200,000	10,506,000	10,821,180	11,145,815	11,480,190	11,824,596	12,179,333	12,544,713	12,921,055	13,308,686	13,707,947
1	14,749,000	15,191,470	15,647,214	16,116,631	16,600,129	17,098,133	17,611,077	18,139,410	18,683,592	19,244,100	19,821,423
Total	**39,817,040**	**41,011,551**	**42,241,898**	**43,509,155**	**44,392,364**	**45,724,134**	**47,095,858**	**48,508,734**	**49,963,996**	**51,462,916**	**53,006,804**
Min target 0.8 per cent											**424,054**
Regular premium (0.0828 per cent; 0.24 per cent)	32,988	33,977	34,996	36,046	**106,542**	**109,738**	**113,030**	**116,421**	**119,914**	**123,511**	**127,216**
Borrowing from the resolution fund				**271,765**							
DIF	**32,988**	**66,965**	**101,961**	**-271,765**	**-165,223**	**-55,486**	**57,545**	**173,966**	**293,879**	**417,390**	**544,606**
DIS liquid funds before repayment					**106,542**	**177,456**	**251,662**	**329,259**	**410,348**	**495,035**	**583,428**
Loan repayment					**-38,824**	**-38,824**	**-38,824**	**-38,824**	**-38,824**	**-38,824**	**-38,824**
DIS liquid funds after repayment					**67,718**	**138,632**	**212,838**	**290,435**	**371,524**	**456,211**	**544,604**
Actual coverage ratio, per cent	0.08	0.16	0.24	-0.62	-0.37	-0.12	0.12	0.36	0.59	0.81	1.03

Table 7.7 Calculation of funding costs for banks, using NPV at 5 per cent

Comparison of costs for banks	In €000
Banks pay extraordinary premium of 0.5 per cent in Year 3 and annual regular premium of 0.15 per cent in the period from Year 4 to the end of Year 10	636,892
Banks pay annual regular premium 0.24 per cent in the period from Year 4 to the end of Year 10	670,955

addition, in order to repay the loan arranged at the market, the DIS must increase the annual regular premium up to 0.15 per cent over seven years (the first considered option).

When the national competent authority doesn't give the consent for the collection of an extraordinary premium, the DIS must increase the annual regular premium over seven years up to 0.24 per cent.

Applying the net present value (NPV) calculation on both future cash flows at a 5 per cent interest rate, the DIS compares the net cost for banks in both cases. As presented in Table 7.7 it is less expensive for the banks if the DIS chooses the first option that is applying the extraordinary premium in Year 3 at 0.5 per cent and increasing the regular annual premium up to 0.15 per cent over 7 years, as they would provide €637 million in total, whereas the second option of borrowing from the resolution fund would cost more.

In real-case scenarios, the DIS may combine several financing options, and if possible borrow from other DISs, if the conditions prescribed in the DGSD Article 12(1) are met.

7.3.2 Use of the DIS' Funds for Financing Bank's Resolution

Details of how DIFs should be used for resolution purposes are not prescribed in the DGSD. Instead, Article 109 of the BRRD prescribes the rules and procedures for the use of DIFs for financing resolution. The decision of the EU policy makers to disburse the logical components into two legal acts resulted in the complexity for readers. In addition, authorities of the member countries must also be careful in the use of funds in order to comply with both Directives.

The DIS funds are used in the bank resolution process when:

(i) The bail-in resolution tool is applied and
(ii) Other resolution tools, other than bail-in, are applied.

If the bail-in tool is applied in resolution or another resolution tool is applied, and if insured depositors absorb any losses, the DIS is liable for the amount by which insured deposits would have been written off and for the amount of losses suffered by the creditors. However, in all cases, such liability should not be greater than the amount of losses that the DIS would have to bear had the bank been resolved under normal insolvency proceedings, that is, the amount of insured deposits that would have been paid to depositors. In such cases, however, the DIS is not liable to finance the costs of establishment or recapitalization of a bank or a bridge bank. In simple words, if using the mentioned resolution tools, the DIS is liable to finance the expenses in an amount that would alternatively be financed if the particular bank failed and the DIS had to repay the covered deposits.

In a way, it represents a new way of thinking in regard to the solidarity participation in resolution costs. In the past, the DISs with paybox mandates were not liable to finance bank rehabilitation. The DISs would use their funds only if the bank was closed, for deposit payout or to supplement the transfer of assets and liabilities onto another bank. Now, it is expected from the DIS to participate in the resolution; otherwise, the bank would fail and the DIS would bear all the costs.

When a failing bank is sold as a whole or when a bridge bank is sold, depositors don't have claims toward the DIS as long as their insured deposits are transferred in the amount equal to or higher than the aggregate coverage amount ensured by the DGSD, that is, €100,000. In simple words, the DIS' funds will be used in the resolution of a particular bank, but only up to the amount of the covered deposits in that bank.

In addition, the liability of the DIS in financing bank resolution is limited up to 50 per cent of its target level. This limitation is set at BRRD, Article 109. However, in accordance with their banking sectors specifics, the national authorities have discretionary rights to increase the prescribed limit for the usage of the DIS' financing resolution.

Although the wording is not clear, it may be concluded, if the DIS has not yet reached the prescribed minimum target level and before the prescribed deadline of July 2024, that the DIS should use the projected proportional minimum target fund size level in July 2024 as a reference point for its maximum financing of bank resolution. *In addition, it is not clear whether the limit responds to the minimum target fund size level of 0.8 per cent or an actual legal minimum target fund size level prescribed in a member country.* Some member countries prescribed the target fund size at a higher level than the EU minimum. For the purpose of this book, we will assume that the limit applies to the minimum target fund as prescribed by the EU, that is, 0.8 per cent.

If there is a partial transfer of insured deposits into a bridge bank or another bank, the DIS is liable toward the insured depositors up to the maximum prescribed coverage level. Similarly, if in the case of bail-in, some insured deposits are converted into bank's capital, the DIS is liable toward the insured depositors for same amount. For example, in the case of transfer of insured deposits and assets into another bank, due to the difference between the book and market values of the assets at the time of the transaction (discounted by losses and non-performing loans), the resolution authority may decide to transfer the insured deposits only partially so that the transaction can be executed. If covered deposits are not transferred to another bank in the full amount of €100,000, the DIS is liable to compensate depositors for the full amount of insured deposits.

If the DIS' funds are used for resolution purposes and if, consequently, these funds reduce to less than two-thirds of the prescribed target level (0.8 per cent of total insured deposits), Article 109(5) of the BRRD prescribes that the premium paid by banks must be set at a level which would allow for reaching the target level within six years (Directive 2014/59/EU 2014, L 173/331–332). The same rule applies if the DIS funds are used for the payout. Therefore, the usage of the DIS' funds either for the deposit payout or for bank resolution has the same treatment regarding the compliance with a minimum target level.

There is one discrepancy in the regulation that relates to the depletion of the DIFs below two-thirds of the targeted level of 0.8 per cent in two Directives.

Article 10(2) paragraph 3 of the DGSD (2014/49/EU 2014, L 173/164), however, prescribes that 'if, after the target level has been reached for the first time, the available financial means have been reduced to less than two-thirds of the target level, the regular contribution shall be set at a level allowing the target level to be reached within six years.' It is not clear whether the EU regulators intentionally prescribed the two articles differently or it was a mistake (oversight), but the wording of the two articles (Article 109 of BRRD and Article 10 of DGSD) do not have the same meaning.

What is written in the BRRD means that if *the DIS' money is used for resolution purposes* and *if the balance of the DIS' funds falls below two-thirds of target funds* (at any point of time, not only if the DIS once reaches the target level), banks must pay a regular premium at a level which would allow reaching the prescribed target level in six years.

While what is written in the DGSD means *that if the DIS the reached the prescribed target level (0.8 per cent) for the first time and if its funds fell below two-thirds of it* (regardless of what caused the fall—don't forget that any payout of insured deposits would cause decrease of funds), the premium should be set at the level which would allow reaching again the target level in six years.

Careful reading raises a question, what would happen if the DIS has not reached the prescribed target level of 0.8 per cent yet (e.g. the DIS' funds are at 0.6 per cent of total covered deposits) but if the funds have been used for the purposes as prescribed by Article 109 of the BRRD? Does this mean that in such a case the premium should be set at such a level to reach the target within six years (as prescribed by the BRRD) or not (because Article 10 of the DGSD prescribes it only if the target level has already been reached for the first time)?

The BRRD prescribes that in all cases the financial liability of the DIS toward insured depositors, as prescribed by Article 109 of the BRRD, is limited up to 50 per cent of its target level as prescribed by Article 10 of the DGSD. Member states may use discretionary rights to increase the prescribed limit of the DIF use for financing bank resolution.

7.3.2.1 Example: Use of DIS' Funds for Financing Bank Resolution

The following example illustrates some open questions on the usage of DIS' funds for financing bank resolution, using the following assumptions:

- The DIS plans to reach the minimum prescribed target fund size of 0.8 per cent of total covered deposits by Year 10 in the amount of €422 million.
- At the end of Year 2, its financial resources amounted to more than €100 million.
- In Year 3, Bank number 9 is resolved using the resolution tool of transfer of assets and liabilities into another bank, where the first valuations and calculations indicate that the DIS would need to provide €80 million. If the bank is going to fail, the total covered deposits are above €98 million. Therefore, the costs for the DIS, expressed as an immediate outflow of liquidity, would be lower if the funds were used in the bank's resolution, compared to deposit payout.

However, the DIS has still not reached the target level of 0.8 per cent of the covered deposits in Year 3. At the time of Bank number 9 resolution, the level of the DIF's coverage ratio is 0.24 per cent with funds in the amount of €101 million, as evidenced from Table 7.8.

Therefore, theoretically, the DIS may engage all of its collected funds for the purpose of financing the bank's resolution since the required amount of €80 million is lower than 50 per cent of the DIS's target, that is, €210 million.

After financing the resolution of the Bank 9 with €80 million, the coverage ratio drops to 0.13 per cent of the covered deposits.

In cases when a larger bank is resolved, which may be a realistic assumption, and where 50 per cent of the DIS's target funds would not be sufficient to finance the total required amount, it is not clear how the remaining financing gap amount would be financed if the national authorities don't use the discretionary right and increase the legal limit.

In such a case, if strictly following the rules prescribed by the DGSD, the DIS would finance resolution only partially, up to 50 per cent of its

Table 7.8 Use of DIS' funds for financing bank's resolution, in €000

Banks	Year 0	Year 1	Year 2	Year 3	Year 4	Year 5	Year 6
10	3,040	3,131	3,225	3,322	3,422	3,524	3,630
9	90,000	92,700	95,481	98,345	0	0	0
8	375,000	386,250	397,838	409,773	422,066	434,728	447,770
6	1,100,000	1,133,000	1,166,990	1,202,000	1,238,060	1,275,201	1,313,458
7	1,300,000	1,339,000	1,379,170	1,420,545	1,463,161	1,507,056	1,552,268
5	1,600,000	1,648,000	1,697,440	1,748,363	1,800,814	1,854,839	1,910,484
4	4,000,000	4,120,000	4,243,600	4,370,908	4,502,035	4,637,096	4,776,209
3	6,400,000	6,592,000	6,789,760	6,993,453	7,203,256	7,419,354	7,641,935
2	10,200,000	10,506,000	10,821,180	11,145,815	11,480,190	11,824,596	12,179,333
1	14,749,000	15,191,470	15,647,214	16,116,631	16,600,129	17,098,133	17,611,077
Total	**39,817,040**	**41,011,551**	**42,241,898**	**43,509,155**	**44,713,134**	**46,054,528**	**47,436,163**
Premium 0.0828 per cent	32,988	33,977	34,996	36,046	37,044	38,155	39,300
DIF financing resolution				80,000			
DIF	**32,988**	**66,965**	**101,961**	**58,008**	**95,051**	**133,206**	**172,506**
50 per cent of target	210,926	210,926	210,926	210,926	210,926	210,926	210,926
Actual coverage ratio, per cent	0.08	0.16	0.24	0.13	0.21	0.29	0.36

target fund level or up to the limit which would be prescribed using its discretionary right.

Contrary to the payout of depositors, in the case of financing the resolution, the DIS does not need to collect extraordinary premium or arrange alternative funding options, in order to collect sufficient funds for the purposes of resolution. Thus, although the use of the DIS funds in bank resolution is mandatory, it is still limited up to 50 per cent (or more) of the target level.

7.3.2.2 Example: DIS' Funds Are Insufficient to Finance Bank Resolution

The following example illustrates the situation in which the DIS is not able to finance the resolution of a larger bank. In reality, there may be such situations since the resolution, by default, will be applied to larger banks, if conditions for the resolution are met.

The example below uses the following assumptions:

- The DIS's target fund size is set at 0.8 per cent by the end of Year 10, approximately in the amount of €428 million;
- In Year 3, Bank number 6 is about to fail and the resolution authority decides to apply the bridge bank resolution tool;
- Total covered deposits of Bank number 6 are €1.17 billion at the end of Year 2;
- Initial valuation of the bank's assets and liabilities confirms that the DIS should provide €600 million in order to transfer the covered deposits into a newly established bridge bank;
- However, the DIS's total funds at the end of Year 2 are at €101 million;
- How much could and should the DIS provide to finance the resolution of Bank number 6?

Before giving any answer, authorities should conduct an assessment of funds and compare it with the liabilities and limitations prescribed by the DGSD and the BRRD.

The DIS's upper limit for the use of funds in the bank resolution process is equal to 50 per cent of its target fund level and, in this case, is €214 million. However, the DIS has only €101 million. Therefore, the DIS is not able to provide the total amount of funds required to finance the transfer of the covered deposits into the bridge bank (€600 million). The question for authorities is whether the DIS should provide all of its available funds in the amount of €100 million or even less. Whatever the authorities decide, it is not sufficient to finance the resolution of Bank number 6. If the DIS participates with funding, it should recalculate its target fund size level again and establish a new annual regular premium.

If Bank number 6 fails (instead of being resolved) and if normal insolvency proceedings are used, the DIS will face a large financing gap and will need to provide the whole amount of €1.17 billion by arranging different financing options such as extraordinary premium and alternative funding arrangements.

7.3.3 Use of the DIS' Funds for Alternative Measures

The DGSD also prescribes that the DIS' funds may be used for financing other measures in order to prevent bank failure. The use of the DIS' funds for deposit payout and for financing bank resolution are of mandatory nature, whereas financing alternative measures is based on a voluntary approach.

The use of the DIS' funds for alternative measures is still under discussion among the national jurisdictions of member countries. Many see this option as a limiting one compared to the previously existing practice in the EU member countries in early interventions. Some (Boccuzzi 2016b, 1) even consider it a 'mission impossible' to use it effectively due to two constraints, such as the least cost rule (under the depositors' preference hierarchy regime) and the state aid rules.

The DGSD uses the term 'alternative measures' but does not provide the definition of alternative measures, although from other sources it may be assumed that alternative measures stand for early interventions in the form of recapitalization, liquidity loans, guarantees and similar support to a problem bank. Some argue (Polis 2015, 10) that the DIS's support may also be non-financial such as the provision of consultancy and audit functions, assistance with the implementation of recovery plans, facilitating and supporting banks to carry out private sector solutions. However, it may be argued further whether the DIS's initial involvement in financing a problem bank is a facilitating signal for private investors to ensure financing of the bank in need (e.g. to provide recapitalization of the bank) or a possible trigger for moral hazard. This would depend on the level of development of the banking sector and whether there are successful examples in the past which then serve as a model.

In any case, especially when the DIS finances early intervention measures, its mandate and the role are expanded from paybox to loss-minimizer through the prevention of the bank's failure whereas the two important rules must be followed, such as the least cost and state aid rules.

Given the purpose of these measures, it may be assumed that the DIS may use its funds for the financial assistance to a 'problem bank', that is, a bank that qualifies for early intervention measures but as long as the conditions for resolution, as prescribed by the BRRD, have not been met, which must be confirmed by the competent authority after consulting the resolution authority.

If the DIS' funds are used for financing alternative measures, there are six conditions that must be met which are set in Article 11 of the DGSD (2014/49/EU 2014, L 173/166):

(i) that the resolution authority has not taken any resolution action under Article 32 of the BRRD;
(ii) that the DIS possesses appropriate systems and procedures for selecting alternative measures and monitoring affiliated risks;
(iii) that the costs of the measures do not exceed the costs of fulfilling the statutory or contractual mandate of the DIS;
(iv) the use of alternative measures is linked to conditions imposed on a bank, involving at least more stringent risk monitoring and greater verification rights for the DIS;
(v) the use of alternative measures is linked to commitments by a bank with a view to securing access to insured deposits;
(vi) the ability of a bank to pay the extraordinary premium is confirmed in the assessment of the competent authority.

The first condition allows the DIS to use alternative measures as long as the resolution authority has not taken any resolution action under Article 32 of the BRRD (Directive 2014/59/EU 2014, L 173/249–250). By carefully reading Article 32 of the BRRD it is clear that it prescribes that the resolution authority should take a resolution action only if it considers that all the listed conditions for resolution are met. There are three listed conditions for resolution actions to be taken, such as:

(i) the bank is failing or likely to fail, which has been determined by a competent authority;
(ii) there is no reasonable prospect that any alternative private sector measures or supervisory actions would prevent the bank's failure;
(iii) a resolution action is necessary in terms of the public interest.

Now, returning to the DGSD's condition, it may be concluded (but this is not clearly prescribed), that *the DIS should not provide alternative measures to a failing bank or to a bank that is about to fail.* Determining whether a bank is failing or about to fail is not straightforward which may result in many qualitative opinions and discretionary decisions (EBA 2015a, 12–18). Therefore, authorities must ensure as much as possible a standardized approach and minimize the possibility of an unjustified use of funds.

If the DIS is to provide alternative measures, the timing is important and the financing must occur prior to the bank's resolution that is in the pre-resolution period.

However, a further reading of Article 11 point 4 of the DGSD states that alternative measures should not be applied where the competent authority, having consulted the resolution authority, considers the conditions for the resolution actions have been met, that is, *if the bank qualifies for an early intervention but as long as the conditions for the resolution have not been met.*

It is critical for the national authorities to prescribe as clearly as possible conditions for the qualification for alternative measures from the DIS to avoid financing a non-viable bank, which would end up in liquidation or possibly in resolution.

Undoubtedly, the bank receiving financing from the DIS during the period of early intervention measures should still be viable; otherwise, the financial intervention provided by the DIS would be a waste of money. In addition, the DIS and the bank supervisor must coordinate on a daily basis to ensure that the financing is necessary, justifiable and that it would contribute to the improvement of the bank's financial position.

Article 27 point 1 of the BRRD prescribes early intervention measures toward a bank with a rapidly deteriorating financial condition, including liquidity situation, increasing the level of leverage, non-performing loans or concentration of exposures and other (Directive 2014/59/EU 2014, L 173/244–245). In other words, Article 27 lists the characteristics of a problem bank where the line between a problem and a failing bank is very thin. In addition, the EBA issued Guidelines where prescribing characteristics and conditions for banks qualifying for early intervention measures (EBA 2015b, 9–14).

Two conditions such as the least cost intervention and non-collision to state aid rules would be hard to meet. Not all costs related to the bank failure are easily calculated such as, for example, indirect costs related to the bank's liquidation. Interestingly, with the depositors' preference rule, as prescribed by the BRRD, the cost test may result in the liquidation of a bank being the least cost option (when the DIS has the highest priority in claims, its net cost of deposit payout may be much lower than the actual liquidity payout).

In the past, many jurisdictions within the EU used some form of early interventions taken or authorized by the national bank supervisors (Boccuzzi 2016a, 154–164), whereas the DGSD would move the focus from an early intervention, that is, alternative measures to resolution and liquidation, due to the complexity and rigorousness of compliance with the least cost test and state aid rules.

Namely, the European Commission argues that the use of the DIS' funds for alternative measures is considered state aid because the banks' contribution to the DIF is mandatory and as such may be considered as 'public (not private) funds' which fall under the control of the state aid rules and the decision as to the funds' application is attributed to the State Aid (EC 2015, 1–2). The BRRD also states, in its Preamble (47), that 'State aid may be involved where resolution funds or deposit guarantee funds intervene to assist in the resolution of failing institutions' (Directive 2014/59/EU 2014, L 173/198).

Whether the arguments are correct or not, if state aid rules apply, there are numerous conditions that must be met (EC 2013, C 216/1–15). If a public intervention occurs, it first triggers bank resolution (in accordance with Article 56 of the BRRD) after all other resolution options have been exhausted. In addition, public stabilization tools trigger the burden sharing principle (in their attempt to increase the level of the capital and obligatory conversion or a write-off of the subordinated debt banks first must seek private solutions). Therefore, it does not make sense for the DIS to use alternative measures, as prescribed by the DGSD and the BRRD for financing problem banks, if the state aid rules apply at the same time.

Some countries, like for example Italy, which had a successful experience in the past in intervening in problem banks rather than in executing the payout of insured deposits, consider that alternative measures, as prescribed by the DGSD, the BRRD and the state aid rules, are not effective and are limiting options resulting in higher costs of bank resolutions.

On the other hand, there are countries which do not have a strong supervision or supervisors delayed actions on banks which resulted in high liquidation costs and almost no value of the banks' assets once the license has been revoked, where the possibility to use discretionary DIS funds during the bank's early intervention may actually camouflage the condition of the bank and enable the use of the DIS' funds to keep a non-viable bank alive for some time.

As from the existing evidence, it is hard to use the DIS' funds without the qualification of being state aid. If the use of the DIS' funds is qualified as being state aid, the bank's restructuring plan envisioning its long-term viability must be approved by the EC, in addition to a number of other conditions that must be met.

Therefore, the question is whether and how to apply the alternative measures mechanisms and whether their implementation is realistic at all and how to prevent paying higher, instead of lower, costs which was the initial goal.

It is unfortunate that the EU regulator prescribed such important issues leaving room for speculations and interpretations, thus leading to a possible misuse of the DIS' funds on the one hand, while on the other hand making it almost impossible to use them at all due to the prescribed limitations of the state aid rules.

If alternative financial measures are implemented, the DIS may provide a liquidity loan or other form of financial assistance, even increase of capital, to a bank without a deteriorating financial condition, but with the objective of preventing its failure, in which case the state aid rules would most likely apply and trigger strict conditions for its implementation.

The DIS may use its funds for financing alternative measures on banks if it has appropriate systems and procedures in place for the selection of measures and monitoring risks. This entails that the DIS should have prepared procedures for approving financial assistance, as well as mechanisms, and is able to monitor risks related to it. The DIS should never provide financial assistance to an unviable bank, if it is likely that the bank might fail in the near future, if there is no control over the usage of funds and so on.

The DIS may use its funds for financing alternative measures on banks if the costs of the measures do not exceed the costs of fulfilling the statutory or contractual mandate of the DGS; that is, the costs should not exceed the total amount of insured deposits. Again, the wording of the DGSD is not sufficiently clear since the word 'cost' is used. If the DIS primarily uses its funds for deposit payout, it will also recover some, but most likely not all, of those funds from the insolvency procedure, that is, from the bankruptcy or liquidation (or receivership) procedure.

The cost for the DIS in the payout is the final non-recovered amount of paid insured deposits and not the liquidity amount initially paid for the insured deposits. This may be illustrated with an example. If a bank has €10mil of covered deposits and if that particular bank fails, the DIS has to pay insured depositors in the amount of €10mil. However, the paid amount is not a cost for the DIS because the DIS will recover some funds in the liquidation (bankruptcy or receivership) process. If the DIS recovers €9mil, its final cost is only €1mil. If, however, the DIS provides a loan to the bank in the same amount of €10mil, it expects the loan to be repaid in full, under certain conditions. The DIS would entail costs only if a bank recipient of such loan does not repay it in full. Therefore, it would be better if the words 'paying amount' are used instead of the word 'cost'. Another option is to clearly prescribe a uniform methodology for the least cost test that must be applied every time before deciding on alternative measures financing.

The DIS may use its funds for financing alternative measures on banks if those measures are linked to the conditions prescribed to a bank, the recipient of financial assistance. If approving some form of financial assistance to a bank, the DIS should impose certain conditions to the bank, involving a more stringent risk of monitoring and greater verification rights for the DIS. The DGSD does not provide details on the conditions but it may be assumed that the DIS should at least use the same conditions otherwise used by the supervisor when providing a similar form of financial assistance to a problem bank. The DGSD actually prescribes that the DIS must consult both the resolution authority and the competent authority on the measures and conditions imposed on the credit institution.

In addition, the use of alternative measures provided by the DIS to the bank must be linked to the bank's commitment to securing access to insured deposits. Therefore, it *may be assumed that the DIS must provide financial assistance to the bank for the purpose of depositors' accessibility to their deposits.*

Article 11 of the DGSD prescribes that if the DIS employs its funds for alternative measures, and if there is a need to pay out insured deposits, the affiliated bank will immediately provide the DIS with the funds received, where necessary in the form of an extraordinary premium if the DIS' funds are less than two-thirds of the target level and if there is a need to compensate the depositors, and if total funds fall below 25 per cent of the target level. On the other hand, the controversy is that the DGSD does not prescribe the limit for financing alternative measures with the DIS' funds, so it seems that the DGSD may engage as many funds as needed.

7.3.3.1 Example: Use of the DIS' Funds for Alternative Measures Preventing Bank Failure

The following example illustrates a possible use of the DIS' funds for financing a problem bank under the following assumptions:

- in Year 1 the DIS provided a liquidity loan in the amount of €50 million Bank number 6 for the period of one year.
- at the end of Year 1, the DIS still has €101 million of total funds, although only €51 million are readily available funds at its disposal.
- at the beginning of Year 2, Bank number 9 failed and the DIS must repay €98 million of covered deposits.
- during Year 2, the DIS is planning to collect a €36 million regular premium over the year.

The DIS conducts a cash flow projection and analysis of its funds. As evidenced from Table 7.9 at the time of the failure of Bank number 9, during Year 2, the DIS only collected one-fourth of its annual premium for that year, that is, €9million, resulting in funds at the DIS's disposal in the amount of €60 (51 + 9) million, which is below 25 per cent of the target funds (€106 million).

Therefore, the DIS is entitled to request from Bank number 6 to return the funds immediately. Bank number 6 returns at minimum the whole amount of €50 million, during Year 2.

Given all unclear wording and non-existing crucial definitions of alternative measures, it is necessary that national regulators prescribe clear conditions for the use of the DIS' funds for both resolution and alternative measures and coordination between the DIS and the bank supervisor in order to ensure that the bank is viable, under the early intervention measures and that the financing by the DIS would improve its financial condition and possibly facilitate private solutions.

However, due to the strict state aid compliance rules, once the DIS' funding is used and characterized as state aid, the restructuring plan must first be approved by the European Commission and the resolution authority must restructure the bank under the BRRD terms, assuming it is of public interest; otherwise, it must initiate bank's insolvency proceedings. Considering all the above mentioned, it may be concluded that the use of alternative measures makes sense only for large problem banks in case of liquidity problems but prior to meeting the conditions for resolution.

In addition, it would be necessary for national jurisdictions to prescribe, at least in subordinate laws, clear procedures for the use of funds for allowed purposes in relation to the DIFs.

Table 7.9 Use of DIS' funds for alternative measures, in €000

Banks	Year 1	Year 2	Year 3	Year 4	Year 5	Year 6	Year 7	Year 8	Year 9
10	3,225	3,322	3,422	3,524	3,630	3,739	3,851	3,967	4,086
9	95,481	98,345	0	0	0	0	0	0	0
8	397,838	409,773	422,066	434,728	447,770	461,203	475,039	489,290	503,969
6	**1,166,990**	1,202,000	1,238,060	1,275,201	1,313,458	1,352,861	1,393,447	1,435,251	1,478,308
7	1,379,170	1,420,545	1,463,161	1,507,056	1,552,268	1,598,836	1,646,801	1,696,205	1,747,091
5	1,697,440	1,748,363	1,800,814	1,854,839	1,910,484	1,967,798	2,026,832	2,087,637	2,150,266
4	4,243,600	4,370,908	4,502,035	4,637,096	4,776,209	4,919,495	5,067,080	5,219,093	5,375,666
3	6,789,760	6,993,453	7,203,256	7,419,354	7,641,935	7,871,193	8,107,329	8,350,548	8,601,065
2	10,821,180	11,145,815	11,480,190	11,824,596	12,179,333	12,544,713	12,921,055	13,308,686	13,707,947
1	15,647,214	16,116,631	16,600,129	17,098,133	17,611,077	18,139,410	18,683,592	19,244,100	19,821,423
Total	**42,241,898**	**43,509,155**	**44,713,134**	**46,054,528**	**47,436,163**	**48,859,248**	**50,325,026**	**51,834,776**	**53,389,820**
Target 0.8 per cent									**427,119**
Premium 0.0828 per cent	34,996	36,046	37,044	38,155	39,300	40,479	41,693	42,944	44,232
Alternative measures	**50,000**								
DIF	**101,961**	**39,662**	**76,706**	**114,861**	**154,161**	**194,640**	**236,333**	**279,277**	**323,509**
DIS liquidity	**51,961**	**-10,338**	**76,706**	**114,861**	**154,161**	**194,640**	**236,333**	**279,277**	**323,509**
ex post Bank 6		**50,000**							
50 per cent of target	213,559	213,559	213,559	213,559	213,559	213,559	213,559	213,559	213,559
Two-thirds of target	284,746	284,746	284,746	284,746	284,746	284,746	284,746	284,746	284,746
25 per cent of target	**106,780**	**106,780**	**106,780**	**106,780**	**106,780**	**106,780**	**106,780**	**106,780**	**106,780**

7.4 Borrowing Between the DISs

The DGSD envisaged the possibility of a mutual borrowing between two or more national deposit insurance schemes on a voluntary basis, if certain conditions are met. As an idea, it is welcomed, but it is questionable whether it would be used as a standard borrowing 'option' or on an isolated basis. It is unlikely that, unless another DIS has a strong interest, such as in case of a cross-border bank failure, it would place its excess of liquidity to assist a DIS that is struggling to repay the covered deposits.

The DIS, as the potential creditor, must assess the credit risk of the DIS, the potential borrower, and of the offered collateral. In addition, the potential creditor wants to ascertain that its member banks are in a good shape and that there are no possible payouts in the foreseeable future at home.

In order to apply for a loan to the 'fellow' deposit insurance authority, several conditions must be met, as prescribed by Article 12 of the DGSD (2014/49/EU 2014, L 173/167):

(i) the borrowing DIS is not able to repay its depositors and undertakes a legal commitment that the borrowed funds will be used for deposit payout;
(ii) extraordinary premium had already been imposed;
(iii) the borrowing DIS is not subject to any obligation to repay a loan to another DIS;
(iv) the total amount of the loan is limited to 0.5 per cent of the covered deposits of the borrowing DIS;
(v) the borrowing DIS must inform the EBA on the conditions and the reasons for requesting the money.

Clearly, the DIS can't borrow from several DISs, but only from one. The total amount of the loan is limited to total covered deposits of the borrowing DIS and not to the target level. At the same time, the level of use of the DIFs for resolution is limited to the target fund size level, but the level of use of DIFs for lending to another DIS is not limited to target fund size. However, it is questionable whether the DIS would rather provide funding to another DIS to ensure the deposit payout in another country or for bank resolution in its own country.

The loan is also subject to specific conditions, as prescribed by Article 12 of the DGSD:

(i) the loan must be repaid within five (5) years, with interest due at the time of repayment;
(ii) the interest rate can be arranged but not lower than the interest rate for the marginal lending facility of the European Central Bank.
(iii) The lending deposit insurance entity must inform the EBA about the duration of the loan and interest rate.

When deciding on a loan, the lending deposit insurance authority should take into the account that premiums paid by member banks to the borrowing deposit insurance entity must ensure the loan repayment and re-establishment of the target level as soon as possible.

7.4.1 Example: Mutual DISs Borrowing

The following example illustrates mutual EU DISs borrowing under the following assumptions and the DGSD limitations:

- at the beginning of Year 1, bank number 6 fails and the DIS must conduct a deposit payout in the amount of €1.2 billion;
- the DIS collects 0.0828 per cent annual regular premium from its member banks in order to comply with 0.8 per cent minimum target fund size level by the end of Year 7;
- At the beginning of Year 1, the DIS has available only €138 million.

Initial calculations, as illustrated in Table 7.10, indicate that the DIS could collect 0.5 per cent of the extraordinary premium, which is €224 million. The remaining financial gap is in the amount of €840 million.

The two EU member DISs are ready to provide €840 million and the borrowing DIS closes a borrowing deal with a neighboring DIS, for a term of five years and at the ECB the marginal lending facility rate at 0.25 per cent annually, paid along with the last principal installment in Year 5.

Table 7.10 DIS borrowing and adjustment of annual premium, in €000

Banks	Year 1	Year 2	Year 3	Year 4	Year 5	Year 6	Year 7
10	3,422	3,524	3,630	3,739	3,851	3,967	4,086
9	101,296	104,335	107,465	110,689	114,009	117,430	120,952
8	422,066	434,728	447,770	461,203	475,039	489,290	503,969
6	1,238,060	0	0	0	0	0	0
7	1,463,161	1,507,056	1,552,268	1,598,836	1,646,801	1,696,205	1,747,091
5	1,800,814	1,854,839	1,910,484	1,967,798	2,026,832	2,087,637	2,150,266
4	4,502,035	4,637,096	4,776,209	4,919,495	5,067,080	5,219,093	5,375,666
3	7,203,256	7,419,354	7,641,935	7,871,193	8,107,329	8,350,548	8,601,065
2	11,480,190	11,824,596	12,179,333	12,544,713	12,921,055	13,308,686	13,707,947
1	16,600,129	17,098,133	17,611,077	18,139,410	18,683,592	19,244,100	19,821,423
Total	**44,814,429**	**44,883,661**	**46,230,171**	**47,617,076**	**49,045,588**	**50,516,956**	**52,032,464**
Min target 0.8 per cent							**416,260**
Regular premium (0.0828 per cent; 0.52 per cent)	37,128	233,395	240,397	247,609	255,037	262,688	43,083
ex post premium 0.5 per cent; 0.0828 per cent	224,072						
DIF	**–838,852**	**–605,457**	**–365,060**	**–117,452**	**137,585**	**400,274**	**432,857**
Borrowing from other DIS	840,000						
DIS liquid funds	**1,148**	**234,543**	**306,940**	**386,548**	**473,585**	**568,274**	**432,857**
Loan repayment (5 years, 0.25 per cent)		**168,000**	**168,000**	**168,000**	**168,000**	**178,500**	
DIS' liquid funds after the loan	**1,148**	**66,543**	**138,940**	**218,548**	**305,585**	**389,774**	**432,857**

The DIS conducts a projection of the funding needs and ex post funding repayment commitments as presented in Table 7.10. As a result of the deposit payout and liquidity loan in the amount of €840 million, the borrowing DIS ends Year 1 with –€838 million DIF and €1,148 million of liquid funds.

The DIS must adjust its annual premium in order to be able to repay the borrowed funds to the 'fellow' DIS on time and to rebuild the DIF, in compliance with the DGSD.

More precisely, the borrowing DIS must collect a sufficiently high annual premium over the next five years in order to:

- repay the loan, as envisaged by the loan contract
- pay the interest rate in the amount of 0.25 per cent annually at the end of the Year 5
- comply with the minimum target fund size of 0.8 per cent by the end of Year 7, as initially envisaged.

The given calculations, as presented in Table 7.10, confirm that the DIS has several options available:

- The DGSD Directive allows to the borrowing DIS to comply with the minimum target fund size over a prolonged period (additional six years), as prescribed by Article 10 of the DGSD (2014/49/EU 2014, L 173/164–165). Initial calculations show that the annual regular premium over the five years of loan repayment should be at least 0.35 per cent in order to ensure the repayment of the loan and minimum liquidity. After the loan repayment, within six years of the prolonged period, it should comply with the minimum target fund size of 0.8 per cent.
- Another option is to collect the annual regular premium to repay the total loan payment (€840 million principal and €10.5 million interest in Year 5) and to build an ex ante DIF at 0.8 per cent by the end of Year 7. In order to do so, the DIS must apply a 0.52 per cent annual regular premium over five years. After the loan repayment, the DIS assesses the riskiness of its banking sector and sets the annual regular premium at 0.0828 per cent again.

Table 7.11 Recalculation of the annual regular premium, in €000

Projected target DIF by mid-2024	416,260
Actual DIF after the payout in 2018	−838,852
Target DIF gap to be collected over 5 years	1,255,112
Minimum required annual premium over 5 years	251,022
Average covered deposits over 5 years	49,000,000
Minimum annual premium level, in percentage	0.512290724
New annual premium level, in percentage	0.52

The DIS opted for a higher annual premium during the loan repayment period which allowed compliance with the target fund within the initial timeframe, that is, by the end of Year 7.

Table 7.11 illustrates recalculation of the annual regular premium, where the DIS has almost €1.3 billion of the total financial gap to ensure repayment of the loan over five years and compliance with the established 0.8 per cent target over the remaining seven years. Thus, the DIS must charge approximately 0.52 per cent annual regular premium over the next seven years.

Having taken into consideration all conditions prescribed by the DGSD, it is very optimistic to expect a borrowing between the deposit insurance schemes on a larger scale.

7.5 Conclusion

Funding the DIS for EU member countries is even more challenging than for the DIS elsewhere in the world due to the strict provisions on funding and use of DIFs. All EU DISs must establish an ex ante DIF with a minimum target at 0.8 per cent of covered deposits by mid-2024. Banks must pay their contributions to the ex ante DIF regularly and in accordance with their risk profiles and up to 30 per cent of their premium liability may be in the form of ex post payment commitments. In case when the DIS faces insufficient liquidity, it may impose ex post premium and ensure borrowing arrangements, including a borrowing from another DIS from another EU member country, under certain conditions. DIFs are used for deposit payout and for financing bank resolution processes, with limitations related to the target fund. In addition, the DIS' funds may be used for alternative financing provided to problem banks that is part of early interventions program but under the prescribed conditions. However, imposed strict rules on funding and use of DIFs in EU member countries in combination with dynamics of legislative changes represent challenges for EU member DISs in their attempt to comply with all established rules and, at the same time, ensure sufficient financial resources to fulfill the given mandate efficiently and more cost-effectively.

Bibliography

Boccuzzi, Giuseppe. 2016a. *The European Banking Union: Supervision and Resolution.* Palgrave MacMillan Studies in Banking and Financial Institutions.

———. 2016b. The New European Framework for Banking Crisis Management. Will It Be Enough? https://openreviewmbf.org/2016/03/12/the-new-european-framework-for-banking-crisis-management-will-it-be-enough/. Accessed 2016.

Directive 2014/49/EU. 2014. Directive 2014/49/EU of the European Parliament and of the Council of 16 April 2014 on Deposit Guarantee Schemes. http://eur-lex.europa.eu/legal-content/EN/TXT/?uri=CELEX:32014L0049. Accessed 2016.

Directive 2014/59/EU. 2014. Directive 2014/59/EU of the European Parliament and of the Council of 15 May 2014 Establishing a Framework for the Recovery and Resolution of Credit Institutions and Investment Firms and Amending Council Directive 82/891/EEC, and Directives 2001/24/EC, 20. http://data.europa.eu/eli/dir/2014/59/oj. Accessed 2016.

EBA. 2015a. *Guidelines on the Interpretation of the Different Circumstances When an Institution Shall Be Considered as Failing or Likely to Fail Under Article 32(6) of Directive 2014/59/EU.* EBA.

———. 2015b. *Guidelines on triggers for use of early intervention measures pursuant to Article 27(4) of Directive 2014/59/EU.* EBA.

EC. 2013. 2013/C 216/01 Communication from the Commission on the Application, from 1 August 2013, of State aid rules to Support Measures in Favour of Banks in the Context of the Financial Crisis ('Banking Communication'). http://eur-lex.europa.eu/legal-content/EN/ALL/?uri=CELEX%3A52013XC0730(01). Accessed 2016.

———. 2015. Fact Sheet: State Aid to Italian Banca Tercas and the Financial Sector in General – Frequently Asked Questions. http://europa.eu/rapid/press-release_MEMO-15-6394_en.htm. Accessed 2016.

Polis, Stefano de. 2015. DGS Alternative Measures in Banking Crises Under the New EU Framework. https://www.bancaditalia.it/pubblicazioni/interventi-vari/int-var-2015/depolis-260615.pdf?language_id=1. Accessed 2016.

Glossary

Bank bankruptcy (insolvency proceedings) Legal proceedings, usually run by a court or another authority, on an insolvent bank when its debts are higher than its assets, usually initiated by the supervisory authority or any bank's creditor, with the aim to liquidate the bank's assets and repay the debt to the creditors, in line with the established credit hierarchy.

Bank liquidation (winding up, insolvency proceedings) Legal proceedings, run by a court or another authority, initiated as a consequence of a bank's license withdrawal or owners' decision to close down the business, resulting in the sale of assets and compensation of creditors from the assets estate. The main difference between bankruptcy and liquidation in some jurisdictions is that in liquidation there should have been sufficient assets to repay all creditors.

Bank resolution (traditional US approach) Disposition plan and processes related to a non-viable (failing) bank. Resolution includes liquidation/bankruptcy of a bank with the deposit payout, transfer and/or sale of assets and liabilities (i.e. purchase and assumption), establishment of a bridge bank and the write-down or conversion of debt to equity (bail-in). The final step is the closure of the bank.

D. Ognjenovic, *Deposit Insurance Schemes*,
DOI 10.1007/978-3-319-51143-6

Bank resolution in the European Union Regime for a failing bank or a bank about to fail, prior to its balance sheet insolvency, other than normal insolvency proceedings, exercised by the national resolution authority applying resolution tools and resolution principles, with objectives to ensure the continuity of the bank's critical functions, avoid adverse effects on financial stability, protect public funds and protect covered deposits, resulting in the bank's continuation as a going-concern where it is possible to liquidate parts of the bank. Within the European Union resolution does not imply closure of a failing bank.

Bank resolution authority Entity established by the law with a bank resolution mandate.

Bank resolution tools in the European Union The sale of business, the bridge institution, the asset separation and the bail-in.

Bank restructuring Bank's reorganization process with restructuring of an entity and its business operations.

Bridge Bank Bank established under special terms and conditions, on a temporary basis (with a prescribed limited life timeframe), with a special license for the purpose of acceptance of assets and liabilities from a failing bank, to bridge the time needed to finalize the resolution process, that is, to bridge the gap between the bank's failure and a permanent resolution option. This tool is mostly used for the resolution of large/systemically important banks

Coverage level (coverage amount) Maximum prescribed level (amount) of eligible deposits per depositor (or per deposit) insured by the deposit insurance scheme. In the European Union, the prescribed coverage level is €100,000.

Coverage ratio The level of total collected deposit insurance fund expressed as a percentage of total covered deposits (payout liability).

Coverage scope Prescribed types of deposits insured by the deposit insurance scheme.

Covered (insured) deposits Eligible deposits up to the prescribed amount, the sum of all eligible deposits of eligible depositors up to the prescribed coverage amount.

Deposit Insurance Scheme (Deposit Protection System, Deposit Guarantee Scheme) Implicit or explicit, established and legally recognized insurance of certain categories of deposits up to the prescribed amount, collected by deposit-taking institutions from insured depositors, provided by the deposit insurance authority in case of deposits' unavailability and occurrence of insured event.

Deposit Insurance Authority (Deposit Insurance Entity) Authority (mostly a legal entity or part of another legal entity) empowered with a deposit insurance mandate. Depending on the national legal framework, it is often called agency, fund or corporation.

Deposit Insurance Fund (capital, reserves) Total deposit insurance financial resources (funds) collected in advance (ex ante) on a regular basis with the main purpose to build up the 'fund' of a significant size for the purpose of deposit payout.

Deposit Insurance Funds All available funding options for the DIS. Funds (cash) collected in advance (ex ante) or ex post to the insured event, classified as initial, regular and extraordinary, administered by the deposit insurance authority and used for payout (repayment, reimbursement, compensation) of covered deposits upon the occurrence of the insured event.

Deposit Insurance Premium (Fee, Contribution, Levy) Legally prescribed amount, expressed as a percentage applied to the premium basis, collected and paid by the insured deposit-taking institutions to the deposit insurance authority. In some jurisdictions, contributions are in the form of claims on the deposit-taking institutions' payment commitments (low-risk securities usually held on a special account in the central bank which can be liquidated when necessary)

Eligible (insurable, protected, covered) deposits Deposits insured and protected by the deposit insurance scheme, that is, deposits which are not excluded from the deposit insurance.

Eligible (insured, protected, covered) depositors Depositors whose deposits are not excluded from the deposit insurance scheme.

Extraordinary (backup, emergency) funding Non-regular funding options available to the deposit insurance authority in cases when regular ex ante funds are insufficient to pay insured deposits.

Initial funding (seed, start-up) Funds collected upon the establishment of the deposit insurance authority from insured deposit-taking institutions, government, central bank or donors.

Linear (flat) premium Premium percentage that is equal for all banks regardless of their risk profile.

Paybox DIS Deposit insurance scheme whose mandate is limited to the payout of covered deposits upon the occurrence of the insured event, without any supervisory or resolution functions.

Paybox plus DIS A deposit insurance scheme whose mandate is limited to paybox but it may use its funds for financing bank resolution.

Payout (repayment, compensation, reimbursement) Action of covered deposits payout by the deposit insurance authority upon the occurrence of the insurance event.

Purchase and Assumption A resolution tool (method) when a sound (healthy) acquiring bank or a bridge bank purchases some or all assets (usually at market value) and assumes some or all liabilities (at book value) from a failing bank.

Receivership Formal closure of a bank, similar to bankruptcy and liquidation in Anglo-Saxon legal frameworks, as practiced in common law legal systems; for example, the FDIC, after the evaluation of the failing bank and determined least cost resolution strategy, becomes the receiver, closes down the bank, takes control of its assets, records and premises, terminates any management or shareholders' operation and conducts the resolution process.

Regular funding Funds collected by the deposit insurance authority from the deposit-taking institutions, on an ongoing basis, as linear (flat) premium or risk-based premium.

Risk-based (differential) premium Premium that is assessed on the basis of the bank's risk profile, according to the prescribed risk-based methodology.

Risk-minimizer DIS A deposit insurance scheme with a mandate to minimize the risks for the banking system such as control over entry and exit of banks from the market and examination and supervision of banks.

Set-off Depositors' claims are deducted by the amount of his or her liability; that is, the covered deposit is decreased for the due or total liability of the depositor toward the bank.

Target fund size level (target fund, target ratio) Desired ratio of targeted ex ante deposit insurance funds to total covered deposits, often used as a benchmark for payout capacity.

Temporary Administration (Conservatorship, Provisional Administration) Temporary management of the bank established by a supervisor as part of supervisory measures, in order to preserve (conserve) bank's asset from further deterioration or illegal management and owners' actions, usually precede formal resolution; during the temporary administration the bank is still open and operates on a going-concern basis.

Index

D. Ognjenovic, *Deposit Insurance Schemes*,
DOI 10.1007/978-3-319-51143-6

The manufacturer's authorised representative in the EU is Springer Nature Customer Service Centre GmbH, Europaplatz 3, 69115 Heidelberg, Germany. If you have any concerns regarding our products, please contact ProductSafety@springernature.com

Printed and bound by CPI Group (UK) Ltd, Croydon, CR0 4YY
25/09/2026
02222854-0011